cultural relativism
PERSPECTIVES IN CULTURAL PLURALISM

BOOKS BY MELVILLE J. HERSKOVITS INCLUDE:

The Human Factor in Changing Africa
Dahomean Narrative (with Frances S. Herskovits)
Cultural Anthropology
Man and His Works
The Myth of the Negro Past
Life in a Haitian Valley
The American Negro

melville j. herskovits

EDITED BY FRANCES HERSKOVITS

cultural relativism

PERSPECTIVES IN CULTURAL PLURALISM

RANDOM HOUSE   NEW YORK

Herskovits, Melville Jean, 1895–1963.
Cultural relativism.

Includes bibliographical references.
1. Cultural relativism—Addresses, essays, lectures.
I. Title.
GN405.H4   301.2   72–6102
ISBN 0–394–48154–2

Grateful acknowledgment is made to the following sources for permission to reprint articles:

American Anthropological Association: "Some Further Comments on Cultural Relativism" from *American Anthropologist,* Vol. 60, No. 2, 1958.

Danforth Foundation: "A Cross Cultural View of Bias and Values," Danforth Lectures No. 7, 1958–1959.

Duke University Press: "Economic Change and Cultural Dynamics" from *Tradition, Values and Socio Economic Development,* edited by Ralph Braibanti and Joseph J. Spengler. Copyright 1961 by Duke University Press.

Royal Institute of Linguistics and Anthropology, Holland: "Review: Symposium on Relativism and the Study of Man" from *Bijdragen tot de Taal-hand-en Volkenkunde,* Vol. 118, 1962.

Science: "On the Values in Culture" from *Scientific Monthly,* Vol. 54, June 1942.

University of Chicago Press: "Rear-Guard Action—Review" from *Perspectives in Biology and Medicine,* Vol. V, No. 1, Autumn 1961. Copyright 1961 by the University of Chicago. "The Problem of Adapting Societies to New Tasks" from *The Progress of Underdeveloped Areas,* edited by B. Hoselitz, 1952.

Wayne State University Press: "Social Selection and the Formation of Human Types" from *Human Biology,* Vol. 1, No. 2, May 1929.

Manufactured in the United States of America
by The Book Press, Brattleboro, Vermont

2 4 6 8 9 7 5 3
First Edition

introduction

herskovits, cultural relativism, and metascience

From those who are offended by the cultural-relativist position comes a steady stream of books (e.g., Edel, 1959; Schoeck and Wiggins, 1961; Moser, 1968; Rudolph, 1968; Tennekes, 1971) and articles (Nowell-Smith, 1971). Those who favor it are either reinventing it under other labels (emics, ethnoscience, hermeneutics, sociology of knowledge, opposition to intellectual imperialism and scientific neocolonialism, etc.) or asserting it without crediting primary sources. While the general acceptance of the cultural-relativist position is probably increasing, there is a lack of any consolidated advocacy of it. So it is particularly appropriate at this time that Frances Herskovits and Random House are making available this collection of Melville Herskovits' essays on cultural relativism and related topics; here are collected in full those papers most frequently cited (often out of context) by the critics and most usable by advocates.

This is, of course, far from being the book on cultural relativism Melville Herskovits intended. It is put together from presentations made in the course of a variety of vigorous debates, and not fully interpretable apart from their specific contexts. They are, however, precious fragments, and I hope their presentation here will inspire one of his intellectual heirs to do the job he would have done in the relative leisure of his impending retirement had he survived to do it.

This introduction attempts to provide some perspectives and testimony that may help future students of these problems, as well as the general reader.

cultural uniqueness and cross-cultural generalization

Before relating cultural relativism to recent developments in the philosophy of science, the history of science and the social psychology of science, i.e., the metascience of the title, it seems appropriate to say something about Herskovits' position on a number of related issues. During the years I knew him (1953 to his death in 1963) he was a vigorous advocate of treating anthropology as one of the humanities, rather than as a science. Most practitioners of the humanistic approach in history, political science, sociology, philosophical psychology and anthropology are by their training incapable of practicing a scientific approach even if they were to be convinced of its value. It seems important to note that Herskovits was an exception to this rule—he had the option of either mode, and had indeed practiced both. He chose the approach of the humanities on the grounds of intellectual conviction. Moreover, unlike many of the more recent converts to a humanistic approach, he had not changed goals. He retained his aim of discovering the truth about man. He made his choice for reasons of superior objectivity in a search for truth shared with the whole of science.

Early in our acquaintance I encountered in a most round-about fashion the quantitative research side of his career. In the course of preparing a theoretical paper on the concept of validity as it relates to psychological measures, I was surveying the kinds of research evidence that had accumulated to invalidate once-popular personality tests. Among the first and most adequate of the studies that eventually undermined the Downey Will-Temperament test (the most popular personality test of the 1920's) was a study by M.J. Herskovits (1924). He described the history of this paper as follows. He was at the time doing anthropometric studies of race crossing in the United States and the Caribbean. He wanted to add personality measures, and was attracted by the claims of this test to measure innate differences through nonlinguistic samples of behavior. E.L. Thorndike warned him that before he invested a lot of time and energy in collecting such data, he should check out the test's claims. This Herskovits did by having persons who knew each other well provide quantitative ratings of each other on each of the six personality-trait polarities the test claimed to measure. The relations of these ratings to the test scores were then computed as product-moment correlation coefficients, producing a dismal array of zero-order insignificant results. (His methodology is still standard in studies of test validity.) As I learned, he had had excellent training in statistics and anthropometrics—from Boas, Thorndike and others—and had used these skills in numerous anthropometric studies of the late nineteen-twenties and early thirties.

His field experience convinced him of the overwhelming importance of culture in determining human personality. With this shift of emphasis came a shift in method, but his goal remained that of a true description of the conditions of human existence, achieved through whatever means were optimal. He was able to argue persuasively that humanistic anthropology was more objective, more intersubjectively verifiable than conventional anthropology focused on "scientific laws." It is well to remember that the an-

thropology of the generations preceding Boas had been
dominated by an interest in cross-cultural generalizations,
and that these theoretical preoccupations had led to biased
observation and to collections of fragmentary observations
misinterpreted out of context. Against such shoddy science
came the demand for extended field work, thorough learning of the local language, detailed notes written up daily
while in the field, and a prohibition on premature or uncritical generalizations so strong that it often seemed to pre-
clude generalization at all. All this in the service of superior
loyalty to the truth. It was Herskovits' own experience, and
in his view the experience of all serious ethnographers, that
field work regularly showed complex interrelationships one
had not anticipated. The cross-cultural laws offered by the
generalizers time after time proved untenable in the light of
the thorough study of individual cultures. Supposedly similar
or identical aspects of separate cultures turned out to be,
upon careful examination, profoundly different. As a result
of such experience, he was deeply skeptical of the approach
of Murdock and the Human Relations Area Files, in which
aspects of ethnographies written for heterogeneous purposes
are coded, categorized, and tabulated in a search for statistical correlations. It was Herskovits' conclusion from his
primary and secondary ethnographic experience that items
so categorized as similar or different on some conceptual
dimension were almost always uninterpretable out of the
context of the total local culture.

Herskovits' arguments against cross-cultural generalization were, I must insist, factual and methodological, rather
than critical of matters of style or ideology. They sprang out
of a hard-headed attention to the facts rather than from the
choice of some nonscientific or poetic goal. He was not
against quantitative multicultural comparison when the data
from each culture were collected for that purpose by ethnographers who knew both the local culture and the purposes
of the study. Under such conditions the possibility was created for the observations to be properly embedded in both

the context of each local culture and the context of cross-cultural comparison. Thus he furthered our joint study of cultural differences in susceptibility to optical illusions (Segall, Campbell and Herskovits, 1966), making the contacts that produced the data from fourteen of the seventeen cultures involved. Similarly, he provided initial support for Robert LeVine's and my cross-cultural study (1972) of ethnocentrism, in which the data from each group were to be collected by an ethnographer familiar with that area.

Not only was he sympathetic to cross-cultural comparison and generalization when done under conditions that gave at least the possibility of adequate interpretative contexts, he was also a gifted generator of theories appropriate to such testing. I will give one illustration of particular interest to me as a psychologist, which I designate to my students as the "Herskovits' Oedipus Complex." The problem area is the irrational emotional attitudes that find expression in parent–child interaction. Whereas in the Freudian version it is the child who brings the irrational, projective attitudes to the interaction, the Herskovits' theory (1958) proposed that the parent brings at least part of the irrational hostility. According to this hypothesis, based on an analysis of the mythology and family patterns of Dahomey, the newborn child reactivates the parents' childhood sibling rivalry. In Dahomey the practice of polygamy is accompanied by a household arrangement in which each wife has her own hut, and in which each child has a monopoly of the mother's attention during the day and on the sleeping mat at night until displaced from this Oedipal monopoly by a younger sibling. This creates an extreme sibling hostility which is reflected in mythology, along with an extreme intergenerational conflict. In each case, it is the older sibling or older generation that initiates the hostility, as indeed did Laius.

While I must refer the reader to the original presentation for that richness of detail which makes the theory plausible, I can note its compatibility with a wide range of psychological theories which predict the transference of attitudes learned in one situation to novel persons or objects on the basis of perceptual similarity. It is well worth an extended cross-cultural study, in which myths, dreams and quarrels would be studied in cultures of widely differing family patterns. I believe Herskovits would have supported such a study with enthusiasm.

But his general emphasis was upon the uniqueness of each culture, on the uninterpretability of any culture item apart from its cultural context and upon the unlikely validity of every simple law regarding cultural human nature. This can be stated quite appropriately in a statistical language, and it is offered here as the first of the metascientific propositions this essay will delineate. It is most convenient to explain this proposition in terms of a statistical method called *analysis of variance* which is much used in experimental psychology and agriculture. In this approach one uses multiple dimensions of experimental variation, A, B, C, D, etc., each of which occurs in several degrees of strength, with (in the simplest of design) each combination of strengths being employed. (Thus if there were four dimensions, A, B, C, and D, each of which had three levels, the total number of different treatment packages would be 81.) In addition to these treatment variables, there is at least one dependent variable in terms of which the results of the treatment are measured— let us call this X. For our present purposes, two major types of outcome need to be distinguished: *main effects* and *interactions*. If a main effect for A is found on X, then we have what could be called a *ceteris paribus* law: B, C, D being held constant at any level, the same rule relating A to X is found, e.g., the more A, the more X. Where *interactions* are found, the relations are complexly contingent. For example, in an A – B interaction, there may be a separate rule relating A and X for each different level of B (e.g., if B is high the more A the more X, but if B is low the more A the less X). Much more complex (higher order) interactions can also occur, such as an A– B– C interaction in which the A to X rule is different for each combination of B and C.

Interactions, where they occur in the absence of main effects, represent highly limited and qualified generalizations. Typical of the history of the physical sciences is the discovery of generalizations conceivably true that are independent of time, place and the status of other variables. Although these laws are more complex than this, nonetheless there was a rich nourishment of "laws of nature" which could be stated without specifying the conditions on the infinitude of other potentially relevant variables.

There is no compelling evidence so far that the social sciences are similarly situated. If we take the one social science, experimental social psychology, that uses the analysis-of-variance approach, the general finding is of higher-order interactions in abundance, and rarely of main effects. Even where we get main effects, it is certainly often due to the failure to include dimensions E, F, G, etc., which would have produced interactions. We are rarely able to replicate findings from one university laboratory to another, indicating an interaction with some unspecified difference in the laboratory settings or in the participants. Stated in these concepts, Herskovits' orientation amounts to a generalization about the kinds of generalizations that will be found tenable, a general law about what sort of specific laws, a metascientific induction based upon firsthand experience and the anthropological literature. For the social and psychological issues that concern the students of culture, higher-order interactions are the rule, and main effects, *ceteris paribus* generalizations, the rare exception. Complex interdependencies, highly contingent relationships and context dependencies characterize the relationships among the aspects of culture and personality.

This metahypothesis is one which we social scientists who attempt the natural-science strategy are reluctant to accept because of its pessimistic implications for our venture. But it is nonetheless one which we should find comprehensible in our own scientific terms. And while the asymptotic evidence is not yet in, it is one whose credibility we should also respect. We should certainly not do as many do and reject it as antiscientific obscurantism.

culture as a source of scientific paradigms and presuppositions

Hume taught us that scientific inference was logically un-justified. In the current generation the exciting intellectual developments in the philosophy of science represent redis-coveries of that truth in a much more specific and descriptive form. Science and ordinary knowing are now seen to be based upon deep-seated presumptions about the nature of the world. These presumptions, or others to take their place, are necessary prerequisites to perceiving and sciencing, but they are unconfirmable. Thus Popper, Polanyi, Quine, Hanson, Russell after 1948, Toulmin, Kuhn, Feyerabend, and other modern philosophers of science emphasize that science is radically underjustified and attempt to describe the pre-suppositions on which such knowing depends. Furthermore, the belief and communication system of scientists has been shown to constitute a self-perpetuating society with many of the features of tradition, authority, conformity pressure, unique ingroup language, etc., shared with other human social systems.

As a part of this same development, Toulmin (1961) and Kuhn (1962) have provided dramatic reinterpretations of the history of science, pointing to fundamental changes in presuppositions, in the kind of phenomena treated as natural or as needing no explanation, and in the more general para-digms of the sciences. The result is a kind of cultural rela-tivism of historical periods within the history of science.

Such relativisms cut two ways. There is the greatest con-sensus when relativism is used to dethrone a specific established erroneous absolutism. Pointing to the arbitrary nature of the presumptive paradigms of the old science helps establish a new one with fewer and more appropriate pre-sumptions. Relativism is in this instance a tool in the service of a critical approach to a superior objectivity. This is cer-tainly how Einstein saw his relativism, and how Popper sees his critical approach to the philosophy of science. But relativism may also be used to argue not for a superior objectivity but for the abandonment of the goal of objectivity entirely. This is what Kuhn and Feyerabend seem to do, and what makes many of us who agree with their facts unwilling to accept their view in its entirety.

The major thrust of Herskovits' cultural relativism fits right into this view of science, although it was developed in an earlier period of scientific absolutism, the remnants of which are still a major source of opposition to it. Cultural relativism points to the fact that among the peoples of the world there are many different belief systems. The anthropologist or any other social scientist is a product of one of these cultures. He inherits from this culture a set of primitive unconscious assumptions about the world and its categories which affect not only his everyday life in his home culture but also his activities as a scientist when he goes to study another culture. Without realizing it, he is a culturally biased observer. If he augments his study with measuring instruments, such as I.Q. tests or projective techniques, these too are permeated with culturally specific content and categories.

In considerable part, these enculturated paradigms and presumptions will be specific to the culture of origin. But the direction of another large part can be stated in advance when the task is one of describing another culture. The general term for these biases is ethnocentrism. Usually when Herskovits is presenting cultural relativism, he accompanies it with a warning against ethnocentrism. I take this pairing to be essential to his major message and is the part of it I myself find most persuasively true. This ethnocentrism provides the anthropologist and tourist with the following biases. He mistakes his own cultural categories as universally correct, as a part of nature rather than a more or less arbitrary convention of his own people. When he encounters different patterns of judgment in another culture, he cannot help seeing them as erroneous. Consciously or unconsciously, he regards his home culture as superior, the people he studies as inferior. The acts his culture has taught him to be immoral and unclean he sees as immoral and unclean when done by others. The anthropologist, being himself an example of an enculturated human, is not exempt from these human failings related to cultural identity.

Herskovits (indeed like most anthropologists since Boas and Malinowski) believed that extended and thorough participation in another specific culture was the most available therapy for this natural ethnocentrism of the ethnographer. He believed that in this experience sensitive anthropologists regularly discover themselves to be much more ethnocentric than they had anticipated—even those who went into the field with a prior feeling of alienation from their own culture. Such experience, plus an intellectual understanding of enculturation, ethnocentrism and cultural relativism, were the methodological curbs he recommended to increase the objectivity of anthropology.

He, of course, did not believe that ethnocentric bias would ever be completely removed. He would not have been surprised at the extreme hostility to the Trobriand culture and the longing for his own culture which the private diaries of Malinowski now reveal. It would be informative to have a thorough comparison of the diary material and the public science Malinowski published on the same topics and episodes. Are not the published works more valid as descriptions of the Trobrianders than the ethnocentric reactions of the diaries? Was Malinowski's guilty awareness of his own tribally human reaction an asset in reducing this bias? Could we not even yet find Trobrianders with a European-style education who also remember the culture that Malinowski tried to understand? Whereas we as Europeans see only the contrast between his two accounts, would not these Trobrianders find in Malinowski's public works strong residual biases shared with the diaries? Even though Malinowski leaned over backward to avoid the outsider's perspective and to adopt the insider's, was he still not too much the European to achieve full understanding? Such research on the role of the ethnographer's own culture in biasing his work has high priority in continuing to develop the critical methodological aspects of cultural relativism.

Express opposition to scientific colonialism and intellectual imperialism is rapidly increasing—in the scholarly journals of the third world if not yet in ours. Much of it is political in a purely European idiom: socialist versus capitalist, anti-imperialist, anti-colonialist. In this, both what is advocated and what is opposed is expressed in category systems developed in Europe in that common culture which produced both Adam Smith and Karl Marx. Even here, however, something of a cultural-relativist insight is available. When a young anthropologist of the third world helps us look at a classic ethnographic description of his area, we are surprised how much of it can now seem to be slanted toward justifying the colonial relationship, a possibility we had entirely failed to notice on earlier readings. He may react similarly to our preference for studying his exotic precontact culture rather than the way his people now live. The participation of large numbers of U.S. anthropologists in counterinsurgency research illustrates the continuing nature of the problem.

There is also in this literature a more subtle theme that is perhaps more important for our critical approach to the objective study of cultures. This theme argues cultural misunderstanding rather than the master–serf, exploiter–exploited bias available within European culture. From this perspective, Russia and the United States are as alike as peas in a pod: compulsive workers and hard drinkers, builders of dams and bombs, evangelical exporters of their own culture, etc., whose tourists, engineers and military advisers are profoundly unable to understand the third-world cultures in which they work. We Western intellectuals share their view of our tourists, overseas engineers and military advisers. What hurts is the assertion that we anthropologists, sociologists and cross-cultural psychologists —emancipated or alienated from our own culture as we feel ourselves to be—still retain a similar bias, though better disguised and probably to a smaller degree. What the science of culture needs is, first, the recognition of the possibility of such bias—indeed, its inevitability to some subtle degree. That is, we should accept the cultural-relativist message. But more than that, we need details, specific corrections of existing ethnographies and alternative holistic descriptions. Some of this, but too little, is in the present anti-intellectual imperialist literature. We need much more.

In recent years some anthropologists have been recruited from non-European cultures, and are providing studies of their own as well as other cultures of the third world, as when an Igbo studies the Navajo, or a Hindu the Embu. This will help, but it will not entirely solve the problem. For these scholars often come from Westernized families and have undergone twenty years of intensive indoctrination in the process of acquiring Western academic credentials. Furthermore, they have until recently been recruited from among the most deferent of their age mates, and from among those most convinced of Western cultural and moral superiority. For the sake of objective scholarship, a still further step should be taken: these young anthropologists should act as interpreters in taking the Western ethnographic descriptions back to the older and less Westernized survivors of their traditional cultures for the purpose of recording the critical reactions of the only remaining genuine authorities on this topic. Nor is there enough genuine deference to these aging custodians of the precious local traditions to sustain the task even if there were the available indigenous anthropologists.

Thus even anthropologists are ethnocentric, more or less, to some irreducible residual degree. Given the proper scrutiny, the works of Herskovits himself will show residues of his U.S. enculturation in Belleview, Ohio; El Paso, xviiIntroduction

Texas; the University of Chicago; and Columbia University. He would have agreed to the general assertion of such residues and blind spots. No one, not even the anthropologist, is immune to the pervasive effects of enculturation. As to each specific bias discovered, he would have been surprised, but such effects are blind spots and do operate without awareness even in one who has set as his goal their elimination insofar as possible.

In closing this section it seems well to raise again the issue of the goal of objectivity. In my judgment, Herskovits' whole career was focused upon making the anthropological record more accurate, doing ethnography that was sensitive to the values and categories of the people whose views he was trying to record, and criticizing the work of others, particularly when it seemed biased by their own ethnocentrism. Thus he stubbornly challenged the orthodoxy of U.S. sociological scholarship which denied any heritages of African culture in contemporary Black culture in America. In this regard it is well to read John Szwed's appreciation (1972). As I see it, his emphasis on cultural relativism is integrally related to this same goal of increased objectivity.

I should like to state my own orientation toward Thomas Kuhn's relativism of scientific periods and paradigms. If, as some fear, Kuhn is advocating that we should give up the goal of objectivity and scientific progress as illusory, I do not follow him. If, instead, he is saying that we are overconfident, that we exaggerate the degree to which external truths have been revealed and underestimate the extent to which scientific decisions are made on biasing grounds of tradition, authority, ingroup solidarity, conformity pressures and the like, I agree, and see in his work the kind of criticism of our foundations which can increase the objectivity of science and help purge it of an irrational and self-delusional absolutism, although that task will never be perfectly completed. For the sciences of culture, the theory of cultural relativism can and should play a similar role.

enculturation and phenomenal absolutism

Herskovits' view of cultural relativism and ethnocentrism is intimately related to his understanding of enculturation. And this involves a hypothesis about the psychology of enculturated perceivers which we have found convenient to label phenomenal absolutism (Segall, Campbell and Herskovits, 1966). It is a hypothesis about the phenomenology of both the ordinary members of a culture and the social scientists.

A part of enculturation is direct, an inculcation of notions of right and wrong by focused punishment and exhortation. While in this type of learning process there is awareness of both norm and counternorm, in the end the result is a phenomenal absolutism, in which wrong acts appear immoral, abnormal, against the natural order of things. This is perceived not as a secondary subsequent act of judgment but, instead, phenomenally, as an immediately present objective attribute of the act. An example from another culture may help. In much of Africa, including the Arabic cultures, children are systematically trained to use their left hands after urination and defecation, and their right hands for eating. Harsh punishment and scandalized rejection may be used in such training, so that absent-minded substitution of the wrong hand is entirely eliminated. When such a person for the first time sees a European or an American put food in his mouth with his left hand, the sight is vividly disgusting, fully as revolting as it would be for us, for example, to see someone wipe his mouth with dirty toilet paper. Culture comes to be built into the automatic, uncritical, immediate contents of ordinary perceiving. We are unaware of the cultural sources of these judgments, unaware in fact that "judgments" are involved at all. Instead, the immorality is seen as a part of the event, as a part of the real world rather than an observer's judgment.

This understanding of the effects of enculturation is an

anthropological extension of the epistemological criticism of naïve realism. Plato's parable of the cave has this moral: such prisoners would of course take the shadows to be the real world, and we are in an analogous situation—our vision too is of shadows, not reality itself. For Herskovits, culture provides a part of the cave. Locke and Berkeley used the relativity of the perception of hot and cold—dependent upon the hand's prior adaptation—to similarly criticize our naïve realist tendency to perceive temperature as an attribute of things directly perceived. Here too we have the alternative uses of relativism, either to justify a total skepticism or solipsism, as in the case of Berkeley, or to support a critical realism, as in the case of Locke.

Enculturation, as I have said, proceeds in part by direct reward and punishment for reinforcing the pattern of performed alternatives, but most of the effect is still more subtle. Most of our knowledge of the world is vicarious, acquired through the observations and reports of others. For such knowledge there is no awareness of alternatives, such as the punished responses, for they have been eliminated from both the model's and mentor's repertoire. For such knowledge the channeling and the narrow limits provided by culture is totally invisible, but nonetheless profoundly important in molding our enculturated perceptions. Just as we are unaware of the wide bands of electromagnetic radiation excluded from our eyes, so are we oblivious to the alternative categorizations, evaluations and behavioral modes that our particular culture excludes or neglects.

It is perhaps appropriate to include some general comments on Herskovits' relations to psychology. He was in the 1920's an early anthropological user of psychological tests, and one of the first to challenge the psychologist's confident assumption that intelligence tests were measuring an innate, unlearned ability. Even though the most effective intelligence-test item was already recognized to be simple knowledge of vocabulary, few psychologists of that day were willing to acknowledge that individual differences in this obviously learned ability reflected individual differences in the opportunity to learn. Those who were aware of this possibility put on the cultural blinders again by regarding nonverbal intelligence tests as culture-free even if verbal ones were not. In fact, the nonverbal ones are probably more culturally biased. The Army Beta was the commonest example, and looking at it today, one feels that those who judged it culture-free must have been focusing only upon the intent and claims of the test without looking at all at the items. Herskovits made the following comments as early as 1927:

> Environmental background, cultural as well as natural, plays a tremendous part in whatever manifestations of innate intelligence an individual may give us through the results from the application of standardized tests to him. Thus it has been found that the American Indians usually rate somewhat lower in psychological tests than whites, and that this holds true when the tests are of a non-language variety, where the use of words is reduced to a minimum. But the consideration of the fact that the tests ordinarily used have been constructed by persons of a background different from that of the subjects is usually overlooked; and were there to be presented, for consideration as to what is wrong with a given picture, a six-clawed bear rather than a net-less tennis court, one wonders whether the city-dwelling white might not be at a loss rather than the Indians.

As we have noted above, with regard to the Oedipus complex, and in other essays (e.g., 1934; 1952), Herskovits made creative use of Freudian problems and themes. He was interested in and sympathetic to the use of projective tests, although he was full of illustrations as to how cultural specifics led inevitably to the presence of certain kinds of responses judged pathological by European norms.

Our joint work on cultural differences was preceded by an interesting debate on psychology. I argued that an underlying tenet of cultural relativism was the biological uniformity of man, and since all cultural differences were to be explained by different enculturation, these biological uniformities would include the processes of learning and perception. Herskovits did not disagree with my general line of argument but thought that I greatly underestimated the degree to which these basic psychological processes were influenced by culture. He would not have been surprised at the discovery, for example, that some groups in fact use quite different strategies of learning and teaching, to the extent that we require different learning theories for their accurate description. These learning strategies he would have seen as themselves the product of enculturation. In the case of visual perception, his own experience had convinced him—correctly, as it turned out (Segall, Campbell, and Herskovits, 1966)—that there were substantial differences. While the proper interpretation of these differences is still of lively concern in the literature of cross-cultural psychology, we were able to interpret them plausibly as being due to a uniform human nature interacting in lawful ways with different visual environments, that is, in a way consistent with both cultural relativism and the empiricist tradition in perception of Helmholtz and Brunswik.

ethical relativism

Herskovits' cultural relativism has received the most extensive opposition when applied to ethics and esthetics. There is a need for a thorough study of his critics by someone sympathetic to cultural relativism, one who is convinced of the ethnocentrism of anthropologists and philosophers and who has also mastered modern philosophical analysis of ethics and values. I am not so skilled, and can only offer my undereducated judgments in these regards as a temporary stopgap.

In the nineteenth century both the common man and philosophers in Europe and America assumed a specific form of ethical absolutism. This absolutism presumed the universal and absolute truth of the "highest" ethics of their Victorian-Hapsburgian culture. The task of the philosopher was to validate this judgment with perfected logic and philosophical systematization, but this task was never completed. Instead, the more meticulous standards of logical analysis and the greater sensitivity to points in the argument where questions were begged, or where unverifiable assumptions were made, turned the analysis of ethics into a negative discipline whose conclusions were that no analytic grounding of "oughts" or values was possible. The reasons for such a negative conclusion constitutes the major content of the course on ethics in the most rigorous philosophy departments today. Philosophers now back off a bit from this conclusion by affirming that it is not their concern to determine the correctness of any ethical or moral statement but rather to display what kind of a statement it is. They conclude that it is a statement of preference or of exclamation, not a descriptive statement for which the question of true or false is relevant.

This sounds much like the message of cultural relativism. At least, it should have a similar curb on ethnocentric moral absolutism. What is frustrating is that even philosophers of ethics who have this modern training forget it when mounting an attack on cultural relativism. They do so in a way that seems to reinforce the ethnocentric moral absolutism which persists in our culture by neglecting to mention the elegant if negative analyses within technical philosophy that point in the same direction. Their unsympathetic logical and linguistic nit-picking misses the intent of Herskovits' message.

Herskovits was neither an ethical nihilist, nor a thoroughgoing ethical relativist (such as technical philosophy can produce). Nor did he claim for his own or anyone else's ethical judgments an entailed truth, logical or revealed.

But he was a vigorous opponent of ethnocentric ethical absolutism, and as an anthropologist saw Western ethical prescriptions as ethnocentric even when offered by philosophers as the result of pure logic. Thus he was against all existing forms of ethical absolutism in practice. For his critics then to accuse him in turn of an ethical absolutism seems to me fundamentally misleading.

He regarded the burdening of European ethical absolutism on African ethical systems as a colonial imposition which deeply and wrongfully humiliated the conquered cultures and personalities. As a corrective—for well-intentioned anthropologists and world citizens—he recommended the guiding rule that one judge no culture's values and ethics as intrinsically superior to another's. This seems quite consistent with modern philosophical analysis. Yet his critics accuse him of believing he had analytically proven that the ethical systems of each culture were exactly equal in value. A better interpretation of his position is that such comparing was impossible and that ethnocentric pretenses to having done it in one's own culture's favor were to be rejected.

While I have scarcely begun to deal with all the issues and what seems to me to be mistaken criticisms of Herskovits' application of cultural relativism to the problems of ethics, I feel that they can be resolved by the recognition that he was an opponent of the still too pervasive ethnocentric moral absolutism. The message needs restating, both for the social scientist and for the general public, as there are no signs of abatement in the cultural and moral arrogance of those cultures with the greatest military and economic power.

Donald T. Campbell

Northwestern University
Evanston, Illinois
July 1971

Frances Herskovits died on May 4, 1972. The circumstances make it seem as though she had postponed dying until the editorial work on these pages was completed and they were safely in the mail to Toni Morrison at Random House. While she often protested her lack of formal training in anthropology, she had been in fact her husband's full-time fully professional colleague in research and writing since the 1930's. She allowed herself to be acknowledged as a coauthor only occasionally, as when the subject was literature or folklore in which she felt she had a trained competence (e.g., *Dahomean Narrative*).

In the nine years since Melville Herskovits' death, Frances continued a full-time scholarly career, devoted primarily to collecting, publishing and reprinting her husband's works, and to editing their unpublished Brazilian materials. She gave courses and lectures on the modern African novel, and intended a book on the subject once her husband's literary estate was completed.

D. C.

contents

one

culture:
definitions
and
values

on cultural values

. . . Before the turn of the century, . . . there were few doubts in the minds of scholars, and less among others, to disturb the conviction that our own way of life was superior to all others. . . . As time went on, however, and more knowledge of other civilizations became available, this complacency began to be challenged. . . . It would seem that a change of direction in our thinking is called for.

Many reasons have been advanced to account for the widespread critical discussion of our political and social system during the past year or two, especially the search for ultimate values and understandable goals by which to order our lives. That the war has had an unsettling effect on our thinking is self-evident; and this is the reason most often brought forward by those who attempt to account for the phenomenon. Yet in itself the war is not enough, for two decades ago a war of equal magnitude failed to produce either the kind of questions or the intensity of questioning of institutions and ways of life which confront us on all sides today. Mr. Archibald MacLeish has suggested[1] that blame must be laid on the scholars and

[1] "The Irresponsibles," *The Nation,* May 18, 1940, and "Postwar Writers and Pre-war Readers," *The New Republic,* June 10, 1940.

writers for the current uncertainties reflected in skepticism
as to the ends of democracy and the meaning of "an American way of life," and questions raised concerning the kind
of world order that is to be sought and the sort of social and
economic system that can best function so as most effectively to further human happiness. That blame may not go
unrecognized, though to lay it is also not enough; for the
confusion of issues and aims is too widespread to refer to
such *ad hoc* explanations. We must be alive to the deeper
currents, which, unheeded these many years, have affected
the movement of thought in our society in the same way as
we can see such currents to have influenced other societies
than our own, or to have been significant in earlier periods
of our own history. To emphasize that such deep currents
do most of their work before they bubble to the surface is
merely to underscore the importance of understanding their
nature and significance when they appear in our lives.

An analogy to be drawn between our present situation
and the experience of many primitive peoples during the
initial phases of their contact with European colonial expansion may be helpful in aiding us to comprehend the
urgency of our present quest for values. The explanation of
the reaction to conquest of such folk is sometimes phrased
by the native peoples themselves in terms of the superior
strength of foreign gods; sometimes in terms more familiar
to our own way of thought. This latter point of view, for
example, is expressed by a proverb of the West African
Dahomeans, which says: "War never goes against the
Whites, for they have the cartridges." Whatever the native
reason, it is not difficult to understand why primitive peoples
so often become demoralized at the onset of an assault by
an aggressive, differing ideology that does not neglect to
make the most of the sanctions that derive from the greater
effectiveness of their armaments. And it is just this situation
that is today faced by those who, in our society, are witness-
ing the underlying values of their own political and social
system assailed by an opposing ideology which validates

the way of life based on it by a vaunted superiority of power. Our analogy holds further, and in some detail. We may consider, for example, the techniques of aggression that have been employed by European governments during the years their empires were building. In some parts of the world, of course, it was merely a matter of establishing an administration to rule unresisting tribes. In a far greater number of cases, however, control over a reluctant people was preceded by an infiltration of European nationals—missionaries and traders, in the main—who, having settled in the far parts of the earth, became, perhaps unwittingly, the instruments of expansion. Sooner or later, certain prerogatives claimed by these persons came to be resented by the natives; protest eventuated in mistreatment or death of the Europeans; a punitive expeditionary force was dispatched; and the members of what had been an independent, local group found themselves members of a world empire. A third technique was of a similar efficacy; in these cases a group who were the rivals of those in power were encouraged to appeal to a ruler across the far waters for aid in establishing a régime of their own. In most instances, a protectorate followed on aid given, with eventual absorption as a colonial possession.

It is obvious that these are precisely the methods that have been employed in recent years by the totalitarian governments. The case of Ethiopia is a marginal one as concerns attitudes toward these events, since here it was a question of African expansion. But when in Albania, Czechoslovakia and Poland the method of rescuing an oppressed minority—the equivalent of the traders and missionaries among primitive peoples—was employed to implement territorial aggrandizement; or, as in Spain and Rumania, a faction other than that in power was aided in establishing itself as a prelude to physical or ideological infiltration, it began to be realized that what was possible in the remote corners of the world was also possible near to home. And those who in Europe experienced the overthrow of their countries and the accompanying attack on their traditions, or those who looked on at these events from afar, unable to stem the hostile drive, experienced the same sense of frustration that primitive folk experienced as they were absorbed into the empires of Europe and America.

As far as our own society is concerned, this kind of reaction is discernible in most of the questions that, though today asked more often and with greater insistence than in earlier years, have been increasingly raised ever since the onset of fascism eighteen years ago. In essence, they are to be subsumed in the question, "Can democracy work?"—a question that has appeared with ever greater frequency as the totalitarian governments, pressing their ideological warfare, have come to be recognized as less and less amenable to the international procedures that had rooted more deeply in our thinking than we had realized. It must also be remembered that an increasingly important precept in our belief has concerned efficiency in the industrial field. Yet in organization for war, and what seems to be organization for survival itself, nations which are openly hostile to our manner of life have manifested a degree of efficiency that has seemed impossible to achieve by those whose values are under attack.

Let us turn again for a moment to those underlying currents of thought, already referred to, whose power has gone unrealized but which have, nonetheless, always been potent in the historic stream of our culture. One of the proudest achievements of our civilization is the development of the scientific approach to the problems of life. Yet the essence of a philosophy based on the scientific method is constant questioning, continuous analysis, never-ending skepticism. Students of human civilization have with others given themselves to this stream of thought, and since the turn of the century all cultural values have been subject to constant investigation. This is in sharp contrast to what obtained before the turn of the century, when our culture had achieved a condition of stability that was only beginning to be disturbed. At that time, there were few doubts in the minds of scholars, and less among others, to disturb the conviction that our own way of life was superior to all others. Varying civilizations were coming to be known, but knowledge of them was principally useful as documentation of the hypothesis of an evolutionary development of culture, in terms of which the traditions of Euro-American societies were held to be the flowering of human experience in much the same way as man himself was held to represent the ultimate product of biological evolution.

As time went on, however, and more and more knowledge of other civilizations became available, this complacency began to be challenged. The defects in our own way of life were coming in for ever wider recognition; the adjustments made by individuals and groups constituting other societies came increasingly to be stressed. The theory of cultural evolution was the chief object of criticism, and with it the point of view that human civilizations could be evaluated on a scale of better and worse. By the end of the last war, reaction to this had reached its peak in the denial of the existence of all laws of social development. This position, and the related stress on the impossibility of evaluating cultures at all, received what was perhaps their ultimate expression in the following passage:

> If inherent necessity urges all societies along a fixed path, metaphysicians may still dispute whether the underlying force be divine or diabolic, but there can at least be no doubt as to which community is retarded and which accelerated in its movement toward the appointed goal. But no such necessity or design appears from the study of culture history. Cultures develop mainly through the borrowing due to chance contact. Our own civilization is even more largely than the rest a complex of borrowed traits. The singular order of events by which it has come into being provides no schedule for the itinerary of alien cultures. Hence the specious plea that a given people must pass through such and such a stage in *our* history before attaining this or that destination can no longer

be sustained. . . . In prescribing for other peoples a social programme we must always act on subjective grounds; but at least we can act unfettered by the pusillanimous fear of transgressing a mock-law of social evolution. Nor are the facts of culture history without bearing on the adjustment of our own future. To that planless hodge-podge, that thing of shreds and patches called civilization, its historian can no longer yield superstitious reverence. He will realize better than others the obstacles to infusing design into the amorphous product; but in thought at least he will not grovel before it in fatalistic acquiescence but dream of a rational scheme to supplant the chaotic jumble.[2]

The recognition of the impossibility of evaluating different cultures is today firmly established, and represents a great advance toward clarity of thought as concerns the nature and functioning of human civilization. Yet it would nonetheless seem that the pendulum, in swinging toward the position that it is impossible to evaluate differing cultures, has overshot its mark, since it has caused us to overlook how important are the values of a given culture to the people who live under it. Our civilization may indeed be recognized as in no way inherently superior to another when the two are compared in terms of what each means to its carriers; but this does not signify that every body of tradition is not regarded by those who live according to it as embodying the best way of life for them. And this is why the imposition of a foreign body of custom, backed by power, is so distressing an experience. A people may recognize ever so clearly that their own customs are best for them, yet no matter how deep their conviction of this, it is supremely difficult for them to meet the immediate argument posed by the possession of superior force.

Folk thus challenged are, moreover, caught between two conflicting points of view after their secondary adjustment to conquest has been achieved. They may recognize certain

2 R. H. Lowie, "Primitive Society," pp. 440–41.

benefits from the situation in which they are subject to a
foreign ruler, yet it continuously rankles that the direction
of their own affairs has been taken away from them. They
may recognize certain values in the ideology being pressed
on them, or to which they are otherwise exposed, and yet
cannot but feel that for them their own way of life must be
best. An example may be given from West Africa, as an
instance of a point of view that could also be cited from
many other parts of the primitive world. To the objective
observer—at least, to the objective observer from our
society—there can be little doubt that the imposed rule of
the French and British empires has brought many material
benefits. Slavery has been put down, and human sacrifice,
and warfare; and it is thus possible for a man to live and
trade where he will without fear of losing his personal
liberty or his life. The introduction of European medicine
has gone far to reduce the many deaths in childbirth, infant
mortality and such pernicious and widespread diseases as
sleeping-sickness, leprosy, and the like, which prevailed in
earlier days. Granting the economic exploitation of the
natives, it is at the present time neither as direct, as brutal
nor as extensive as was that of the displaced native dynas-
ties. Yet despite all this, the native African speaks longingly
of older times. He will grant that much has been brought
him by the European; yet he will nevertheless, when speaking frankly to one not connected with government, missions
or trading companies, express a nostalgia for the days when
European control was not present, if he is an old man; or,
if he is young, look forward to experiencing freedom from
that control. There is, indeed, some reason to feel that the
concept of freedom should be realistically redefined as the
right to be exploited in terms of the patterns of one's own
culture.

   It would seem that a change of direction in our thinking
is called for. Those who are seeking to understand the
nature of human civilization and its effect on the men and
women who live under it must separate the evaluation of

different cultures from the problem of value in culture. Granting that our own body of tradition is but one of many such bodies—just as we today recognize that man is but one unit of the biological series—it must not be forgotten that our society has developed values whose importance for us must be recognized and sustained if we are not to be bested in the ideological struggle that goes on about us, whether or not physical conflict accompanies it. Such analyses of fundamental values in our life as that contained in the recent discussion by Professor Carl Becker[3] indicate the kind of realization our society must come to, and quickly. It must be made clear that this does not imply that the constant questioning which is the essence of the scientific approach need be given over, or that we must abandon the constant search for better methods of social and economic adjustment, or the struggle against the inequalities and injustices that mark our social order. But in terms of the present world situation, we must clearly understand that it is possible to reaffirm in positive terms the fundamental tenets by which we live, even while we recognize the shortcomings in the organization and functioning of our society. On the ideological front, such a realization is essential if the values and goals by which we order our lives are to be maintained in the face of the present assault on them.

[3] "Some Generalities that Still Glitter," *Yale Review,* Vol. XXIX, No. 4, Summer, 1940.

cultural relativism and cultural values

Cultural relativism, in all cases, must be sharply distinguished from concepts of the relativity of individual behavior, which would negate all social controls over conduct. . . . The very core of cultural relativism is the social discipline that comes of respect for differences —mutual respect. Emphasis on the worth of many ways of life, not one, is an affirmation of the values in each culture. Such emphasis seeks to understand and to harmonize goals, not to judge and destroy those that do not dovetail with our own.

All peoples form judgments about ways of life different from their own. When systematic study is undertaken, comparison gives rise to classification, and scholars have devised many schemes for classifying ways of life. Moral judgments have been drawn regarding the ethical principles that guide the behavior and mold the value systems of different peoples. Their economic and political structures and their religious beliefs have been ranked in order of complexity, efficiency, desirability. Their art, music, and literary forms have been weighed.

It has become increasingly evident, however, that evaluations of this kind stand or fall with the acceptance of the premises from which they derive. In addition, many of the criteria on which judgment is based are in conflict, so that conclusions drawn from one definition of what is desirable will not agree with those based on another formulation.

A simple example will illustrate this. There are not many ways in which the primary family can be constituted. One man may live with one woman, one woman may have a number of husbands, one man may have a number of wives. But if we evaluate these forms according to their function of perpetuating the group, it is clear that they perform their essential tasks. Otherwise, the societies wherein they exist would not survive.

Such an answer will, however, not satisfy all those who have undertaken to study cultural evaluation. What of the moral questions inherent in the practice of monogamy as against polygamy, the adjustment of children raised in households where, for example, the mothers must compete on behalf of their offspring for the favors of a common husband? If monogamy is held to be the desired form of marriage, the responses to these questions are predetermined. But when we consider these questions from the point of view of those who live in polygamous societies, alternative answers, based on different conceptions of what is desirable, may be given.

Let us consider, for example, the life of a plural family in the West African culture of Dahomey.[1] Here, within a compound, live a man and his wives. The man has his own house, as has each of the women and her children, after the basic African principle that two wives cannot successfully inhabit the same quarters. Each wife in turn spends a native week of four days with the common husband, cooking his food, washing his cloths, sleeping in his house, and then making way for the next. Her children, however, remain in their mother's hut. With pregnancy, she drops out of this routine, and ideally, in the interest of her child's health and her own, does not again visit her husband until the child has been born and weaned. This means a period of from three

[1] Cf. M. J. Herskovits, 1938b, Vol. I, pp. 137–55, 300–51.

to four years, since infants are nursed two years and longer. The compound, made up of these households, is a co-operative unit. The women who sell goods in the market, or make pottery, or have their gardens, contribute to its support. This aspect, though of great economic importance, is secondary to the prestige that attaches to the larger unit. This is why one often finds a wife not only urging her husband to acquire a second spouse but even aiding him by loans or gifts to make this possible.

Tensions do arise between the women who inhabit a large compound. Thirteen different ways of getting married have been recorded in this society, and in a large household those wives who are married in the same category tend to unite against all others. Competition for the regard of the husband is also a factor, when several wives try to influence the choice of an heir in favor of their own sons. Yet all the children of the compound play together, and the strength of the emotional ties between the children of the same mother more than compensates for whatever stresses may arise between brothers and sisters who share the same father but are of different mothers. Cooperation, moreover, is by no means a mere formality among the wives. Many common tasks are performed in friendly unison, and there is solidarity in the interest of women's prerogatives, or where the status of the common husband is threatened.

We may now return to the criteria to be applied in drawing judgments concerning polygamous as against monogamous families. The family structure of Dahomey is obviously a complex institution. If we but consider the possible lines of personal relations among the many individuals concerned, we see clearly how numerous are the ramifications of reciprocal right and obligation of the Dahomean family. The effectiveness of the Dahomean family is, however, patent. It has, for untold generations, performed its function of rearing the young; more than this, the very size of the group gives it economic resources and a resulting stability that might well be envied by those who live under different systems of family organization. Moral values are always difficult to establish, but at least in this society marriage is clearly distinguished from casual sex relations and from prostitution, in its supernatural sanctions and in the prestige it confers, to say nothing of the economic obligations toward spouse and prospective offspring explicitly accepted by one who enters into a marriage.

Numerous problems of adjustment do present themselves in an aggregate of this sort. It does not call for much speculation to understand the plaint of the head of one large compound when he said: "One must be something of a diplomat if one has many wives." Yet the sly digs in proverb and song, and the open quarreling, involve no greater stress than is found in any small rural community where people are also thrown closely together for long periods of time. Quarrels between co-wives are not greatly different from disputes over the back fence between neighbors. And Dahomeans who know European culture, when they argue for their system, stress the fact that it permits the individual wife to space her children in a way that is in accord with the best precepts of modern gynecology.

Thus polygamy, when looked at from the point of view of those who practice it, is seen to hold values that are not apparent from the outside. A similar case can be made for monogamy, however, when it is attacked by those who are enculturated to a different kind of family structure. And what is true of a particular phase of culture such as this, is also true of others. Evaluations are *relative* to the cultural background out of which they arise.

2

Cultural relativism is in essence an approach to the question of the nature and role of values in culture. It represents a scientific, inductive attack on an age-old philosophical problem, using fresh, cross-cultural data, hitherto not available to scholars, gained from the study of the underlying value-systems of societies having the most diverse customs.

The principle of cultural relativism, briefly stated, is as follows: *Judgments are based on experience, and experience is interpreted by each individual in terms of his own enculturation.* Those who hold for the existence of fixed values will find materials in other societies that necessitate a re-investigation of their assumptions. Are there absolute moral standards, or are moral standards effective only as far as they agree with the orientations of a given people at a given period of their history? We even approach the problem of the ultimate nature of reality itself. Cassirer[2] holds that reality can only be experienced through the symbolism of language. Is reality, then, not defined and redefined by the ever-varied symbolisms of the innumerable languages of mankind?

Answers to questions such as these represent one of the most profound contributions of anthropology to the analysis of man's place in the world. When we reflect that such intangibles as right and wrong, normal and abnormal, beautiful and plain are absorbed as a person learns the ways of the group into which he is born, we see that we are dealing here with a process of first importance. Even the facts of the physical world are discerned through the enculturative screen, so that the perception of time, distance, weight, size, and other "realities" is mediated by the conventions of any given group.

No culture, however, is a closed system of rigid molds to which the behavior of all members of a society must conform. The psychological reality of culture tells us that a culture, as such, can *do* nothing. It is but the summation of the behavior and habitual modes of thought of the persons who make up a particular society. Though by learning and habit these individuals conform to the ways of the group into which they have been born, they nonetheless vary in their reactions to the situations of living they commonly meet. They vary, too, in the degree to which they desire change, as whole cultures vary. This is but another way in

2 E. Cassirer, 1944, p. 25.

which we see that culture is flexible and holds many possibilities of choice within its framework, and that to recognize the values held by a given people in no wise implies that these values are a constant factor in the lives of succeeding generations of the same group.

How the ideas of a people mediate their approach even to the physical world can be made plain by a few examples. Indians living in the southwestern part of the United States think in terms of *six* cardinal points rather than four. In addition to north, south, east and west, they include the directions "up" and "down." From the point of view that the universe is three dimensional, these Indians are entirely realistic. Among ourselves, even in airplane navigation, where three dimensions must be coped with as they need not by those who keep to the surface of the earth, we separate direction from height in instruments and in our thinking about position. We operate, conceptually, on two distinct planes. One is horizontal—"We are traveling ENE." One is vertical—"We are now cruising at 8000 feet."

Or take a problem in the patterning of sound. We accept the concept of the wave length, tune pianos in accordance with a mechanically determined scale, and are thus conditioned to what we call true pitch. Some persons, we say, have absolute pitch; that is, a note struck or sung at random will immediately be given its place in the scale—"That's B flat." A composition learned in a given key, when transposed, will deeply trouble such a person, though those who are musically trained but do not have true pitch will enjoy such a transposed work, if the *relation* of each note to every other has not been disturbed. Let us assume that it is proposed to study whether this ability to identify a note is an inborn trait, found among varying but small percentages of individuals in various societies. The difficulty of probing such a question appears immediately once we discover that but few peoples have fixed scales, and none other than ourselves has the concept of true pitch! Those living in cultures without mechanically tuned and true instruments are free to enjoy notes that are as much as a quarter-tone "off," as we would say. As for the patterned progressions in which the typical scales and modal orientations of any musical convention are set, the number of such systems, each of which is consistent within its own limits, is infinite.

The principle that judgments are derived from experience has a sure psychological foundation. This has been best expressed by Sherif in his development of the hypothesis of "social norms." His experiments are fundamental, and his accessory concept of the "frame of reference," the background to which experience is referred, has become standard in social psychology. Because of its importance for an understanding of cultural differences, we shall briefly describe the work he did in testing his hypothesis that "experience appears to depend always on *relations*."

The subjects were introduced into a dark room where a dim light appeared and disappeared when an electric key was pressed. Some subjects were brought into the room, first alone and later as members of groups, while others were exposed to the group situation before they were tested individually. Though the light was fixed, the autokinetic response to a situation like this is such that the subject perceives movement where there is none, since being in a room that is perfectly dark, he has no fixed point from which to judge motion. Judgments obtained from each subject *individually* conclusively demonstrated that individuals subjectively establish "a range of extent and a point (a standard or norm) within that range which is peculiar to the individual" when no objective standard is available to them, and that in repetitions of the experiment the established range is retained. In the group situation, diversity of individual judgments concerning the extent of movement by the light became gradually less. But each group establishes a norm peculiar to itself, after which the individual member "perceives the situation in terms of the range and norm that he brings from the group situation."

The general principle advanced on the basis of these

results and those of many other relevant psychological experiments may be given in the words of Sherif:

> The psychological basis of the established social norms, such as stereotypes, fashions, conventions, customs, and values, is the formation of common frames of reference as a product of the contact of individuals. Once such frames of reference are established and incorporated in the individual they enter as important factors to determine or modify his reactions to the situations he will face later—social, and even non-social, at times, especially if the stimulus field is not well structured.[3]

—that is, if the experience is one for which precedents in accustomed behavior are lacking.[4]

In extending Sherif's position in terms of the cross-cultural factor, but with stress laid on the influence of culture on the perceptive processes in general, Hallowell has stated:

> Dynamically conceived, perception is one of the basic integral functions of an on-going adjustment process on the part of any organism viewed as a whole. . . . In our species, therefore, what is learned and the content of acquired experience in one society as compared to another constitute important variables with reference to full understanding, explanation or prediction of the behavior of individuals who have received a *common* preparation for action.[5]

And he quotes from a paper by Bartlett, the psychologist: "Everybody now realizes that perceptual meanings, which

[3] M. Sherif, 1936, pp. 32, 92–106.

[4] A psychological basis for relativism, deriving from gestalt psychology, has been proposed by S. E. Asch, 1952, pp. 364–84. He fails to consider in this connection Sherif's critical experiment cited above. He does not seem adequately to have distinguished (1) between intracultural and cross-cultural relativism, and (2) between absolute values and universal aspects of culture.

[5] A. I. Hallowell, 1951, pp. 166–67.

have an enormous influence upon social life, vary from social setting to social setting, and the field anthropologist has a golden opportunity to study the limits of such variation and its importance."[6]

Numerous instances of how the norms posited by Sherif vary may be found in the anthropological literature. They are so powerful that they can flourish even in the face of what seems to the outsider an obvious, objectively verifiable fact. Thus, while recognizing the role of both father and mother in procreation, many peoples have conventions of relationship that count descent on but one side of the family. In such societies, it is common for incest lines to be so arbitrarily defined that "first cousins," as we would say, on the mother's side call each other brother and sister and regard marriage with one another with horror. Yet marriage within the same degree of biological relationship on the father's side may be held not only desirable, but sometimes mandatory. This is because two persons related in this way are by definition not considered blood relatives.

The very definition of what is normal or abnormal is relative to the cultural frame of reference. As an example of this, we may take the phenomenon of possession as found among African and New World Negroes. The supreme expression of their religious experience, possession, is a psychological state wherein a displacement of personality occurs when the god "comes to the head" of the worshipper. The individual thereupon is held to be the deity himself. This phenomenon has been described in pathological terms by many students whose approach is non-anthropological, because of its surface resemblance to cases in the records of medical practitioners, psychological clinicians, psychiatrists, and others. The hysteria-like trances, where persons, their eyes tightly closed, move about excitedly and presumably without purpose or design, or roll on the ground, muttering meaningless syllables, or go into a state where their bodies achieve complete rigidity, are not dfficult to equate

[6] *Ibid.*, p. 190.

with the neurotic and even psychotic manifestations of ab-
normality found in Euroamerican society.

Yet when we look beneath behavior to meaning, and
place such apparently random acts in their cultural frame
of reference, such conclusions become untenable. For *relative to the setting in which these possession experiences
occur, they are not to be regarded as abnormal at all,* much
less psychopathological. They are *culturally* patterned, and
often induced by learning and discipline. The dancing or
other acts of the possessed persons are so stylized that one
who knows this religion can identify the god possessing a
devotee by the behavior of the individual possessed.
Furthermore, the possession experience does not seem to be
confined to emotionally unstable persons. Those who "get
the god" run the gamut of personality types found in the
group. Observation of persons who frequent the cults, yet
who, in the idiom of worship "have nothing in the head"
and thus never experience possession, seems to show that
they are far less adjusted than those who do get possessed.
Finally, the nature of the possession experience in these cultures is so disciplined that it may only come to a given
devotee under particular circumstances. In West Africa and
Brazil the gods come only to those who have been designated in advance by the priest of their group, who lays his
hands on their heads. In Haiti, for an initiate not a member
of the family group giving a rite to become possessed at a
ceremony is considered extremely "bad form" socially and
a sign of spiritual weakness, evidence that the god is not
under the control of his worshipper.

The terminology of psychopathology, employed solely
for descriptive purposes, may be of some utility. But the
connotation it carries of psychic instability, emotional im-
balance, and departure from normality recommends the use
of other words that do not invite such a distortion of cultural reality. For in these Negro societies, the meaning this
experience holds for the people falls entirely in the realm
of understandable, predictable, *normal* behavior. This be-

havior is known and recognized by all members as an experience that may come to any one of them, and is to be welcomed not only for the psychological security it affords, but also for the status, economic gain, aesthetic expression, and emotional release it vouchsafes the devotee.

3

The primary mechanism that directs the evaluation of culture is *ethnocentrism*. Ethnocentrism is the point of view that one's own way of life is to be preferred to all others. Flowing logically from the process of early enculturation, it characterizes the way most individuals feel about their own culture, whether or not they verbalize their feeling. Outside the stream of Euroamerican culture, particularly among nonliterate peoples, this is taken for granted and is to be viewed as a factor making for individual adjustment and social integration. For the strengthening of the ego, identification with one's own group, whose ways are implicitly accepted as best, is all-important. It is when, as in Euroamerican culture, ethnocentrism is rationalized and made the basis of programs of action detrimental to the well-being of other peoples that it gives rise to serious problems.

The ethnocentrism of nonliterate peoples is best illustrated in their myths, folk tales, proverbs, and linguistic habits. It is manifest in many tribal names whose meaning in their respective languages signifies "human beings." The inference that those to whom the name does not apply are outside this category is, however, rarely, if ever, explicitly made. When the Suriname Bush Negro, shown a flashlight, admires it and then quotes the proverb: "White man's magic isn't black man's magic," he is merely reaffirming his faith in his own culture. He is pointing out that the stranger, for all his mechanical devices, would be lost in the Guiana jungle without the aid of his Bush Negro friends.

A myth of the origin of human races, told by the Cherokee Indians of the Great Smoky Mountains, gives another

instance of this kind of ethnocentrism. The Creator fash-
ioned man by first making and firing an oven and then,
from dough he had prepared, shaping three figures in human form. He placed the figures in the oven and waited for
them to get done. But his impatience to see the result of
this, his crowning experiment in the work of creation, was
so great that he removed the first figure too soon. It was
sadly underdone—pale, an unlovely color, and from it
descended the white people. His second figure had fared
well. The timing was accurate, the form, richly browned,
that was to be the ancestor of the Indians, pleased him in
every way. He so admired it, indeed, that he neglected to
take out of the oven the third form, until he smelled it
burning. He threw open the door, only to find this last one
charred and black. It was regrettable, but there was nothing
to be done; and this was the first Negro.[7]

This is the more usual form that ethnocentrism takes
among many peoples—a gentle insistence on the good qualities of one's own group, without any drive to extend this
attitude into the field of action. With such a point of view,
the objectives, sanctioned modes of behavior, and value
systems of peoples with whom one's own group comes into
contact can be considered in terms of their desirability, then
accepted or rejected without any reference to absolute standards. That differences in the manner of achieving commonly sought objectives may be permitted to exist without
a judgment being entered on them involves a reorientation
in thought for those in the Euroamerican tradition, because
in this tradition, a difference in belief or behavior too often
implies something is worse, or less desirable, and must be
changed.

The assumption that the cultures of nonliterate peoples

[7] This unpublished myth was told F. M. Olbrechts of Brussels,
Belgium, in the course of field work among the Cherokee. His having made it available is gratefully acknowledged. A similar tale has
been recorded from the Albany Cree, at Moose Factory, according
to information received from F. Voget.

are of inferior quality is the end product of a long series of developments in our intellectual history. It is not often recalled that the concept of progress, that strikes so deep into our thinking, is relatively recent. It is, in fact, a unique product of our culture. It is a part of the same historic stream that developed the scientific tradition and that developed the machine, thus giving Europe and America the final word in debates about cultural superiority. "He who makes the gun-powder wields the power," runs a Dahomean proverb. There is no rebuttal to an argument, backed by cannon, advanced to a people who can defend their position with no more than spears, or bows and arrows, or at best a flint-lock gun.

With the possible exception of technological aspects of life, however, the proposition that one way of thought or action is better than another is exceedingly difficult to establish on the grounds of any universally acceptable criteria. Let us take food as an instance. Cultures are equipped differently for the production of food, so that some peoples eat more than others. However, even on the subsistence level, there is no people who do not hold certain potential foodstuffs to be unfit for human consumption. Milk, which figures importantly in our diet, is rejected as food by the peoples of southeastern Asia. Beef, a valued element of the Euroamerican cuisine, is regarded with disgust by Hindus. Nor need compulsions be this strong. The thousands of cattle that range the East African highlands are primarily wealth to be preserved, and not a source of food. Only the cow that dies is eaten—a practice that, though abhorrent to us, has apparently done no harm to those who have been following it for generations.

Totemic and religious taboos set up further restrictions on available foodstuffs, while the refusal to consume many other edible and nourishing substances is simply based on the enculturative conditioning. So strong is this conditioning that prohibited food consumed unwittingly may induce such a physiological reaction as vomiting. All young animals provide succulent meat, but the religious abhorrence of the young pig by the Mohammedan is no stronger than the secular rejection of puppy steaks or colt chops by ourselves. Ant larvae, insect grubs, locusts—all of which have caloric values and vitamin content—when roasted or otherwise cooked, or even when raw, are regarded by many peoples as delicacies. We never eat them, however, though they are equally available to us. On the other hand, some of the same peoples who feed on these with gusto regard substances that come out of tin cans as unfit for human consumption.

4

Cultures are sometimes evaluated by the use of the designations "civilized" and "primitive." These terms have a deceptive simplicity, and attempts to document the differences implied in them have proved to be of unexpected difficulty. The distinctions embedded in this set of opposed terms are, however, of special importance for us. "Primitive" is the word commonly used to describe the peoples with whom anthropologists have been traditionally most concerned, the groups whose study has given cultural anthropology most of its data.

The word "primitive" came into use when anthropological theory was dominated by an evolutionary approach that equated living peoples, outside the stream of European culture, with the first human inhabitants of the earth, who may justifiably be called "primitive" in the etymological sense of the word. It is quite another matter to call present-day peoples by the same term. In other words, *there is no justification for regarding any living group as our contemporary ancestors.*

The conception implicit in such usage colors many of the judgments we draw about the ways of life of native peoples with whom the expansion of Europe and America has brought us into contact. When we speak or write of the living customs of American Indian or African or South Seas peoples as being in some way earlier than our own, we are treating their cultures as though they were unchanging. As we have seen, however, one of the basic generalizations about culture is that no body of custom is static. No matter how conservative a people may be, we find on investigation that their way of life is not the same as it was in earlier times. Remains of the past dug from the earth give ample evidence that continuous, though perhaps slow, change was the rule. Hence we must conclude that no group that exists today lives either as its ancestry or our own lived.

With time, the word "primitive" gathered other connotations that are evaluative rather than descriptive. Primitive peoples are said to have simple cultures. One widely accepted hypothesis holds that they are unable to think except in terms of a special kind of mental process. Perhaps as a summation of all these, it is asserted that primitive cultures are inferior in quality to the historic civilizations. Such terms as "savage" or "barbarous" are applied to them in this sense, deriving from a presumed evolutionary sequence of "savagery," "barbarism," and "civilization."

One example can be taken from the extended investigation into the nature and processes of change in civilization by the historian A. J. Toynbee. He speaks of those peoples outside the "base-line" of "the modern Western national community" as the "external proletariat," whose contacts with a "civilization" tend to debase it. In the United States, the "external proletariat" was the Indian. The powerful influence exerted by the Indian in modifying the ways of life of the American frontiersmen, through the "barbarization" of European custom, as he terms it, astonishes Toynbee. Many similar instances concern him, as, for example, the influence of the "barbarians of West Africa" on modern art.

> This triumph of a Negro art in the northern states of
> America and in the western countries of Europe represents a
> . . . signal victory for Barbarism. . . . To the layman's eye the

flight to Benin [a center of African art] and the flight to
Byzantium seem equally unlikely to lead the latter-day Western artist to the recovery of his lost soul.[8]

For all the philosophical grounding and immense scholarship in Toynbee's massive work, it is apparent that these
attitudes but demonstrate the biases of the writer. Borrowing is a basic mechanism of cultural interchange, and results
inevitably from any contact of peoples. Quite as often as not
a dominant group are deeply influenced by the customs of
those over whom they rule. Toynbee's astonishment is based
on what he calls the "initial disparity in spiritual culture"
between the "incomers from Europe" and the Indians. Evidence is vast that the portrayal of the savage as a creature
living in anarchism, without moral restraint and without sensibilities, is a vulgar caricature. What happened in America
does not "astonish" the scientific student of culture. The
mutual borrowing by colonists of Indian customs and by
Indians of European custom should be taken for granted,
despite disparity in size of the groups in power and even in
capacity to survive under attack.

Some of the characteristics held to distinguish "primitive"
or "savage" ways of life are open to serious question. What,
for example, is a "simple" culture? The aboriginal Aus-
tralians, customarily held to be one of the most "primitive"
peoples on earth, have a kinship terminology and a method
of counting relationship based on it so complex that for
many years it defied the attempts of students to analyze it.
It puts to shame our own simple series of relationship terms,
where we do not even distinguish between paternal and
maternal grandparents, or older or younger brother, and
call literally dozens of relatives by the same word, "cousin."
The natives of Peru, before the Spanish conquest, made
tapestries of finer weave, dyed in colors less subject to deter-
ioration, than any of the deservedly prized Gobelin tapestries. The world-view of the Africans, which has so much

[8] A. J. Toynbee, 1934–9, Vol. V, pp. 373, 479–80, 482.

in common with the Hellenic world-view, or the epic myths of the Polynesians, impress their complexities on all who take the trouble to become acquainted with them. These, and untold other examples, show that "primitive" folk do not have ways of life that are necessarily simple. Such instances also demonstrate that "primitive" peoples are neither childlike, nor naïve, nor unsophisticated, to cite favored adjectives that are often used by those who have either had no first-hand experience with such peoples, or have not taken the trouble to come to know them through reading contemporary accounts of their ways of life.

That "primitive" peoples fail to distinguish between reality and the supernatural, as the theory concerning their presumed "prelogical mentality," put forward by the French philosopher, L. Lévy-Bruhl[9] held, is similarly proved untenable by the facts. For the facts about many cultures demonstrate that all peoples *at times* think in terms of objectively provable causation, just as *at times,* they indulge in explanations that relate a fact to an *apparent* cause. What the comparative study of culture, based on first-hand contact with many peoples, has taught is that all people think in terms of certain premises that are taken for granted. Granted the premises, the logic is inescapable.

Most of the life of any people is lived on a plane where ideas of causation or explanations of the universe enter but rarely. In these homely aspects of life, what we would call a "hard-headed sense of reality" is manifested. Thus, except for the names, the following passage from the autobiography of a Navaho Indian, telling of the last illness of the

[9] Lévy-Bruhl, 1923, 1926. It is a tribute to the intellectual honesty and greatness of this scholar that when convinced by the data of the invalidity of this concept, he was willing to renounce it, though it had for many years been identified with his name. Before his death in 1940 he set down his reasons why he no longer regarded the idea of "primitive mentality" as valid, in notebooks posthumously published, where he sketched his ideas for his next book. (Cf. L. Lévy-Bruhl, 1949, pp. 49–50, 61–62, 129, 157.)

narrator's father, rings entirely familiar to ears accustomed
to the reasoning of a mechanistic tradition.

> Old man Hat said, "I don't think I'll get well. I don't think
> I'll live long. That's how I feel about myself, because of the
> way I look now. I look at myself, and there's nothing on me,
> no flesh on me any more, nothing but skin and bones. That's
> why I don't think I'll live long. . . . About eating, you know
> I can't eat anything that's hard, only things that are soft,
> something I can swallow. But I don't take much, only two or
> three swallows. But I drink plenty of water." Choclays Kins-
> man said, "Even though you're that way, my older brother,
> you'd better keep eating all the time. By doing that it'll give
> you strength. If you don't you'll surely get weak. Even though
> you're so weak now and not able to eat, try to eat and
> swallow something. Somehow or other you might get over
> your illness. If you quit eating food, then you'll sure be
> gone." That's what he said, and then he left, and I went out
> with the herd.[10]

We readily recognize the common-sense reasoning in this
passage. Let us look at another instance where the explanation of a phenomenon is based on a premise at variance with
what we regard as scientific fact. We take as our instance a
widely spread West African belief that the youngest child
is sharper of wit than his older brothers and sisters. This
belief is based on the observation that children tend to
resemble their parents, and the fact, further observed, that
as a man or woman grows older, he grows in experience.
These facts may seen unrelated to us, but not to the West
African. He reasons that greater age permits them to pass
on to their younger, and especially their youngest child, a
surer, more alert awareness. Such a child is thus expected
to surpass his older siblings in astuteness. The *logic* of this
reasoning is impeccable. It is with the *premises* that we must
differ, if we would challenge the conclusion.

In truth, it must be recognized that all human beings

[10] W. Dyk, 1938, p. 269.

think "prelogically" at times.[11] The pattern of scientific thought on which we pride ourselves is followed by relatively few persons in our culture. Nor do these persons think logically all the time. When they are actually at work in their laboratories, they employ the rigorous logic of science. But outside it, other categories of reasoning come into play, as when a scientist thinks in terms of "luck" in social ventures or pays homage to some symbolic representation of power or grace.

The assumption that all those called "primitives" or "savages" have many characteristics in common when they are contrasted to "civilized" peoples is another expression of the tendency to evaluate cultures. In actuality, the range of behavior among all those many peoples termed "primitive" is much greater than among those few called "civilized." Thus we find "primitive" peoples with money economies like "civilized" ones, others who practice barter, and still others who are economically self-sufficient and do not trade at all. Numerous marriage forms and family types, including monogamy, are found in "primitive" societies. Some have totemism, but more do not. Some have a clan system, many do not. Some count descent through both parents, as we do; some count it only on the father's side; some count it on the mother's. And so we could continue with institutions of all kinds, and much customary behavior, meeting always with variety. Whatever the word "primitive" means, then, it comprehends no unity of custom, tradition, belief, or institution.

In anthropological works, the words "primitive" or "savage" do not have the connotation they possess in such a work as Toynbee's or in other non-anthropological writings. Anthropologists merely use the word "primitive" or "savage" to denote peoples outside the stream of Euroamerican

[11] This point of view was also accepted by Lévy-Bruhl, who in his posthumously published notebooks states: "From a strictly logical point of view, no difference between primitive mentality and our own can be established."—L. Lévy-Bruhl, 1949, p. 70.

culture who do not possess written languages. By reiterating this meaning, it was hoped that it would no longer convey such meanings as simple or naïve, or serve as a catchall to describe, except in the simple matter of absence of writing, such differing civilizations as those of the Siberian reindeer herders or the Lunda Empire of the Congo.

Several terms to replace "primitive" have been suggested. "Non-historic," which is one of these, implies that absence of written history is the equivalent of having no history at all, which, of course, cannot be said of any people who exist in time. "Pre-literate" has found more favor, but here the objection is that the prefix *pre-*, derived from the "contemporary ancestor" concept, implies that peoples without written languages are at a stage antecedent to the one in which, presumably, they will devise, or at least acquire, writing. The third form, *nonliterate,* simply describes the fact that these peoples do not have written languages. It is sometimes confused with "illiterate," but the use of this word should be guarded against, since it carries a distinct connotation of inferiority in ability or opportunity or both. "Nonliterate," because it is colorless, conveys its meaning unambiguously and is readily applicable to the data it seeks to delimit, is thus to be preferred to all the other terms we have considered.

The question that inevitably comes to mind is whether any single criterion such as the presence or absence of writing is adequate to describe the many peoples it seeks to comprehend. Its adequacy has been indicated by its demonstrated usefulness, though it is evident that no one characteristic is ideally satisfactory for designating entire cultures. It is to be recognized that certain other characteristics commonly go with an absence of writing. Nonliterate peoples are found on observation to be relatively more isolated, to have smaller numbers, and to be less addicted to rapid change in their sanctioned modes of behavior than those that have writing. In recent generations, moreover, Euroamerican culture has had to be set off not only from

nonliterate cultures but from the literate cultures outside
Europe and America as well, because of the presence in
European and American culture of a technology based on
power-driven machinery and the scientific tradition. But it
must be recognized that none of these differences, except
perhaps this last, is as clearly manifest as is the presence or
absence of writing.

5

Before we terminate our discussion of cultural relativism,
it is important that we consider certain questions that are
raised when the cultural-relativistic position is advanced.
"It may be true," it is argued, "that human beings live in
accordance with the ways they have learned. These ways
may be regarded by them as best. A people may be so
devoted to these ways that they are ready to fight and die
for them. In terms of survival value, their effectiveness may
be admitted, since the group that lives in accordance with
them continues to exist. But does this mean that all systems
of moral values, all concepts of right and wrong, are
founded on such shifting sands that there is no need for
morality, for proper behavior, for ethical codes? Does not
a relativistic philosophy, indeed, imply a negation of these?"

To hold that values do not exist because they are relative
to time and place is to fall prey to a fallacy that results from
a failure to take into account the positive contribution of
the relativistic position. For cultural relativism is a philosophy that recognizes the values set up by every society to
guide its own life and that understands their worth to those
who live by them, though they may differ from one's own.
Instead of underscoring differences from absolute norms
that, however objectively arrived at, are nonetheless the
product of a given time or place, the relativistic point of
view brings into relief the validity of every set of norms for
the people who have them, and the values these represent.

It is essential, in considering cultural relativism, that we
differentiate absolutes from universals. *Absolutes* are fixed,

and, as far as convention is concerned, are not admitted to have variation, to differ from culture to culture, from epoch to epoch. *Universals,* on the other hand, are those least common denominators to be extracted from the range of variation that all phenomena of the natural or cultural world manifest. If we apply the distinction between these two concepts in drawing an answer to the points raised in our question, these criticisms are found to lose their force. To say that there is no absolute criterion of values or morals, or even, psychologically, of time or space, does not mean that such criteria, in differing *forms,* do not comprise universals in human culture. Morality is a universal, and so is enjoyment of beauty, and some standard for truth. The many forms these concepts take are but products of the particular historical experience of the societies that manifest them. In each, criteria are subject to continuous questioning, continuous change. But the basic conceptions remain, to channel thought and direct conduct, to give purpose to living.

In considering cultural relativism, also, we must recognize that it has three quite different aspects, which in most discussions of it tend to be disregarded. One of these is methodological, one philosophical, and one practical. As it has been put:

As method, relativism encompasses the principle of our science that, in studying a culture, one seeks to attain as great a degree of objectivity as possible; that one does not judge the modes of behavior one is describing, or seek to change them. Rather, one seeks to understand the sanctions of behavior in terms of the established relationships within the culture itself, and refrains from making interpretations that arise from a preconceived frame of reference. Relativism as philosophy concerns the nature of cultural values, and, beyond this, the implications of an epistemology that derives from a recognition of the force of enculturative conditioning in shaping thought and behavior. Its practical aspects involve the application—the practice—of the philosophical principles derived from this method, to the wider, cross-cultural scene.

We may follow this reasoning somewhat further.

In these terms, the three aspects of cultural relativism can be regarded as representing a logical sequence which, in a broad sense, the historical development of the idea has also followed. That is, the methodological aspect, whereby the data from which the epistemological propositions flow are gathered, ordered and assessed, came first. For it is difficult to conceive of a systematic theory of cultural relativism—as against a generalized idea of live-and-let-live—without the pre-existence of the massive ethnographic documentation gathered by anthropologists concerning the similarities and differences between cultures the world over. Out of these data came the philosophical position, and with the philosophical position came speculation as to its implications for conduct.[12]

Cultural relativism, in all cases, must be sharply distinguished from concepts of the relativity of individual behavior, which would negate all social controls over conduct. Conformity to the code of the group is a requirement for any regularity in life. Yet to say that we have a right to expect conformity to the code of our day for ourselves does not imply that we need expect, much less impose, conformity to our code on persons who live by other codes. The very core of cultural relativism is the social discipline that comes of respect for differences—of mutual respect. Emphasis on the worth of many ways of life, not one, is an affirmation of the values in each culture. Such emphasis seeks to understand and to harmonize goals, not to judge and destroy those that do not dovetail with our own. Cultural history teaches that, important as it is to discern and study the parallelisms in human civilizations, it is no less important to discern and study the different ways man has devised to fulfill his needs.

That it has been necessary to consider questions such

---

[12] M. J. Herskovits, 1951, p. 24.

as have been raised reflects an enculturative experience wherein the prevalent system of morals is not only consciously inculcated, but its exclusive claim to excellence emphasized. There are not many cultures, for example, where a rigid dichotomy between good and evil, such as we have set up, is insisted upon. Rather it is recognized that good and evil are but the extremes of a continuously varied scale between these poles that produces only different degrees of greyness. We thus return to the principle enunciated earlier, that "judgments are based on experience, and experience is interpreted by each individual in terms of his enculturation." In a culture where absolute values are stressed, the relativism of a world that encompasses many ways of living will be difficult to comprehend. Rather, it will offer a field day for value judgments based on the degree to which a given body of customs resembles or differs from those of Euroamerican culture.[13]

Once comprehended, however, and employing the field methods of the scientific student of man, together with an awareness of the satisfactions the most varied bodies of custom yield, this position gives us a leverage to lift us out of the ethnocentric morass in which our thinking about ultimate values has for so long bogged down. With a means of probing deeply into all manner of differing cultural orientations, of reaching into the significance of the ways of living of different peoples, we can turn again to our own culture with fresh perspective, and an objectivity that can be achieved in no other manner.

[13] Instances of the rejection of relativism on philosophical grounds, by writers who attempt to reconcile the principle of absolute values with the diversity of known systems, are to be found in E. Vivas, 1950, pp. 27–42, and D. Bidney, 1953a, pp. 689–95, 1953b, pp. 423–29. Both of these discussions, also, afford examples of the confusion that results when a distinction is not drawn between the methodological, philosophical, and practical aspects of relativism. For a critical consideration of relativism that, by implication, recognizes these differences, see R. Redfield, 1953, pp. 144 ff.

tender- and tough-minded anthropology and the study of values in culture

. . . make no mistake, cultural relativism is a "tough-minded" philosophy. It requires those who hold to it to alter responses that arise out of some of the strongest enculturative conditioning to which they have been exposed, the enthnocentrisms implicit in the particular value-systems of their society. . . . The questions raised by the problem of the scientist as citizen are not only being faced by anthropologists, but by all scientists and, indeed, by scholars in the humanities as well. Admittedly, it is especially difficult in the disciplines where man studies man.

The problem of values in culture, long implicit in anthropology, has been precipitated out as a question for analysis and discussion by the formulation of the principle of cultural relativism. The concept, in its undifferentiated state, is really nothing new. Many years ago Boas, for example, writing to the problems of his day, could say, "It is somewhat difficult for us to recognize that the value which we attribute to our own civilization is due to the fact that we participate in this civilization, and that it has been controlling all our actions since the time of our birth; but it is certainly conceivable that there may be other civilizations, based perhaps on different traditions and on a different equilibrium of emotion and reason, which are of no less value than ours, although it may be impossible for us to appreciate their values without having grown up under their influence."[1] Or, in 1934, Ruth Benedict could write: "No man ever looks at the world with pristine eyes. Even in his philosophical probings he cannot go behind these stereotypes; his very concepts of the true and the false will still have reference to his particular traditional customs."[2]

In these terms, the significance of the differences between peoples, as concerns the relation between custom and sanction, reduced itself to a question of cultural superiority or inferiority. To this question, American anthropologists, at least, have given a clear and unequivocal answer; in the vast majority, we are agreed that objective indices of cultural inferiority and superiority cannot be established.

The publication of the "Statement on Human Rights"[3] submitted by the American Anthropological Association to the United Nations in 1947, and the analysis of relative values in culture in *Man and His Works*[4] published a year later, brought to the foreground of consciousness some of the broader philosophical and practical implications of this position, that had come to be accepted without too much questioning. And since, in the world of free scholarship it is through discussion that concept and theory are clarified, this paper represents an attempt to analyze some of the reactions which these presentations stimulated, and thus to carry our thinking on this important problem of values in culture a step farther.

2

Many years ago, William James, with his gift for homely phrasing, suggested that people could be divided into those

[1] *The Mind of Primitive Man* (first edition, New York, 1911), p. 208.
[2] *Patterns of Culture* (New York, 1934), p. 2.
[3] *American Anthropologist*, vol. 49, pp. 539–43, 1947.
[4] Melville J. Herskovits, *Man and His Works* (New York, 1948), pp. 61–78, 653–55.

who are "tender-minded" and who are "tough-minded."[5]
We need not here go into the way in which James char-
acterized the modes of thought of those who fitted his
categories, for he himself set them forth merely to illuminate his concepts. He was too wise a man to accept any
polar type as characteristic of any individual, and he made
this quite clear in his discussion. The initial trait he set
down for each type—the tender-minded "going by 'principle' " (rationalistic) and the tough-minded "going by
'facts' " (empiricist)—is enough for our purpose. For whatever the merits of his specifications, the fact remains that he
did put his finger on two kinds of thought that set off
persons and, as has been increasingly recognized, also set
off ideas from each other—designations so shrewd and vivid
that it is easy to understand why they caught on and moved
into common speech.

They are particularly applicable, it would seem, in considering the problem of cultural relativism; for make no
mistake, cultural relativism is a "tough-minded" philosophy.
It requires those who hold to it to alter responses that arise
out of some of the strongest enculturative conditioning to
which they have been exposed, the ethnocentrisms implicit
in the particular value-systems of their society. In the case
of anthropologists, this means following the implications of
data which, when opposed to our enculturated system of
values, sets up conflicts not always easy to resolve.

There are other reasons why the acceptance of cultural
relativism by anthropologists has meant holding to a tough-
minded point of view. One friendly critic of our discipline,
more witty than wise in his assertion, has defined an anthropologist as a person who respects every culture-pattern but
his own. Like any other *bon mot,* it is true and not true; but
the part that is true is to the point here. That is, anthropologists, as with any members of any society, live in a

[5] *Pragmatism, a New Name for Some Old Ways of Thinking*
(New York, 1907), pp. 11 ff.

climate of opinion whose influence is so strong and yet so
subtle that it is only by an effort of will that one becomes
aware of it. And on this point the present-day climate of
opinion in the United States—and in this paper we are concerned only with American anthropologists, since cultural
relativism has not as yet evoked any responses from elsewhere in the world—is quite confused. For despite the
deep-seated feeling we hold to in this country that the ideas
and ways of the Western world are best for mankind, the
climate of opinion at the same time maintains a firm belief
in the importance and desirability of political freedom for
all people. This duality of sanction has set up powerful
ambivalences that come into play when a relativistic point
of view is put forth concerning the validity of the differing
value-systems to be found in the myriad cultures of mankind.

Moreover, discussions of relativism seem sometimes to be
facing in more than one direction. This is because the relativistic position has of itself three quite different aspects;
distinctions that heretofore have tended to go unrecognized.
One of these aspects, that is, is methodological, one is
philosophical, and one practical.[6]

As method, relativism encompasses the principle of our
science that, in studying a culture, one seeks to attain as
great a degree of objectivity as possible; that one does not
judge the modes of behavior one is describing, or seek to
change them. Rather, one seeks to understand the sanctions
of behavior in terms of the established relationships within
the culture itself, and refrains from making interpretations
that arise from a preconceived frame of reference. Relativism as philosophy concerns the nature of cultural values

[6] Bernard Siegel (*Currents of Anthropological Theory and Value
Concepts,* Southwestern Journal of Anthropology, vol. 4, pp. 199–
210, 1948) adumbrates this tri-partite approach, but did not differentiate relativism in method, philosophy, and practice except by
inference. See especially pages 203–04. This division is also referred to on p. 22.—Ed.

and, beyond this, the implications of an epistemology that derives from a recognition of the force of enculturative conditioning in shaping thought and behavior. Its practical aspects involve the application—the practice—of the philosophical principles derived from the method, to the wider, cross-cultural world scene.

In these terms, the three aspects of cultural relativism can be regarded as representing a logical sequence which, in a broad sense, the historical development of the idea has also followed. That is, the methodological aspect, whereby the data from which the epistemological propositions flow are gathered, ordered, and assessed, came first. For it is difficult to conceive of a systematic theory of cultural relativism—as against a generalized idea of live-and-let-live—without the preexistence of the massive ethnographic documentation gathered by anthropologists concerning the similarities and differences between cultures the world over. Out of these data came the philosophical position, and with the philosophical position came speculation as to its implications for conduct.

3

Kroeber, in a recent summary of developments in anthropology during the last half-century,[7] initially stresses what would seem to be the methodological aspect of the relativistic approach to the study of culture. "Anthropologists now agree," he states, "that each culture must be examined in terms of its own structure and values, instead of being rated by the standards of some other civilization exalted as absolute—which in practice of course is always our own civilization." In the sentences that follow, he moves to the philosophical implications of the methodological precept: "This anthropological principle leads, it is true, to a relativistic or pluralistic philosophy—a belief in many values

---

[7] *Anthropology* (Scientific American, vol. 183, pp. 87–94, Sept., 1950).

rather than a single value system. But why not," he continues, "if the facts so demand? The domain of life is certainly pluralistic, what with a million species on our own
small planet. I have not heard of biologists bewailing the
diversity of species. Rather, they try to find some kind of
order in it."

At this point, however, Kroeber injects a new note, and,
in doing so, exemplifies the need for clarification of the
relativistic approach in its varied implications. For the note
that he injects lies neither in the modality of method, nor
philosophy, nor practice. "Quite correspondingly," he says,
"anthropologists try to treat all cultures, including our own
civilization, as parts of nature—without preferential and
partisan priorities. This may be distasteful to partisans, but
it is certainly the only way of science." This is the note to
which he returns at the conclusion of his article, where, in
describing "the common attitude" that has held anthropologists together, despite their special interests, and has
made for an "integrated attack on the biological, the socio-
cultural and the linguistic phenomena presented by man,"
he says, "This attitude is expressed by the principle of the
relativistic approach. It might equally be called the naturalistic approach."

It is not within the compass of this discussion to consider
whether the study of culture lies in the domain of the
natural sciences or the social sciences—or, indeed, considering the philosophical aspects of the question of our
concern, whether it lies in the realm of the humanities. For
our purpose, it is enough to point out how, in a single
discussion, relativism can variously be conceived.

The important thing to realize is that, in his method, the
present-day field worker accepts the relativistic principle as
a basic postulate. Granting we have not given the attention
to method this important phase of our work deserves, nonetheless such discussions of it as we have are always based on
the premise that objectivity is a primary requirement of our
scientific endeavors. In our field work we ask questions;

and if we challenge a response, it is a calculated challenge, to elicit a reaction that will reveal an underlying value, or a rationalization of the kind that tells one much about a value-judgment. We couch our findings within the frame of reference set by the culture we are studying; in short, the behavior we concern ourselves with is analyzed in terms of its relevance to the total structure of cultural form and sanction of which it is a part.

4

It is inevitable that the area of disagreement between anthropologists should widen as we moved from the methodological to the philosophical implications of cultural relativism, though published statements of disagreement with the relativistic philosophy are not easy to find. We may take as an example the most explicit anthropological demurrer that has thus far appeared as an example of the line criticism has taken.

This demurrer,[8] by Kluckhohn, exemplifies the ambivalence that arises out of the conflicting points of view that, as has been stated, are simultaneously present in the current of contemporary American thought. Its initial statement concerning cultural relativism is as follows: "To understand 'the meaning of a way of life to those who have it' is a significant and indeed a noble undertaking. To understand, however, should not necessarily mean to accept or even to remain content with description." One cannot but speculate on the intent of this passage. Does it signify that if an anthropologist studies the sanctions of a marriage system based on polygyny, he should not accept these sanctions for himself, in his own thinking about values, or in his own behavior, in which case he might become polygynous?

And how, one asks, should an anthropologist manifest his refusal to "remain content with description"? If this implies

8 *Saturday Review of Literature,* Sept. 18, 1948, pp. 11–12.

that he should seek deeper levels of integration in studying a culture, none will dispute the point. But in its context, one cannot but wonder if this does not imply the duty of an anthropologist to seek to change those elements of the culture of which he disapproves—in the case of our example, to advocate monogamy or polyandry for the polygynous people being studied. Kluckhohn does propose, as a "test for extrinsic values" the formula suggested by Thorndike—"are the means effective to the ends?" Yet, at this stage of anthropological sophistication, one would think that it might be taken as self-evident that this so-called test, in actuality, is met by every functioning value-system in every functioning culture.

We may follow this argument further. "The doctrine that science has nothing to do with values," Kluckhohn states, "is a pernicious heritage from Kant and other thinkers. Scientists dare not abdicate the right to study values by scientific means." In some bewilderment, one wonders how the relativistic position, which stresses the understanding of values—something that obviously, under the rubric of anthropological science, can mean only their study and analysis—can be contorted into an "abdication" of the "right" to study them. Does this exemplify how in the search for social "laws" that has occupied so many anthropologists, and the preoccupation with making of anthropology a "science"—as if it were not one—our traditional humanistic concerns have been lost sight of? Is it this latter aspect of our interests, which involves an understanding of the range of the creative drive in man and the value-systems that give point to his living, that we are told is being "abdicated" because some anthropologists have put aside the search for meaning in their preoccupation with form and structure?

"The amnesty which the anthropologist gives to the exuberant variety of cultural patterns," we are told, "must be that which the psychiatrist gives to incestuous dreams." It is difficult to believe that this is more than an exuberant figure of speech. Are anthropologists, working cross-culturally, really to decide what is good and bad in culture and, as social psychiatrists, attempt to cure the bad and promote the good? The psychiatrist, working with individuals who are deviant in terms of their own cultural prescriptions, frames procedures to permit his patient in the everyday round to fill the cultural prescription in a socially approved way. But where are the cross-cultural guides for the anthropologist? He, like all human beings, has undergone enculturative conditionings to the standards of his proper culture. Can his judgments be so Olympian that they are not influenced by these standards? The inevitable basic questions enter: Whose good? Whose bad? Whose means? Whose ends?

Kluckhohn's answer to these questions is found in the final passage of his discussion. "Some values," he says, "may well be regarded as within the realm of taste or choice or circumstance. But other values would seem to be appropriate and necessary to all men—given the nature of the human organism and the conditions to which all men, regardless of race and culture, must adjust." And to achieve this, one must "recognize what must eventually be the most important task" of our science, the "discovery and testing in the scientific crucible of the many values that transcend cultural variation."

One again must ask, however, what are those values that "seem to be appropriate and necessary to all men," and especially those that "transcend cultural variation." Is it possible that this is an attempt to have one's relativistic cake and eat it? Has an ambivalence arising out of conflicting currents of thought made it so difficult to recognize the critical point of the difference, precisely in the cross-cultural study of values, between universals and absolutes?[9] More than this, is it possible we see here a failure to apply the elementary lesson of cultural psychology, that all men are so conditioned in their perceptions, their emotions, and

[9] Cf. *Man and His Works*, pp. 76–78.

their judgments that these are framed, as far as the members
of any group are concerned, within the limits of variation
in belief and behavior sanctioned by the group at a given
moment in its history? One may wish to minimize the difference, for the sake of argument, between the absolute
values on which many peoples, especially ourselves, insist,
and those generalized orientations of culture, the universals,
that we find in all societies. Dialecticians, such as Child,
may wish to apply to relativism the exercise of a sterile logic
which proved, after the manner of Zeno, that one could
never reach a given point in space, or in medieval times,
disputed the choreography of angels. It has indeed occurred
to anthropologists "that the basis of moral judgment might
be found elsewhere than in logic, fact, or custom. . . .";[10]
but this leads us into a realm of mysticism and undebatable
belief with which we cannot be concerned when, as scientists, we follow the facts where they may lead us, after the
tough-minded empiricism of a science of man.

5

Despite the demurrer that has been cited, American anthropologists, on the whole, seem quite prepared to accept the
philosophical implications of their scientific findings. This is
evident, for example, in the criticisms of the American
Anthropological Association's "Statement on Human
Rights" that followed its publication. In all of these, discussion centered on the third aspect of the cultural relativistic position, its applications. In these discussions, indeed,
the objections seemed not so much to rise from reservations
to the philosophical position from which the "Statement"

---

[10] Arthur Child, Review of *Man and His Works* (Ethics, vol.
59, pp. 222–25, 1949). Another critique of cultural relativism by a
philosopher, more extended than that of Child and in the full
philosophical tradition, in contrast, of calm examination of an
intellectual position, appeared too recently to permit any consideration of it here. See Eliseo Vivas, *The Moral Life and the Ethical
Life* (Chicago, 1950), especially Ch. I.

derived as from a feeling that the logic of relativism has not been followed with enough rigor, and that the approach of the "Statement" contained a hidden ethnocentrism that tended to vitiate the position it assumed. Barnett, for example, reminds us[11] that "peoples of all degrees of sophistication will still prefer their opinions to ours despite the quantities of 'evidence' that we can bring to bear." Or Steward[12] says that "a declaration about human rights can come perilously close to advocacy of American ideological imperialism."

The point at issue here would not seem to be relativism, as such, but whether anthropologists, as scientists, can speak as scientists on matters of practical concern. This is the point to which Bennett wrote[13] in discussing the two comments on the "Statement" that have just been cited, when he says, "The criticisms of Steward and Barnett *could* lead to this: Because of the possibility of . . . disagreement, we must blind ourselves to the implications of our work. This, however, virtually denies a social humanity to the scientist. We would appear to need debate and argument over the implications of anthropological research—not a pretense at purity."

Of similar import are certain reactions to the implications of relativism as set forth in *Man and His Works*. Thus Hoebel, writing to the point made that, in practice, the philosophy of relativism is a philosophy of tolerance, and recognizing "that a larger measure of tolerance is needed in this conflict-torn world needs no arguing," feels that relativism fails to "give due consideration to the need for selectivity and integration in the formation of culture. It is a social need," he continues, "for any society to select but

[11] *On Science and Human Rights* (American Anthropologist, vol. 50, pp. 352–55, 1948).

[12] *Comments on the Statement on Human Rights* (American Anthropologist, vol. 50, pp. 351–52, 1948).

[13] *Science and Human Rights: Reason and Action* (American Anthropologist, vol. 51, pp. 329–37, 1949).

a few, and reject many, out of all possible lines of behavior. . . ." And because a "world society means a world
culture with a certain measure of integration, and all present
cultural systems are most certainly not compatible with
each other," then "some social norms will have to give along
the way. Not all can be tolerated."[14]

On the other hand, Bennett's position on the "Statement"
that we are justified, while speaking as scientists, in using
only those findings of our science that contribute to the ends
we, as citizens desire,[15] would seem to be far too cynical for
most scientists. This is scarcely the answer to the problem
the scientist must face as citizen, if the franchise of science
as a means of achieving an objective analysis of experience
is to be maintained. It is simply not true, as Bennett asserts,
that in discussions of racism, anthropologists suppressed the
known facts concerning the existence of differences between
human groups in their desire to stress similarities. It would
be exceedingly difficult to document the statement he makes
in this connection, that "Scientifically, we know that differences between human varieties can and do exist; ideo-
logically, it serves our purpose to deny them." It is apparent
that Bennett has forgotten the difference between a scientist's ordering of known fact for the layman so as to place
them in scientifically valid perspective and the propagan-
dist's suppression of facts to attain a given end.

These discussions, with their varying emphases, also have
to do with the broader problem of the relation between the
research aspect of our science and its applications, a topic
that is outside the scope of this paper. This is clear, for
example, when Steward states, "As a scientific organization,
the Association has no business dealing with the rights of
man." Barnett, likewise, is writing to this same problem
when he says, "It is an inescapable fact that we cannot at
the same time be moralists (and policy makers) and scien-

[14] *American Anthropologist,* vol. 51, pp. 473–74, 1949.
[15] *Op. cit.,* p. 334.

tists." The questions raised by the problem of the scientist as citizen are not only being faced by anthropologists, but by all scientists and, indeed, by scholars in the humanities as well. Admittedly, it is especially difficult in the disciplines where man studies man. Here we may only call attention to the fact that, as has been pointed out elsewhere,[16] many of these difficulties would be resolved if social scientists would recognize the difference between what has been called the curiosity function of their work—"pure science"—and the application of their findings—engineering. This would not resolve all the problems, as the exact and natural sciences have learned, but it would greatly reduce the number of them that would have to be faced.

Only one more point may be made of the criticism leveled at the attempts that have been made to point the practical implications of the relativistic findings of anthropology. It is difficult to see how the recognition of a cultural difference is the same as an advocacy of it. There can be no question as to the selectivity of cultures; the primary lesson of cultural diffusion teaches this. It would seem that what cultural relativism implies in its recognition of the existence of cultural pluralism is just this: that the values every human group assigns to its conventions arise out of its own historical background, and can be understood only in the light of that background. Relativism establishes the fact, and forces the recognition of the process as a continuing one; and on the level of application, stresses the importance of allowing, rather than imposing acceptances of cultural elements newly experienced.

Steward's doubt that "in urging that values be respected because 'man is free only when he lives as his society defines freedom,' we really mean to approve the social caste system of India, the racial caste system of the United States, or many of the other varieties of social discrimination in the world" only confuses the issues. To recognize the force of con-

[16] *Man and His Works*, pp. 649–53.

ventions in cultures other than one's own that are not congenial to one's enculturated patterns of thought is one thing;
to insist on suppressing them is quite another. In addition,
it is something entirely different when we, as Americans,
try to do something to correct "the racial caste system of
the United States" of which we, as members of the society
of whose culture this is a part, do not approve. In recognizing the validity of all ways of life for those who live in
accordance with them, cultural relativism does not deny
the dynamics of culture by insisting on an unchanging
acceptance by a people of their pre-existing ways of life, or
by failing to take into account the influence of cultural
transmission in making for cultural change. It accepts these,
and in its acceptance achieves the most fruitful approach to
the problem of the nature and significance of differential
values in culture that has yet been devised. For, as scientists
concerned with the problem of value, we will deny our pro-
fessed methodological assumptions and the empiricism of
our scientific point of view if we do not move from the facts
as we have established them in arriving at generalizations
regarding this phase of culture which we realize is so important for us to understand.

further comments
on cultural
relativism*

There is no cultural relativist, as far as I know, who
asserts that his doctrine is based on, describes, or
implies behavioral anarchy. . . . In fact, the need for a
cultural relativistic point of view has become apparent
because of the realization that there is no way to play
this game of making judgments across cultures except
with loaded dice.

      During the past five years, the
implications of cultural relativism have been considered at
length in at least two books by philosophers and two by
anthropologists; some of its specific points have been analyzed in papers by psychologists, economists, and semanti-
cists; it has been the subject of one of the Huxley Lectures
of the Royal Anthropological Institute; it has received
formal discussion by the Eastern Division of the American
Philosophical Association and by the Humanities Panel of
Oberlin College.

      This is not the place to analyze the reasons for this inter-
est, since to do so would take more time than is available
here and would necessitate moving far beyond the terms of

* Reprinted from *American Anthropologist,* Vol. 60, No. 2, April,
1958. Read before the V International Congress of Anthropological
and Ethnological Sciences, Philadelphia, 1956.

reference of this paper. It is enough, for the moment, to recognize that an important factor in its development is the increasingly felt need to expand the base of formal philosophical thought so as to include the entire range of human culture, rather than to continue its focus on the Graeco-Roman tradition which, from the point of view of the total cultural inventory of mankind, has limited its resources and its findings.

One is tempted, also, to assess these responses to relativism in terms of ethnopsychology and cultural dynamics. Like the analysis of anthropological reactions I made a few years ago (Herskovits 1951), this could be drawn in terms of "tough-minded" and "tender-minded" orientations. Because whether we consider the metaphysical and axiological implications of relativism, or its relation to perception, cognition, and motivation as manifest in ethical systems, many of these analyses are to be thought of as representing honest but tortuous attempts to surmount deeply inculcated, even subliminal, ethnocentrisms. They represent, in terms of a far-reaching reexamination of preexisting commitments, a very real struggle between the intellectual and emotional components in attitudes long accepted and convictions long held.

One manifestation of this conflict is found in the attempts that are made to separate the fact of relativism and its philosophical implications. Thus Schmidt (1955:782), in his critique, says, "I wish to assert now and reaffirm later that I think the fact of cultural relativism is a well established empirical truth. . . ." Or Hartung, insisting that a "sharp distinction must be maintained" between cultural variation and cultural relativity—though just where these two have been confused is not stated—explains that "cultural variation refers simply to the differences . . . in the cultural patterns serving the same or similar ends. . . . The form and degree of this variation are almost endless, and need no further documentation here" (1954:120). In this context, certain satisfactions seem to be gained from pointing out that relativism is nothing new. Schmidt, for example, ends the sentence just quoted by adding ". . . although I can't resist remarking that it was known by the Sophists of the fifth century B.C. in Athens"; and Hartung finds it necessary to note that "cultural relativity as we know it . . . is a good two hundred years old, dating as it does at least from David Hume."

Yet, to my knowledge, no present-day cultural relativist has assumed that this philosophy has leaped, full-blown, from the head of an anthropological parent. What is new is the massive documentation that derives from the great body of comparative data bearing on variation in custom, and the implications of these data when they are considered in the light of older theories. It may be noted that antiquity can be called on to support a claim to respectability or to show how well-worn a concept may be. In the cases cited, and in others that could be given, the ambivalences would seem to have achieved a certain degree of resolution by utilizing the claim in its pejorative sense.

One of the most interesting aspects of the reaction to cultural relativism, whether by anthropologists or others, is the almost exclusive stress that has been laid on the problems of value and ethics. Thus the central question in Ginsberg's discussion is "the connexion between the diversity of morals and the relativity of ethics" (1953:117); and he speaks of "ethical relativity or, as the American anthropologists call it, cultural relativism" (ibid:127). Asch opens his discussion of the topic, "The Thesis of Cultural Relativism," by stating, "That ideas of what is right and wrong differ poses a sharp problem for a theory of human nature" (Asch 1952:367). Edel (1955) and Vivas (1950) restrict their analyses to the relativity of ethics and morals, while Bidney (1953:425) states the two alternatives presented by cultural relativism in this way: "One must either accept a doctrine of fixed absolute values or deny objective norms in favor of historic relativity and the relative validity of values." According to Redfield (1953:144), "Cultural relativism means that the values expressed in any culture are to be both understood and themselves valued only according to the way the people who carry that culture see things."

This tendency to restrict relativism to morals, ethics, and values has the unfortunate result of throwing the problem at issue out of focus, since it undercuts the enculturative factor in cultural learning in general. As a matter of fact, among critics of relativism, only Schmidt has faced the implications of the fact that relativism applies to judgments of time and space and volume as well as of conduct. But this is not the place to consider the problem of the nature of truth, however tempting it may be to explore the many paths down which such an analysis, in relativistic terms, would lead us. Let us rather return to the point we are considering, the importance of the nonethical dimensions of relativism. Here we find ourselves, for one thing, on a plane where differences in perception and cognition can be assessed in terms of mensurable standards to a far greater degree than would ever be possible where only ethical judgments are taken into account.

An example of how the enculturative experience shapes perception may be drawn from the West African country of Ghana. An electrical contractor was explaining a problem with which he was constantly confronted. "When a trench for a conduit must be dug, I run a line between the two points, and tell my workers to follow it. But at the end of the job, I invariably find that the trench has curves in it." The answer was simple, when sought in terms of the culturally influenced patterns of perception of his workers. For these were men from the northern part of the country, where circular forms predominate and where the straight line plays a minor role. They do not live in what has been called a carpentered world, so that to follow a straight line marked by a cord is as difficult for them as it would be for those of us whose learning experience stresses the perception and allocation in space of rectangular forms to describe, freehand, a perfect circle.

Over the years, Hallowell has accumulated such material showing Saulteaux Indian patterns of orientation in their spatial and temporal world. Some of his observations are pertinent to our discussion. "While it remains an open question of how far the purely psychophysical dimensions of perception may be influenced by culturally constituted experiential factors," he writes, "schematic perception, involving the meaningful aspects of experience, can hardly be understood without reference to an articulated world of objects whose relations and attributes become meaningful for the individual, not simply through the innate psychological potentialities he brings to experience but, above all, through the significance for experience that the develop ment, patterning, transmission, and accumulation of past experience, in the form of a cultural heritage, have come to imply." Or, again, "The human individual is always provided with some culturally constituted means that are among the conditions which enable him to participate with his fellows in a world whose spatial attributes are, in part, conceptualized and expressed in common terms. Ontogenetically, self-orientation, object-orientation, and spatio-temporal orientation are concomitantly developed during the process of socialization" (Hallowell 1955:184, 185).

This broader approach to relativism involves a reexamination of some of the phenomena of human behavior that have been categorized in terms of the application of culture-bound concepts to societies other than those in which they have been developed. Thus, in a number of places (e.g., 1948:66–67) I have pointed out that to regard spirit-possession in African and Afroamerican societies as being directly comparable to psychopathological seizures found in Europe and America is to neglect the all-important fact of cultural definition. Recently, Ribeiro has adduced some important data bearing on this point (Ribeiro 1956; cf. also Stainbrook 1952:passim; Linton 1956:90–95). Himself a psychiatrist, Ribeiro has had long experience in studying the Afrobrazilian cult groups in Recife. Not only has he reduced the overall concept of "spirit-possession" to categories drawn in accordance with the degree of volition involved in a given instance, but he has pointed out that the cult-priests themselves recognize the difference between normal and pathological cases. For, as he describes it, certain cult-members are from time to time brought to him by these priests for treatment, with the explanation that their possessions are not proper ones, and that they are "sick" and in need of help.

Even where the relativity of ethics is under discussion, however, it is interesting to see how a psychologist tends to project his particular problem against the broader background. Defining culture as "essentially a common pattern of learned significances," Cantril stated, "Experience, then, has implicated within it: some impingements from the environment, physiological sensory processes, learned significances that have somehow become registered in us from the consequences of our past action, assumptions of constancy concerning both inorganic and organic events, choice purposeful action, value satisfaction, some degree of faith." And he warns, "All of these aspects of reality can be negated if there is sharp and consistent lack of correspondence between them and the consequences of purposeful action with respect to them" (Cantril 1955:681, 682).

Relativism will remain a subject for sterile debate if we are content to permit its applicability to anything less than the total range of human thought and conduct. We must subject the problem of the force of enculturative experience to study under conditions of as careful control as possible, if we are to move from logical argumentation to scientific analysis. Some work . . . in the field of the perception of color (Ray 1952, 1953; Conklin 1955), concomitant with the revival of interest among psychologists in the study of perception in general. Cross-cultural studies of visual illusions and of the perception of differences between angles, based on the use of experimental, controlled techniques, are to be initiated by the Program of African Studies at

Northwestern University. It is anticipated that the results of this research will afford a less subjective, less anecdotal body of data dealing with the influence of culture on perception than has hitherto been available, and will thus further test the validity of basic relativistic assumptions.

We may move to certain other points that have marked the discussion of relativism. One of these not found in anthropological publications, since anthropologists are much too aware of the cross-cultural factor to fall into this trap, is the failure to distinguish between intracultural and crosscultural relativism. This confusion is particularly striking where problems of ethics and values are under discussion, and represents the logical confusion that results when ideas from different historical strata in the development of philosophical thought are not sharply distinguished. Perhaps the most unequivocal statement of this confusion is that of Hartung, which Kluckhohn (1955:688) has quite correctly denoted as coming "close to the popular vulgarization of the doctrine." For Hartung says, "This plea for tolerance of all customs makes ethical concepts, for the individual, completely a matter of personal taste and preference. For example, arguing on the basis of tolerance and equal validity, I could just as logically adopt the conventions of any other culture I chanced to learn about, because I would then have no possible way of concluding that my own culture's conventions are right, and furthermore, I would at the same time be convinced that the rules of another are just as valid as mine" (Hartung 1954:122).

On a somewhat more sophisticated level, Edel falls into similar confusion when he tells us that, "Not all relativity is self-centered. It may be culture-centered or nation-centered" (1955:23). "If morality is man-made and if it is changing, there is no purpose metaphysically or theologically imposed. If egoism is correct, there are no morally mandatory social obligations not subject to individual veto. . . . If cultural relativity is a sociological truth, then your morality is a function of your domicile. If moral assertions are simply expressive, it all depends on what you feel" (ibid:27–28). Yet even granting that "the design that is formed is one of arbitrariness in ethics," is not the important point, quite disregarded in these passages, whether "arbitrariness" exists on the individual or the cultural level?

What is consistently forgotten by those who fail to distinguish between intra- and cross-cultural phenomena is the power of the enculturative experience in shaping conduct and ideas. There is no cultural relativist, as far as I know, who asserts that his doctrine is based on, describes, or implies behavioral anarchy; there is no one who does not recognize that every society has rules of conduct, an ethical system, a moral code, that the individual members rarely question. Intraculturally, any act that falls outside the limits of accepted variation will be adjudged in terms of preexisting standards, and either rejected or reconciled with them. Those who make up a society have no more difficulty in defining reality than they have in defining good conduct and bad. But this is within a society. Cultural relativism developed because the facts of differences in these concepts of reality or in moral systems, plus our knowledge of the mechanisms of cultural learning, forced the realization of the problem of finding valid cross-cultural norms. In every case where criteria to evaluate the ways of different peoples have been proposed, in no matter what aspect of culture, the question has at once posed itself: "Whose standards?" The force of the enculturative experience channels all judgments. In fact, the need for a cultural relativistic point of view has become apparent because of the realization that there is no way to play this game of making judgments across cultures except with loaded dice.

This brings us to another point, which also seems to give difficulty to those who criticize relativism: the distinction between universals and absolutes. Whether, with Schmidt, we wish to speak of "cultural invariants" (1955:783) or, with Edel, couch the problem as one of reducing "indeterminacy," matters but little, since the difficulty would appear to be no more than a semantic one. The problem would rather seem to be analogous to that of ascertaining the most adequate basis for deriving general principles of human behavior, in terms of the relation between form and process. Here the issue is clear (cf. Herskovits 1948:619), with the particular experience of each society giving historically unique formal expression to underlying processes, which are operative in shaping the destiny of all human groups.

The discussion of this point has tended to underscore the swing of the pendulum from emphasis on similarities among human cultures to one laid on differences. In truth, however, the dichotomy exists more in argumentation than in fact. Early students of man, it is true, stressed the concept of "human nature," but this was essentially to allow them to bring observed divergences under a single head. Later, more emphasis was laid on these differences, but again this was to show how diverse the manifestations of common human tendencies might be. It should be recalled that those who most strongly urged the unique historical position of each culture also insisted on the unity of *homo sapiens* in opposing doctrines of racial determinism.

As far as I know, there is no relativist who would exclude from the anthropological repertory the study of values, or who would deny to human behavior its common psychophysical base. Nor do relativists deny the importance of research which would refine our knowledge of the nature and functioning of this common base, or the investigation of the relation between belief and behavior. Cultural relativism, which has arisen out of the empirical study of the historical and psychosocial springs of human behavior and the macroethnographic analysis of its range, is thus committed to the investigation of any question which bears on the epistemological and ontological problems implicit in its position. It may be true that "modern empirical science," as Bidney states, systematically excludes "values, such as the good and the beautiful, in its pursuit of scientific truth" (1953:405), but this in no sense raises the question whether "there may be a science of cultural values" (ibid:416). The continuous growth of anthropological interest in the study of values is the best answer to such a suggestion.

But this is something quite different from postulating a "normative science of human culture," which, in its very essence, substitutes prescription for analysis and scientific understanding. Cultural ideals are indeed "social facts" (Bidney 1953:419), and the difference between the cultural ideals of a people and the total range of variation in their behavior has long been recognized. Yet to project this into the realm of the universal is to express a wish rather than to follow the leads of scientific investigation, and the difference between the two must be recognized. Perhaps, as Edel and others maintain, it may be possible empirically to establish certain specific manifestations of moral behavior found everywhere. It may be, but one is struck in these writings with the heavy loading of such phrases as "if we do this, we should be able to . . ." and the rarity of specific suggestions as to ways of going about finding what is sought. It is well enough to speak, as Bidney does, of the importance of the Platonic concept of "ideal truth," and to make the "metaphysical, or metacultural" postulate of "objective reality, independent of the observer." This may exist, but in terms of the framework of our knowledge of the psychocultural processes of enculturation, the relativist can only once again pose his basic query: "*Whose* objective reality?"

Finally, we come to the question of practical relativism. What are we to do when a people openly interfere, for whatever end, with the life of another human group? Redfield has put the matter very clearly: "It was easy to look with equal benevolence on all sorts of value systems so long as the values were those of unimportant little people remote from our own concerns. But the equal benevolence is harder to maintain when one is asked to anthropologize the Nazis, or to help a Point Four administrator decide what to do for those people he is committed to help" (1953:145–

46). Yet Redfield himself, unlike many of those who reject cultural relativism or whose acceptance of it is limited, has analyzed with admirable candor and insight his own ethnocentric evaluations of culture (ibid:163–65), and goes on to say, "I should like to point out that the doctrine of cultural relativism . . . is not a doctrine of ethical indifference" (ibid:146).

The answer to the problem raised by practical relativism remains one which cannot be resolved on the philosophical level. It must be repeated, there is no living in terms of unilateral tolerance, and when there is the appeal to power, one cannot but translate enculturated belief into action. An economist (Kovisto 1955:57; cf. also Simpson 1954:5) has phrased this position succinctly: ". . . the wages of the sin of ethnocentrism is open conflict. If no agreement on values can be reached, we can only try to develop social controls to minimise the conflict over ends, provided we can find sufficient consensus against the existence of a high level of overt conflict."

---

references

Asch, Solomon E.
    1952   Social psychology. New York, Prentice Hall.
Bidney, David
    1953   Theoretical anthropology. New York, Columbia University Press.
Cantril, Hadley
    1955   Ethical relativity from the transactional point of view. The Journal of Philosophy 52:677–687.
Conklin, Harold C.
    1955   Hanunóo color categories. Southwestern Journal of Anthropology 11:339–344.
Edel, Abraham
    1955   Ethical judgment, the use of science in ethics. Glencoe, The Free Press.

GINSBERG, MORRIS
    1953   On the diversity of morals. Journal of the Royal An-
            thropological Institute 83:117–135.
HADDON, ALFRED C. (ed.)
    1901   Reports of the Cambridge Anthropological Expedi-
            tions to the Torres Straits, Vol. 2, pt. 1, Cambridge
            (England).
HALLOWELL, A. I.
    1955   Culture and experience, Philadelphia, University of
            Pennsylvania Press.
HARTUNG, FRANK E.
    1954   Cultural relativity and moral judgments. Philosophy of
            Science 21:118–126.
HERSKOVITS, M. J.
    1948   Man and his works. New York, A. A. Knopf.
    1951   Tender- and tough-minded anthropology and the study
            of values in culture. Southwestern Journal of An-
            thropology 7:22–31.
KLUCKHOHN, C.
    1955   Ethical relativity: sic et non. The Journal of Philoso-
            phy 52:663–677.
KOVISTO, W. A.
    1955   Moral judgments and value conflict. Philosophy of
            Science 12:54–57.
LINTON, RALPH
    1956   Culture and mental disorders, George Devereux ed.
            Springfield, Illinois, Thomas.
RAY, VERNE F.
    1952   Techniques and problems in the study of human color
            perception. Southwestern Journal of Anthropology
            8:251–259.
    1953   Human color perception and behavioral response.
            Transaction, New York Academy of Sciences, Ser. 2,
            16:98–104.
REDFIELD, ROBERT
    1953   The primitive world and its transformations. Ithaca,
            Cornell University Press.
RIBEIRO, RENE
    1956   Unpublished communication to the Northwestern
            University of Anthropology Club.
SCHMIDT, PAUL F.
    1955   Some criticisms of cultural relativism. The Journal of
            Philosophy 52:780–791.

SEGALL, MARSHALL
    1956   A review of studies by Rivers among Murray Islanders
            and Todas. MS.
SIMPSON, GEORGE E.
    1954   Cultural relativism. Humanities Panel Discussion,
            Oberlin College, No. 7, Mimeographed.
STAINBROOK, EDWARD
    1952   Some characteristics of the psychopathology of schizo-
            phrenic behavior in Bahian society. American Journal
            of Psychiatry 109:330–335.
VIVAS, ELISEO
    1950   The moral life and the ethical life. Chicago, University
            of Chicago Press.

symposium on relativism and the study of man— a review*

A realistic and flexible approach to the problems of adjustment in a multi-cultural world can be achieved only by accepting the fact of cultural diversity, and granting in principle the worth of each system of values as this is related to the goals of the people who live by it.

It is difficult to believe, in the present climate of thought, that a symposium on the question of relativism in human affairs could be organized without the presence of someone competent to present the anthropological position. Lacking a student skilled in handling cross-cultural data, only a welter of confusions could result. And this is precisely what occurred in the symposium that forms the basis for this book.

Let us see, first of all, the disciplines that were represented in the group. The editors, according to the biographical note about them on the book-jacket, are sociologists, both on the staff of Emory University in Atlanta, Georgia. Of the contributors, one is a psychologist (Carmichael),

---

* The book reviewed is *Relativism and the Study of Man,* Schoeck, Helmut and Wiggins, James M. (editors), Princeton, W. van Nostrand, Co., Inc., 1961.

one is a botanist (Zirkle), one a theologian (Casserly), two are political scientists (Leoni and Strauss), one an economist (von Mises), one a historian (Malin). There were also a philosopher (Vivas), a professor of English (Weaver), an educationalist (Tietz), and a linguist (Pei). There were thus both social scientists and humanists; the group included those whose interests lay in the realm of ideas as well as those whose concern is with practical affairs.

As one reads through the chapters, a certain homogeneity in point of view becomes apparent. There is no member of the symposium who is not disturbed at the developments that mark the present trends of our culture; none who does not view with alarm contemporary changes in morals, modes of behavior, patterns of thought and ways of expression. The book gives the feeling that the discussions at the meetings where these papers were presented must have carried a strong emotional component. One is tempted to raise the question: Is not this book an example of the perennial cry of the elders against the innovations of the oncoming generation? Only in these terms can we explain the note of dissatisfaction that appears again and again when new ways manifest in various aspects of our culture enter into the discussion.

It is perhaps not without significance that the only papers wherein this feeling of dismay at change is subordinated to the intellectual problem are the two final ones on linguistics. Particularly in the chapter written by Pei, one feels the intellectual serenity that comes when the range of variation in any aspect of total human behavior is squarely faced, accepted as a fact to be reckoned with, and its implications objectively analyzed. It is worth noting, moreover, that this is really the only paper that makes a substantive contribution. This is found in its discussion of the roots of linguistic relativism in earlier thinking. Its analysis of relativistic excesses in the field of linguistics are coldly, clearly and convincingly analyzed. One can only say that it deserves a better setting than it has.

Most prominent among the confusions in the book is that between intra-cultural and cross-cultural relativism. It is difficult to understand why such a simple conception should be so hard to grasp. The kind of intra-cultural relativism envisaged by the various contributors—that is, the denial of validity to standards of conduct operating within a society—would not only bring on moral, but perceptual anarchy, and social life would grind to a halt. Every society has its codes; they are stable, and only to those within a given group does change seem important. Change in values and beliefs constantly occur, but with regularity. This is why, when seen in retrospect, we find all ways of life exhibit the phenomenon of cultural drift. The culture of no social entity is marked by the moral disintegration that intra-cultural relativism, if practiced, would bring on.

When we move to value-judgments drawn on a cross-cultural basis—and it is this, and this alone, that is the concern of cultural relativists—we are faced with quite a different problem. This has to do with the question of the existence of absolutes and universals in human culture. The problem is essentially methodological—how any human being, enculturated to the evaluative and perceptual modes of a particular way of life, can avoid the enculturative screening of experience in judging cultures other than his own. That is, since every society has its particular schedule of absolutes, how do we, as human beings who accept the schedule of our own society, attain objectivity in evaluating the schedules of other societies? The cultural relativist is content to withhold judgment until empirical proofs of the existence of absolutes that are also universals can be adduced.

In anthropology, the importance of this question has long been recognized, but in this book it scarcely even enters. Carmichael, one of the few contributors who recognizes the existence of the cross-cultural problem in relativism, like his colleagues in the symposium, becomes enmeshed in the shift from this to intra-cultural applications.

Thus he states, "The idea . . . that there are some established esthetic values in the arts is . . . hard for those who
now like to say that a fashionable non-objective painter who
reports that he experiences great emotional satisfaction as
he paints is necessarily as satisfactory an artist as was
Titian." Or, again, "If we accept the suggestions . . . that
there may be some absolutes in human conduct that can be
discovered, we must have the courage to apply this knowledge in deciding the content of the education that we wish
to furnish for the children of this or any other age" (p. 11).
The statement of Vivas that, "Cultural relativism leads to
individual relativism, which is to say, moral nihilism" (p.
52), flies in the face of everything we have learned from
the comparative study of the processes of cultural conditioning. And these are only samples of the many other
examples of confusion on this point that can be found.

The only chapter in the book which invokes anthropological findings is that of Vivas, who uses the writings of
anthropologists as a stick with which to beat the cultural
relativists. The doctrine of relativism, we are told, holds
that, "The criteria of value judgements are determined by
the culture. From this it follows that it is not possible to
judge the values of one culture in terms of any criteria
except its own, and, therefore, the objective indices of
cultural inferiority or superiority cannot be established. An
American cannot feel superior to Malinowski's savages because they are lousy and dirty. It's just a matter of cultural
difference—although I do not see how we can deny they
are lousy" (p. 46). Granting the validity of the statement
about the Trobriand Islanders, to which no citation is given,
one does not deny the fact; what is puzzling is the assertion
that the American, free of lice, "cannot feel superior" to
the lousy Melanesian. He not only can, but does feel
superior; Vivas obviously does so. However, one could
scarcely hold that our American, in his response, is reacting
as a scientific student of culture.

Vivas bases most of his argument on an enthymeme:

"A culture determines the values acknowledged by its members. Therefore a culture determines the values its members ought to acknowledge."

The "implicit premise," we are told, is that:

"The values determined by a culture are the values that the members of that culture ought to acknowledge."

Yet there is no anthropological relativist, as far as is known, who either as a scientist or in his philosophy would sanction the "ought" in the shift from the first to the second of these propositions. Indeed, if we move from moral to perceptual relativism, the propositions lead to a *reductio ad absurdum*. How "ought" one to divide the continuum of color that makes up the spectrum? Even as stated, the enthymeme vanishes, for the so-called "implicit premise" is but a rewording of the explicit statements out of which it presumably arises. Space does not permit an examination here of how, moving from this distortion of the logic that directs the relativist position, the discussion in this chapter also distorts the position of the anthropologists who are cited. One can only conclude that this symposium would have been the better if it had entirely ignored the anthropological contribution.

The anti-relativist position of the papers reveal other points worthy of remark. Zirkle, accepting the universality of "scientific" relativism, seems to forget scientific objectivity when it comes to the science of man; certainly his discussion exhibits no lack of value-judgments. Most striking is the doctrine of what may be called neo-social-Darwinism, arrived at by an analogy to the biological struggle for survival. Animal behavior patterns, he tells us, "have been preserved and developed by nature to just the extent to which they aid the behaving organism to survive and reproduce" (p. 28). Quite aside from the anthropomorphism found in ascribing will and purpose to the reification of the

concept, "nature," anthropologists must challenge his readiness to argue, from analogy, that survival is a criterion for
evaluating human cultures. We read that "deviant sub-
cultures are . . . checked and controlled almost automatically by natural selection" (p. 32); that "if the test of
survival is applied to the different human cultures, they can
easily be recognized as being fit or unfit" (p. 43). Unfortunately for the argument, all existing cultures have
survived. How, in terms of this analogy, is the worth of
these many surviving cultures to be "scientifically" evaluated?

Casserly, the theologian, gives one answer. He draws a
distinction between "the absolute, which is certainly never
absolutely known, and that which is absolutely known, for
the absolutely known is nearly always not merely a relativity, but even a triviality" (p. 107). Presenting the thesis
that "while it is true that man as we know him is always
man in the context of the local and the temporal, it is also
true that man as he knows himself is always man face to
face with the absolute" (p. 109), he cites the role of the
prophet as "an important criterion" for evaluating cultures.
"There are cultures so placidly successful as almost completely to exclude the prophetic challenges. There are others,
on the contrary, that seem by their very nature to encourage
and foster it. . ." Hence "we may distinguish between relatively closed and relatively open cultures and insist strongly
on the higher value of the open kind of culture" (p. 109–
110). One can but wonder how, in these terms, he grades
the cultures of Africa and North America, which have long
had "prophetic challenges"; to say nothing of the presumably lousy Melanesians, with their prophet movements
called Cargo cults.

It is not possible here to give further examples of the
confusions that mark this book. Because it is one of the
most extended series of statements against cultural relativism, it is important for anthropologists to read it. For those
of us who accept the logical postulates of cross-cultural re-

search, and are willing open-mindedly to abide by the scientific principle of basing our conclusions on facts, the volume will provide many enlightening instances of ethnocentric reactions to the relativistic point of view. That it has proved disturbing to this sampling of students from so many disciplines testifies to the power of cultural relativism, giving evidence of the stimulus which the relativistic principle, willy-nilly, carries even to those who have not been exposed to the cross-cultural methods of anthropology.

two

ethnocentrism, racism and peace

cultural diversity and world peace

The revolution of our day is not the proletarian revolution of Communist ideology; it is the collapse of classical imperialism. . . . From the point of view of our approach to the problem of world peace . . . the most important phenomenon we must consider is ethnocentrism. . . . No culture in its totality is a commodity for export. This is why any people who, by any method, whether by conquest or persuasion, assume that they can cause another group to change its entire way of life, are building policy on a psychological unreality. . . . [Yet] Culture is not a straitjacket. . . . The restlessness of man, the creative drive of the gifted individual, the search for variety in experience, all of these assure us that man is not an automaton, nor ever has been, nor at least while he persists as we know him, will ever be.

Until recent years, the diversities in culture of the peoples of the world presented no great problem. Power rested in countries where modes of life and thought were actually quite similar. All of them belong to the same historic stream; their forms of speech appertain to a single language family. There is certainly nothing of the order of difference in patterned forms of thought and behavior between England and France, let us say, that is apparent when we compare either of these with

China or Indonesia. The differences in any aspect of life between the United States and Germany, to take another instance, are minor compared to those between either country and India, for example, or Nigeria. And Russia, though she was thought of to some degree as a Western Power, was peripheral to the system. It was a commonplace in the chancelleries that in many respects she was different from these others. Russia, as the phrase ran, was as much of Asia as she was European; she was a special case.

Today American diplomats concerned with India meet with the representatives of India, not of England; when they treat of Indonesian affairs, their representations are made at Jakarta, not The Hague. The French deal with the Philippines as one sovereign nation speaking to another, and no longer seek answers in matters of mutual interest in Washington. It was only just before the second World War that the principle of extra-territoriality was abolished in China; the Sudan is now an independent nation; it will be no more than a year or two until certain capitals of the world receive the envoys of the self-governing African state of the Gold Coast.

Nor need we restrict ourselves to the sphere of politics in considering the question of the relation between cultural diversity and world peace. We come even closer to the fundamental problems involved when we consider economic development. On the diplomatic scene, dealings are between individuals who are at least aware that they are facing men with basic orientations that may differ from their own. In the sphere of economic development, it is the ordinary people of a country who are primarily involved. There is no screen of protocol to sift out gross differences in attitude and behavior. The degree of accommodation between donors and recipients of aid or advice must be far-reaching and the potentialities for friendship or hostility between the parties concerned are thereby made infinitely greater.

It is not easy to realize that in many parts of the world "the little brown brother" has grown up and is now politically our equal. It is a fair question whether the perplexity we in the United States experience in our efforts to understand the neutralist policy of India is not related to the difficulty of accommodating our thinking to the fact that India is shaping her own course and making her own decisions. And if we, in the United States, with our traditional opposition to colonialism, and the support we have given to movements looking toward autonomy for non-self-governing peoples everywhere can be taken aback by the forthrightness of a country such as India, so recently in the colonial status, how much more must be the difficulty in understanding the political behavior of former colonial peoples by those who have so recently been their rulers?

Such questions reach far beyond the day-to-day preoccupations of those concerned with international affairs. Both statesmen and scholars are weighed down by a sense of urgency in face of the uncertain world in which we live. It is enough, surely, it is argued, to have to meet the exigencies of the crises with which we are continuously presented without being compelled to anticipate problems that may arise in the far future. But the questions we raise here do not concern the distant future. They are with us now, lurking just behind the headlines that tell of today's tensions, providing the unrealized background for the stories of commentators who speculate on the result of yesterday's conference.

In truth, we are facing a revolutionary situation. The revolution of our day is not the proletarian revolution of Communist ideology; it is the collapse of classical imperialism. It is understandably difficult for those accustomed to a world under the tutelage of the powers of Western Europe and, later, of the United States, to accept as equals those whom, with varying degrees of benevolence, they regarded until quite recently as peoples whom the more advanced nations must guide to higher stages of culture and thus to an eventual future participation in world affairs. It is not easy for those who have sat in judgment to realize that they are being judged; to understand that they can suggest and negotiate, but not order; to comprehend the fact that they must now take into account motivations and patterned responses far different from those of the countries with whom they had been accustomed to deal.

All too commonly, we find our men of affairs facing the revolutionary situation with a philosophy that is outmoded as the horse and buggy in an age of jet propulsion. If it is true that the struggle for peace has its weapons no less potent than those of war, it is also true that the diplomats, no less than the generals, tend to lay their stratagems in terms of the conflict that is over, and not the one ahead. We have left behind a multi-cultural world where only a small segment of the peoples inhabiting it really counted; we are living in the same multi-cultural world, but one in which peoples with the most diverse modes of thought and behavior are in continuous interaction.

That the problems raised by these multi-cultural realities have dimensions of an order of complexity far beyond our contemporary experience should but encourage us to marshal all our scientific skills to their solution. The answer, when it comes, must be realistic and flexible. Above all, it must involve a reorientation in thought that, by giving full weight to the cross-cultural factor, will grant to all peoples their right of choice to identify their future with the continuities of their ancestral heritage.

2

From the point of view of our approach to the problem of world peace, there can be little question that the most important phenomenon we must consider is that of ethnocentrism. For the constrictions of cultural provincialism that result from the active play of ethnocentrism must be taken into account as a major factor in any discussion of conditions essential to the resolution of the tensions that inevitably develop out of the differing values of peoples in ever closer contact.

Ethnocentrism is just what the term, in its literal meaning, implies—the end result of a psychological process by which men center their world in their own group, seeing it in their own dimensions, judging conduct by their own standards, planning so as to achieve in terms of their own ambitions. One reason why it is so important not to neglect the force of ethnocentrism in any consideration of contact across cultures is that, as a universal in human experience, it moves to the deepest levels of individual personality and group identification. Yet just because of this fact, its power tends to be overlooked, even where it is elevated to the status of a virtue in terms of exclusive loyalties. It cannot, however, be negated, for it performs an essential function for human beings. Without it, the kind of orientation in society that is indispensable to man could not be achieved, and the adjustment each individual must make to the world in which he lives would be difficult, if not impossible. It is apparent, then, that we cannot approach the phenomenon of ethnocentrism with any attitude of praise or blame; that we are not dealing with the devil in the world scene. To achieve realism and flexibility we must balance, not judge; our answer must be drawn in terms of more or less, not as a choice between polar opposites.

To understand what ethnocentrism is, we must briefly indicate the nature of culture, and particularly of cultural learning. It is scarcely necessary to define the term here, for recognition of its importance for a comprehension of the ways of man has steadily grown, and with this has come acceptance of the word as signifying the totality of learned human behavior. Culture can be viewed objectively, as by a traveler visiting a people whose ways differ from his own, as an aggregate of institutionalized modes of behavior that, when he comes to know them, will permit him to anticipate how a member of the society he is visiting will react to a given situation. For culture regulates the relationship of one member of a society to his fellows; it orders the concept of the Universe which a people hold; it patterns their aesthetic satisfactions. It conditions the ways in which they perceive and react to time and space; it gives to every man the ethical norms by which he guides his own conduct and judges that of others. There is literally no moment in the life of an individual when the influence of his culture is not felt.

The critical point about culture is this fact that it is learned; and the process of cultural learning is called enculturation. This process is all-pervasive, and for the most part, we are not conscious of its operation. It is carried on by means of the symbols of language, the use of which, unique to man, allows each society, like mankind as a whole, to build on the achievements of past generations. These cultural symbolisms are internalized so that they not only assure adequate response to particular cues to behavior, but set up those enculturated restraints that go under the designations of conscience, the super-ego, guilt feelings and the like. Hence if culture is to be thought of as the ordering of behavior in a society, enculturation is the mechanism which orders for each of its members the form and extent of accepted modes of conduct and aspiration, and also sets the limits within which variation in individual behavior is sanctioned.

The results of the enculturative process are thus both positive and negative. This process equips a man or woman to become a fully functioning member of the society into which he is born, allowing him to "grow into" his culture, as it has been put. It gives him the knowledge of the technological responses of his society so that he can gain a living, socializes him by patterned rewards and punishments so he can function within the group to which he belongs, equips him with a belief system that allows him to face the powers of the natural and supernatural world with a minimum of psychological insecurity, channels his creative drives in music, dance, poetry and art. On the other hand, it provides the complements of "Thou-shalt-nots" which, so to speak, are the governor-bearings to conduct, and are integral parts of the systems of moral values and ethical precepts that are a feature of every culture man has devised.

All these patterns of conduct and thought are so well learned that behavior, to a very considerable degree, is automatic. Much of what we do lies below the level of consciousness; we sing without giving the modal structure of our music a thought, we speak and are quite unconscious of the phonemic system of our language. Most men in our society do not have to contemplate what a shovel is for and how they must use it when faced with a task of digging a hole. Yet in the gold mines of the Union of South Africa, whose labor-force is recruited from the hoe-using cultures, the visitor will see classes of newly arrived workers being instructed in the use of the shovel. Involving, as this does, no more than a simple reorientation in motor behavior, it takes only a few days for the responses to become as automatic as any learned behavioral pattern. And this is as it should be, for if we had to make a case for each item of behavior before we acted at all, we would perish before we reached a decision how even our most elementary needs should be satisfied.

It is, obviously, easier to think and act in accustomed ways than to learn new ones. Not that we do not learn new ways; we do this all the time, and one of the basic questions in the study of culture is how a people come to accept, and why they reject, a given innovation presented to them. This is a matter which we cannot analyze here, since it would lead us into the involved problems of the dynamics of culture. We need but point out that each innovation is projected against the pre-existing cultural mass, and judged in terms of its utility or disutility as these appear in the light of established values. This is why, for instance, efficiency as an end does not necessarily appeal to all peoples as it does to us, for there are many who do not accord time the great value we assign to it. Examples without number could be given of those culturally derived differentials, yet the point is clear—we take over from our experience with other societies those elements of their cultures that appeal to us, in the light of our enculturative background; but for the most part, we move in the accustomed, more comfortable aspects of our enculturated habits.

This leads us to a further point, the very essence of the psychocultural base of ethnocentrism. For the worth we ascribe to the things we have and use and the ways in which we use them; the relationships we sanction; the beliefs by which we live, lodge as deeply beneath the stream of conscious thought as any element in culture. That is, we take these values for granted, which means that when they are challenged, our response is essentially an emotional one. On this plane, we react to challenge; we do not reason. For a challenge to basic values is a challenge to the things that give essential meanings to life. This is why the exercise of power on the international, cross-cultural level, is so hazardous. Time and again we have seen how a people, giving outer expression of acquiescence and submission, have bided their time until they could re-establish their accustomed ways, often with a fury that lays bare the intensity with which they have reacted to the imposition of foreign controls.

Even where force is not in play, the adjustment of differing ways of life to achieve a *modus vivendi* under a single socio-political system presents difficulties. On our own continent, tensions between French- and English-speaking Canadians have still to be resolved; in Europe, we need only think of the adjustments that recurrently have to be made between the Flemish and Walloons of Belgium. We refer such cases ordinarily to language differences, but in this we fail to perceive that here the languages are but symbols of certain emphases in the ways of life of these peoples that differ as well. One recalls the witty comment of Lindsay Rogers, "Nowadays it seems as if every little language must have a nation of its own." In the above instances, the cultural differences between the populations involved are slight indeed when compared with the case of peoples whose cultures belong to different historic streams, as is the case with the American Indian and European-derived groups in the United States. These instances indicate something of the magnitude of the problem when it assumes world-wide dimensions.

Because of its importance for our day, ethnocentrism is a concept that requires redefinition. Its implications are especially difficult for those who live in the countries of Europe or in the United States to grasp, and even more difficult still to take into account in planning programs of action. The expansion of Europe was effected with a minimum of European manpower, bearing in mind the vastness of the areas brought under European control and the size of their populations; more than this, the degree of accommodation to European culture, as it has spread over the world, has been remarkable.

Can we not argue that it is reasonable to conclude that the benefits rendered by scientific knowledge and the machine technology are therefore self-evident, and must accordingly transcend pre-existing differences in cultural values? Why should they not be accepted everywhere? And do they not testify to the quality of our achievement, and give us a further franchise to bring other ways of life into consonance with our own?

Yet, to take the example of attempts to spread the benefits of science at its most humane level, we find, as the sobering experience of technical aid programs all over the world has shown, that even what seem the most obvious answers to direct problems become tortuously complex when applied cross-culturally. One may prolong life and reduce infant mortality, but a tradition of prestige accorded the man or woman with many children will raise new problems that emerge when an increased population presses against the available food supply. Or again, it should not be forgotten that this same scientific methodology has made possible the development of far more effective instruments of warfare and death than the world has ever known. Moreover,

the very peoples who, in earlier years, could not stand
against the musket with spear, or with bow and arrow, have
learned to make effective use of the hand-grenade, the ma-
chine-gun, and the howitzer, as the lessons of Korea and
Indo-China, and to a lesser degree, of Kenya, have taught.

Where the uses of technical power, whether to control the
natural world or establish hegemony over human groups,
has carried its conviction, it does not necessarily follow that
scientific achievement will be identified with enlightenment
and truth. We must not lose sight of the fact that societies
where science and industrialization are most developed differ in religion, in language, in characteristic forms of social
structure, in the forms of their art.

The fact of the matter is that a way of life is a tightly-
knit fabric, and it is most difficult to substitute any one
strand for another without affecting the pattern of the totality. Attempts to achieve political unity on the European
and American model of territorial entities where the self-
identifying cultural and linguistic subgroupings have persisted for many generations must cope with strong resistance
in India, in the Gold Coast, and elsewhere. "It will take
time before we can think of ourselves as WaTanganyika"—
the people of Tanganyika—remarked a member of one of
the tribal groups of this Trust Territory. Certainly no culture, in its totality, is a commodity for export. This is why
any people who, by any method, whether conquest or persuasion, assume that they can cause another group to
change its entire way of life, are building policy on a psychocultural unreality.

For ethnocentrism, which, as we have seen, is a function
of early enculturation, is a force as powerful in recipient as
in donor cultures. Imposition of new ways may be a painful
experience, and a demoralizing one if carried far enough.
But it is rare that the entire value-structure of aboriginal
custom is lost, or that elements of it will not eventually re-
emerge in some form. For though an effective demonstration can be offered of how the machine can conquer time or

distance, lying quite outside readily demonstrable limits are such elements of culture as a kinship structure, a belief-system, or a moral code. And even when the efficiency of a technologically oriented way of life is objectively demonstrated, the question, "To what end?" still needs to be answered.

As a universal phenomenon of human social life, then, ethnocentrism must be assigned a preponderant place if we are realistically to weigh the factors that impinge on efforts to achieve world peace. Is it possible, we must ask, that by understanding the mechanisms that give it the power over the thinking of men, and the processes that allow it to function, its countervalences can be met and its positive values utilized in helping us realize our aim?

It will be recalled that one of the positive contributions to human social life made by ethnocentrism was indicated to be the fact that it provides the individual with a sense of identification with his group. This identification evokes pride in the achievements of the society of which he is a member, so that he experiences its triumphs as his own by a simple process of ego-extension. It is a mechanism, therefore, that makes for social adjustment and, beyond this, for a kind of balance in personality-structure that can only be achieved where convictions of social, no less than personal, worth come into play. Seen from this point of view, the universality of ethnocentrism becomes understandable, and its contribution to the health of the individual, in the psychological sense, is seen to be an important one.

This is its aspect of affirmation, viewed as it functions within a culture. What of its role in cross-cultural situations? We must recognize, first of all, that the manifestations and potentialities of ethnocentrism in the world scene are not the same as in a more restricted sphere. In this it is akin to other social and psychological phenomena, which only present serious problems of adjustment when blown up to world-wide dimensions. Thus, for example, nationalism comes to mind, or religious systems of restricted distribution.

For most peoples, living in a relatively narrow geographical range, ethnocentrism is no more than a conviction that one's own ways are better than those of other peoples one has met with, or has heard of. It is a belief that leads to no aggressive action, for it admits the validity for these others of their own particular tradition.

In no sense, however, does it imply wholesale rejection of these other ways, or drawing comparative evaluations of all aspects of other cultures. People take over cultural items from one another continuously. In those situations where intra-cultural ethnocentrism obtains, to argue that something done or made or used by another people is useful to one's own group does not mean that one's own culture is judged to be deficient. Hence, even where one people conquers another, and the second, recognizing the power of the supernatural beings of their conquerors as manifest through their success in warfare, worships them, no particular disorganization, either of the culture of the group, or the personality of the individual results. This comes only where the exercise of power is accompanied by a claim of total cultural superiority, and where conquest is a part of a movement of cultural evangelism.

It is this latter kind of ethnocentrism that poses one of the major problems to be faced in achieving world peace. This is not only because it has been this variety that, historically considered, has given a rationale for the expansion of Europe and the United States, but because it is today an increasingly virile force in Russia and China, a force whose manifestations are also apparent in the developing nationalisms of Africa and the Near and Middle East. Yet, as students of human behavior, we know that other, less militant aspects of ethnocentrism do exist, and can be called on in developing a realistic and flexible ideological basis for world order. We shall return to this later, after exploring other findings of cross-cultural investigation for such further insights as have relevance for our inquiry.

3

As we take a broad view of the cultures of the world's peoples—all the peoples, that is, and not only those that are usually considered, who are the most numerous, or are the most powerful, or who have written histories—it is the fact of the differences between them that initially impress us. It took generations before the early travelers saw anything more than this, and likewise today it is the difference between his own ways and those of the peoples he visits that strike the traveler with greatest force.

It was not until the middle of the nineteenth century, indeed, that any systematic attempt was made to order those impressions into categories that recognized the existence of unities underlying the welter of observed cultural diversities. This can be said to be the point that marks the emergence of the study of culture as a science, since some kind of classification of data is the first requisite in scientific analysis. The history of cultural anthropology as a science can be traced, since then, in the increasing insights into the unities that underlie the differing manifestations of each phase of human cultural activity, as described in one society after the other.

In broadest form, the generalizations about culture objectively considered have to do with what is termed its aspects. Regarded from the point of view of the behavior of human beings, these aspects represent the institutionalized ways in which different peoples face situations common to all of them. From this point of view the principal least common denominators of culture lodge in the overall physical and psychological problems that every society must solve if it is to survive. These problems fall into three groups.

The first comprises the adjustments men make to the natural setting in which they live, the use of their technological knowledge to produce what they must have, and of their economic system to assure that what they produce becomes available to the society as a whole. The second group of problems centers about the relationship of man to man. Here are included the organization of kin-groups to care for the young and all kinds of associations of a social, economic and political order. The final grouping concerns the relation of man to the Universe and the powers that rule it, manifested in the vast range of world-views that man has developed, each with its ritualistic and magical devices that are calculated to enlist on the side of man forces greater than those at his command. Rituals are reinforced by the use of the aesthetic resources which each society posseses in art, song, dance, poetry and drama.

These are universal in the structure of every culture; but the tale of unities in culture does not end there, for we have gone beyond structure to analyze out the mechanisms that give each form its functioning reality. For one thing, there is the symbolism of language, that provides for an entire cultural system the instrument of communication that is essential to human social life. By means of language, the education of the young, in the broadest sense, is achieved. All societies, too, regularize their ways of life in terms of value systems that, as we have seen, fashion and order the attitudes and the motivations that give each individual culture its describable distinctiveness, just because these values are so taken for granted and so implicitly accepted. And, with time, we have come to see the universality of cultural re-learning as a process, as the very essence of the dynamic quality of cultures, marked as they are by constant changes, whether these innovations come through a discovery or an invention from within a society, or are the result of contact with peoples of different cultural orientations.

Out of all this has come a recognition of the primacy of enculturation in our search for an understanding of the unities and diversities in the ways of life of the world's peoples, an understanding which is an important requisite for the building of world peace. If, as the philosophers tell us, we ourselves can never touch the raw stuff of reality, then it becomes evident that enculturation, which screens our perception and cognition, becomes our essential guide in the efforts we make to meet reality on terms meaningful to us, and effective in attaining the ends we desire. To each of us, that is, the reality of the world in which we live is the enculturated reality, and until a new conception of some aspect of it comes to us, there can be no other. Our evaluations of life, too, are enculturated values, and summon to their support all the power of affect that goes with belief.

From this point of view, each society is to be thought of as living in terms of its own ethnocentrisms, each judging its own way of living as best among all the differing ways its members know. One more step brings this point home. For in these terms, our culture, for all its technological achievement, is but one among many, its values having only the intra-cultural validity that is conceded to the system of values of any society, no matter what its size and the nature of its adjustment to its natural setting.

If we look at the problem of evaluating cultures from the point of view of judgments made of us by those who belong to other societies, we come to realize that their reactions to us must be screened through their own enculturated cognitive and affect responses just as are our own. A distinguished African, Robert Kwaku Gardiner,[1] writing a manual for students of his country who go to England, gives us a glimpse of this, for much of what he says applies to our American customs as much as it does to English ways, since compared to the African scene we differ but little. "The African visitor," we read, "is sometimes shocked at the behavior of the English. In conversation, children do not hesitate to contradict the views of their elders. Not only do they not understand the principle that 'children should be seen and not heard,' but they allow their children to talk even more than their parents. It comes as a great shock to

[1] This reference recurs in several of the discussions to make clear how closely, and critically, the African observes the life style of Europeans, e.g., white men. Though knowing M. Gardiner, one can say it was written in a satiric vein. *Ed.*

an African to hear a child say, 'Don't be silly, Daddy!' In some instances, familiarity between children and parents is so great that children call their parents by their first names." Or again, after commenting on certain incomprehensible aspects of the behavior of women, he says: "The men appear even more mysterious. It may seem to us that they really play the role of children in the house. They are looked after very carefully and told what they are supposed to like, to eat, and to wear, and to do. They hardly ever talk. Often when the mother and children are continuing an argument, one notices that the father has already withdrawn from it. Perhaps it is correct to say that the Englishman's home is a castle in which his wife offers him shelter."

Yet, we may say, this is all very well, but what do judgments by individuals on such homely levels have to do with matters of high policy relating to world peace? The answer is not difficult. Statesmen, like the rest of us, react in terms of their own enculturation, and the judgments they make flow from the value systems of their own cultures. When everyday behavior is translated in terms of overall objectives, and these, in turn, are put to the test of challenge in critical situations, it is inevitable that ethnocentrism comes into play, with the consequent blindness to the force of conviction on the other side of the discussion.

At times, ethnocentrism can give a humorous quality to serious political activity, as when British radio broadcasts to Arabic countries during the last World War began with a cock-crow, and thereby lost much of their effectiveness until it was realized that the crowing of a cock was an obscene symbol to the Arabs. Or it can have more serious consequences, as when the Russian delegates to Liberia on the occasion of the inauguration of its President made a serious diplomatic blunder by ethnocentrically wearing business dress at a formal ceremony. The diplomatic history of all countries is replete with examples of how errors of cross-cultural judgment have impeded the attainment of stated objectives. And with the importance of the colonial revolution of our day in mind, it is not out of order to recall the even more numerous examples of the results of failure to respect the customs of the peoples governed. For, though instances of this kind may be buried deep in the files of the various Colonial Offices, as they lie in the archives of our own Indian Service, telling how such occasions gave rise to "incidents" requiring the use of force to re-establish order, they have by no means been forgotten by those who, impotent to act, saw their cultural values swept aside.

We ask, then, is there a way to harness to constructive objectives this enculturated ethnocentrism of the world's peoples? Or does our cultural conditioning bind us so tightly that, in a world of closer contact, we can look forward only to increased friction, tension and eventual strife? These are fair questions, given the undoubted weight which research has shown the enculturative experience to have in forming the whole personality structure of the individual and shaping the characteristic responses of entire peoples.

Here it is profitable for us to recall our discussion of one of the basic discoveries of the science of culture, that however well men learn the ways of their own group, they do not rule out alternatives that may be developed from within the group by invention, or from without by borrowing. In technical terms, the force of enculturation does not rule out the possibility of re-enculturation. Indeed, the seeds of this lie in every body of custom, and are apparent in the fact of cultural variation. Culture is not a straitjacket. It is a loose garment, and just as no two societies have identical cultural patterns, so no two members of the same society have identical behavior patterns. The restlessness of man, the creative drives of the gifted individual, the search for variety in experience, all of these assure us that man is not an automaton, nor ever has been, nor at least while he persists as we know him, will ever be. Herein lies the essentially humanistic quality of the study of man, and herein lies the clue we are seeking in our attempt to solve the problem of how to break through the ethnocentric restraints to the resolution of cultural diversities into the unities that are essential in the attainment of world peace.

4

A realistic and flexible approach to the problems of adjustment in a multi-cultural world can be achieved only by accepting the fact of cultural diversity, and granting in principle the worth of each system of values as this is related to the goals of the people who live by it. By basing its assumptions on the facts which cross-cultural research has made available to us, this approach provides us with a system of values that takes cognizance of the sensibilities of the peoples who enter newly as protagonists on the international stage. A philosophy of this kind calls for basic reorientation of thought. It is what William James would call a "tough-minded" philosophy, requiring that the force of one's own enculturated points of view be recognized and counter-balanced by granting philosophical parity to systems other than one's own.

We must, however, not confuse this philosophy of cultural relativism with the doctrine of ethical relativity with which it is often mistakenly identified. As should be apparent from our discussion of cultural learning, the facts of relativism in culture go far beyond the analysis of differentials in value-systems. For cultural relativism takes full account of ways in which such fundamental psychological processes as perception and cognition respond to the enculturative experience of the individual, and as well explains the foundations of his moral and ethical behavior.

The difference between cultural relativism, on the one hand, and ethical relativity as it is treated by the philosophers becomes clear when we recognize that cultural relativism has exclusive cross-cultural reference, whereas ethical relativity is essentially intra-cultural in its focus. The first raises the question of the validity of applying the criteria that sanction the behavior and guide the thinking of the people of one society to the standards of another; the second raises the question of whether any standards can be drawn to direct individual conduct. This, presumably, is a logical problem of some importance, but ethnologically it is of minor significance, inasmuch as among the several hundred human societies that have been systematically studied by anthropologists, none has been found which tolerates moral or ethical anarchy. In every group individuals are present who deviate in some degree from the patterns of their society. But we also know that those who, questioning the precepts of the group, go beyond the sanctioned limits of variation in conduct laid down by their society, and, in some societies the sanctioned bounds of thought, do this at their peril.

This brings us to a second *caveat,* the need to distinguish carefully between absolutes and universals in the relativistic approach to culture. Every society, we have just stated, has its moral code, which carries unquestioned sanctions for its members. But once we move into another society, we find a series of values differently conceptualized, differently phrased, but having sanctions of equal force. It is therefore apparent, by extending this observation to human society in general, that while the fact that every culture has an accepted code governing attitudes and conduct has been empirically established, the absolute worth of any one of these codes, except for a given society in terms of its own culture, is amenable to no such empirical validation.

We know of no peoples who do not assign values to life and death, to pleasure and pain, to love and hate, but the precise nature of the value assigned each can be predicted only in the context of the total culture. We know of no societies where there is a complete absence of some form of artistic expression, yet just what form this expression takes among a given group, whether it is graphic or plastic, whether representative or stylized, and if so, the nature of the symbolisms, cannot be foretold. Given a society of which nothing is known, we can say no more than that its members will assign values to life and death, pleasure and pain; and that they will manifest some kind of patterned aesthetic responses. We could continue this process through all the aspects of culture, and in each we could predict with all confidence that some kind of institutional arrangement, with its underlying sanctions, would be present. And while we could not indicate beforehand the form of either the institutions or its sanctions, we could be sure that the people who possessed them would assign them unquestioned validity, and that this, in turn, would dictate their reactions to the ways of other groups with whom they might come into contact. That is, we could be certain of the universals, but we would have to know the details of the total culture before we could indicate the particular forms these universals would take in this particular society.

As I have pointed out elsewhere, we must recognize that our approach is not based on an all-or-none model. It has a number of different levels, which, if we do not distinguish them, will obscure the various facets of the problem of cultural diversity, and lessen our ability to draw scientifically valid conclusions from the cross-cultural materials. This is especially important for us, for the very nature of our approach requires us, so to speak, to move conceptually outside the boundaries of our own deep-set modes of thought and judgment if we are to achieve to any degree the psychological distances that are essential in re-evaluating our own culturally determined values.

The first of these facets is methodological. We here mention it only in passing, since it is essentially the concern of the professional student of culture. It asserts the principle that to understand a people, one must study them in their own terms, and not, as a student, judge them. It is thus an expression of scientific objectivity in cross-cultural research. Though this principle strikes us now as self-evident and indispensable, it took many years of field work to establish it, as a reading of the earlier anthropological works makes apparent. It has required time and scientific discipline to enable us to learn to report, not to evaluate; to understand that the mission of the investigator, which is to accumulate a sound body of fact, will be achieved only to the degree that he frees himself of *a priori* cultural judgments.

More difficult, and at the core of our discussion, is the philosophical aspect of our approach. Here we come to the question of ultimates, which we must face in terms of a searching re-examination of systems of thought that have come down to us through the works of generations of thinkers who were quite unaware of the degree to which their basic assumptions, even concerning the nature of reality itself, were culture-bound. Yet, to take one point which is useful as an instance because it is without implications of value, the wealth of information at our disposal on the differing ways in which men interpret time, and distance, and color, quite aside from the question as to how they variously order their behavior in moral and ethical terms, cannot but give us pause. We base our perception of color on shade; and research in physics, moving from this kind of culturally shaped conceptualization of how color is to be approached, has given us the spectrum as a basic tool. Yet in the Philippines, as Conklin has shown, intensity is the basis of classification, so that identical shades of green in two plants of the forest, one bright and one dull, are held to be quite different in color. This variation in possible interpretations of natural phenomena is found even within a culture. We can draw an example of this in the way we ourselves describe distance. Ideally, we should delimit distance in units of space. Yet all of us will at times indicate how far it is between one place and another by giving the time it takes to traverse the proper distance in a given type of conveyance—so many minutes, or hours, by motor-car, or by train, or by airplane—or on foot!

Everything we have learned through cross-cultural research concerning linguistic differentials, or variant systems of social structure, or of political orientation, to name but a few of the aspects of culture, teaches how effectively the most varied kinds of forms can fulfill a given functional end. Take an example from West Africa, from one culture where every man or woman has one of seven possible names by which he is known, given according to sex and the day of the week on which he was born. In a large population such as is found there, the difficulty of distinguishing which specific member of a group is meant when a given name is pronounced would seem substantial. Yet it works quite as well, let us say, as does our own way of designating kinfolk, whereby we use words such as "brother" or "sister" or "grandmother"—to say nothing of "cousin"—which are anything but specific in reference. Or, again, we get along quite well with the rather simple tense structure of our language. We feel no need, when indicating time, to state whether an act occurred in the recent or distant past as is done in many languages, nor do we trouble to think that systems of gender need not be confined to differentiating the sexes.

Time, and space, and color appertain to the natural world. How much more difficult is it to set up categories of validity for intangibles of belief and conduct, where the hard facts of the ecological and biological bases of human life are not present to yield terms of reference in drawing judgments; or where aesthetic evaluations enter. Provided that fundamental beliefs are not challenged, the greater effectiveness of a newly introduced technical process will be recognized by a people, though whether or not the innovation will be accepted is another question. One has only to recall how tenacious the belief systems of the American Indians have remained despite their long contact with Europeans, to realize that values of this order do not give way so easily. On the positive side, this bespeaks the devotion of every people to its basic philosophy; a point which underscores the difficulty faced by the philosophers when the absolutes in human experience on which they rest their theories of knowledge and value are examined in the light of the cross-cultural facts.

These are problems which we cannot resolve here. They
have significance for our discussion in the way that any
philosophical position which can serve as a guide for action
is relevant. In terms of the problem of resolving issues
arising out of the divergencies of culture so as to achieve
world peace, they are important because they point to the
culturally pluralistic world that can no longer be disregarded when theories of the nature of reality and the ultimate springs of human behavior are advanced. Not that
cultural pluralism has been entirely neglected by the
philosophers, nor that its implications are not considered
in their writings. But in a world where contacts of peoples
having different ways of life are constantly increasing in
duration and intensity, and the potentialities of conflict
arising out of a failure to respect cultural differences are
thereby enhanced, the philosophical questions we have
posed take on a new urgency in quite practical terms.

This brings us to the third facet of our approach, the
implications for practical affairs of a philosophy which holds
that *the values by which men live are relative to the particular kind of cultural learning they have experienced.*
Here questions not only of the philosophical validity of this
interpretation of reality arise, but also those which can be
integrated under the formula of tolerance and, on the cross-
cultural level, non-interference with the ways of other
peoples. Most frequently the question posed is, "Granting
the validity of each people's ways of life, and the respect
to be accorded these ways by peoples whose values are different, what should we do in the face, let us say, of the
Nazi policy of extermination of the German Jews?" The
question has unending variants. It is asked about the Soviet
work-camps, about the headhunters of Borneo, about the
lynching of Negroes in the United States. Alternatively, it
may be asked whether we should reject such a statement of
high purpose as was pronounced by Lord Lugard in 1922
when, in setting the background for his development of the
conception of the Dual Mandate, he described the mission

of Europe in Africa in these words: "It was the task of civilization to put an end to slavery, to establish Courts of Law to inculcate in the natives a sense of individual responsibility of liberty, and of justice, and to teach their rulers how to apply these principles; above all, to see to it that the system of education should be such as to produce happiness and progress."

These are questions not easy to answer, but not because they pose problems that lie outside the philosophical dialectic of cultural relativism, or of practical solutions. To espouse a philosophy based on the scientific findings of cross-cultural study does not imply unilateral tolerance of ideas other than one's own. If one must respect, one must also be respected. What we face is the gigantic task of devising ways of dealing with man's inhumanity to man.

It is important to understand that no approach, no philosophy, offers a method for the resolution of all practical problems. The recognition of the fact of cultural diversity is a statement of opportunity to build realistically on what research has taught us. Professor George Simpson of Oberlin College, in the course of a discussion of the relation between cultural relativism and human ideals, has put the matter cogently. "Scientific knowledge," he says, "is employed for useful and constructive purposes, or for harmful or destructive purposes, according to the beliefs of a particular person or group. A knowledge of cultural relativism does not inevitably lead to tolerance any more than a knowledge of nuclear physics leads inevitably to the use of atomic energy for peaceful purposes. Cultural relativism in and of itself does not provide all the rules or all the answers for living in a modern world. An appreciation of the fact of cultural relativism, plus some knowledge of concrete cultural situations other than our own, may contribute to an understanding of the ways of men. There is no money-back guarantee."

5

Let us now return to our basic question, the integration of cultural diversities as a step toward the achievement of world peace. On the practical level, it will be recalled that the need was stressed for a set of principles that would be realistic and flexible, and that would bring to bear on the problem the findings of scientific research into differences manifest in the cultures of mankind. We have seen how, through the mechanisms of cultural learning, the ethnocentrisms that express the ultimate validity of a culture for those who live by it are inculcated. We have seen how these ethnocentrisms, viewed as a way in which the worth of the individual is compounded for himself by means of his identification with his group, give a leverage for the establishment of a climate of friendliness and trust, and afford a corrective for the hostility and suspicion that is a legacy of the disregard of ethnocentric values that has been outstanding in the events of the past.

On the basis of our scientific knowledge, and of the philosophy that derives from it, four principles can be advanced to shape attitudes and inform policy. They are minimal requirements, if we accept the fact that world peace has to be achieved in a culturally pluralistic and dynamic world. They must be regarded as a beginning, and subject to elaboration in many ways as the world situation changes through their implementation and the possibilities of new applications appear. They are as follows:

First, we must recognize, and strive to have generally recognized everywhere, the fact that different peoples often achieve identical ends by different means. This being the case, we must, secondly, search out the functional unities that underlie the differences in form that are to be observed in the different modes of belief and behavior found among the peoples of the world. Third, we must define our values and goals clearly, so that we and those with whom we have dealings will be conscious of them, and we should strive for a similar delineation from others. And finally, we must in common build on these differing patterns to achieve common ends, accepting the right of choice among peaceful alternatives for all peoples.

a cross—cultural
view of bias
and values

We are not the most ethnocentrically oriented society
the world has known, but we certainly possess one of
the most powerful ethnocentrisms in the experience of
mankind. . . . Even today, it is difficult for us not to do
what I term "thinking colonially" by applying to peoples
whose ways of life differ from our own the dreary
vocabulary of inferiority. . . . We must recognize that
the pluralistic nature of the value systems of the world's
cultures . . . cannot be judged on the basis of a single
system. . . . Unless we realize that perhaps we do not
have the only answers to questions of common concern, and that our biases, though they seem natural
enough to us, cannot be universally accepted, we will
be in for some very difficult times.

What has been called "the
cross-cultural approach" to the understanding of Man is a
major contribution of anthropological science. It means
that any problem of human life must be looked at from the
point of view of the total range of human institutions and
modes of behavior to be found over all the world. Once
stated, the importance of this cross-cultural approach is so
obvious that we can but wonder why it took so long to
discover.

In probing its significance we must, first of all, consider

some of the implications of the concept of culture, a concept that is so basic in the human sciences that its discovery and use in the study of Man has been compared to the importance of the discovery and use of the concept of gravity in understanding the natural world. Culture is something that all human beings, but only human beings, have. It is not related to race, because any human being, given normal capacity—and most members of every race have normal capacity—can learn anything that any human society has developed, provided only that he has the opportunity to do so, and starts at a young enough age. It is thus not inborn; it is learned. Yet while culture is ubiquitous among human beings, the particular mode of life each culture represents carries validity only to the members of the society that lives in accordance with it.

To the ordinary person, the standards by which he lives seem logical, and natural, and even inevitable. But when we discover how differently other peoples act in identical situations, or how differently they meet a common problem, the question is raised: "Are these ways really logical? Are they natural? Are they inevitable?" It then becomes apparent that much of what one group may consider logical and natural and inevitable, another will deem illogical, unnatural and contrived.

An example will make the point. We think of the natural world as something that is fixed, and as being in the "nature" of things, having the character of objective reality arising from contact with it through the ability to touch or feel or hear it. If we assume that biologically, Man is a single species, it follows that perception of the natural world must channel through the same sensory organs in all human beings, with comparable results.

Yet this is not the case, as an incident that happened in West Africa a few years ago will make clear. In the city of Kumasi, in Ghana, I was talking to an English electrical contractor who used African labor. "Why is it," he asked, "that when I have to dig a trench for a conduit, I stretch a line from one stake to another to give me the shortest distance between my two end-points? I tell my workmen to dig the trench following the straight line, but it is always curved. Why can these men never dig a straight trench?"

"Your workmen are from the northern territories?"

"Yes."

"Can you draw a perfect circle?"

He soon got the point. His workmen, who came from the northern part of Ghana, live in what my colleague, Professor Campbell, calls a "noncarpentered world." Their houses are round; the enclosures for their animals are round; their knives are curved. They live in a circular world. A straight line, therefore, is something that they must learn to make.

Numberless anecdotes of this sort give the rationale for an experimental study we are conducting to assess the influence of culture on perception.

Taking a different aspect of perceiving the natural world, we may ask, what is the color blue? If one goes to certain parts of West Africa, he will find that it may be anything from indigo to black. What is red, and when does red stop being red and become orange? When does blue stop being blue and become violet? Those who look at the spectrum as it actually is, soon realize that these colors really merge one into the other, and that it is convention that assigns to a given segment of that spectrum a name, arbitrarily cutting it off and saying "This is red; this is orange; this is blue." To the person who is enculturated to a given system, these arbitrary divisions seem of the natural order of things. Actually, they are culturally determined. They are no more than conventions accepted by the members of the particular society in which they are found.

We can pursue this question further. All human beings get hungry, but a particular individual senses hunger according to the schedule set up by the society of which he is a member. Englishmen feel a need for tea at four o'clock; it suffices an American to eat in the morning, at noon, and

in the evening. This "natural" need is thus manipulated by
the timetable of culture. Some people schedule two meals
a day; some eat five. If one happens to come from a five-
meal society into one- or two-meal groups, a great deal
of readjustment will be necessary. Certainly, there is no
objective reason why one should eat morning, noon, and
night. One of the things that has made for difficulties in the
colonial world is that Europeans, who have developed an
industrial discipline having a time-table of breakfast, followed by a morning given to steady work, a pause for
lunch, then an afternoon of work, after which one has an
evening meal, have imposed this routine on peoples having
different conventions, and they have found this one of the
most difficult things to which they must adjust.

I may once more draw an example out of my experience,
in the industrial city of Durban, in the Union of South
Africa, the manager of a particular plant discovered that
his African workmen were not being properly fed. They
would not eat lunch during the "proper" lunch hour, and
they would tire early in the afternoon. A system was thereupon devised whereby his company would make hot lunches
available to the African workers at very low cost. The
Africans flocked in for two or three days; then the number
decreased rapidly. The manager would periodically call
them in and urge them to take advantage of this. They
would respond, but in a few days the attendance would go
down again. This was puzzling until it was pointed out that
the industrial schedule was out of line with the hunger
schedule of the workers. Aboriginally there was no time in
the morning to make a fire and heat food for breakfast, so
that a man took only a bite of what was left from the preceding night's meal before he went to work in the fields.
About ten o'clock in the morning, the children would bring
him food which would suffice until he went home, when he
would eat a hearty meal in the late afternoon.

I might point out that the imposition of this Euroamerican pattern of organizing the day according to a schedule

essential to the industrial effort is one of the things that has made it difficult for European and American industries operating in various parts of the world to obtain a steady labor supply. Not being accustomed to working at this kind of regular pace, or breaking the day in these particular ways, work is done until money is in hand to buy some commodity he wants; then the worker leaves his job. This is what economists call a "target worker." A man takes a job so that he can get enough money to buy a sewing machine, or a bicycle, or something of that kind, after which he goes back to live as he did before.

Differences of this sort, and the many others that have been revealed by the cross-cultural approach, have led us to a concept technically called "cultural relativism." This concept holds that there is no absolutely valid moral system, any more than there is an absolutely valid mode of perceiving the natural world. The traditions of a people dictate what for them is right and wrong, how they are to interpret what they see and feel and hear, and they live according to these imperatives.

Now this is a very tough-minded point of view. It has proved to be difficult to grasp, let alone accept. This has been particularly the case with the philosophers, who have been trained in terms of the Greek tradition, which brings them to certain conclusions that are based on principles that are not borne out when submitted to the cross-cultural test. One thus takes either the scientific position or the philosophical one. We need not know a great deal about our own intellectual history, however, to predict that the philosophers will, after being given the facts, shift their thinking so as to bring their positions into line with those facts.

Let us now consider the problem of bias, which is intimately related to this matter of the relativistic, cross-cultural point of view. There can be all kinds of bias, and bias can be a very good thing. If bias is defined as having a penchant for the things and ideas one has been taught since childhood are right and proper; if by bias is meant the ordering of behavior in such a way that one is in accord with the traditions of his own society and thereby obtains the satisfactions that come from conformity, then bias can be said to play an important role in promoting social and psychological adjustment.

Technically, we speak of bias as a form of ethnocentrism, a word used to designate the reactions of a person who is centered on the customs of his own people. In these terms, ethnocentrism provides an excellent way of establishing and validating the structure of one's own ego through the simple process of identification. For the individual, it works something like this: I am a member of my society. The way my society does things is right and proper. I do the things that are right and proper, therefore I am a good member of my society. The way my society does things is the best way. I do things in the best way, therefore I am one of the best people. This simple kind of reasoning is not only healthy, but it is an important stabilizing factor in social life. If the infrahuman social forms had the symbolisms of language that Man commands, they might very well phrase their attitudes by saying "We dogs are undoubtedly better than those cows, and dog culture is better than cow culture."

Yet the matter is not quite this simple. One can either say, "My way is best, and anyone that does not follow it is foolish," or he can say, "My way is best, and everyone had better follow it, or else. . . ."

The first of these may be thought of as benevolent ethnocentrism. It permits identification by an individual with the things that everyone he knows or has had contact with thinks is good. Another example out of my own field experience may be cited to make the point. The Bush Negroes of Dutch Guiana, among whom I conducted field research a good many years ago, practice plural marriage. Having come the distance I had come, with the equipment I had and the gifts I brought, I was regarded as a person of some consequence in my own society. In their view, a person of this status must have more than one wife. When I assured them that my wife, who was my collaborator in this study, was my sole spouse, some thought I was not telling the truth, some that I was merely foolish. Some thought I should behave like a proper man, and gave me the opportunity to acquire further wives. But no one said, "Get yourself more wives, or leave."

The difference between this more restrained sort of ethnocentrism and that of Europe and America is obvious. It is one of the reasons that the cross-cultural point of view of which I have spoken is so difficult for us to grasp, enculturated as we are to patterns of militant ethnocentrism. We are not the most ethnocentrically oriented society the world has known, but we certainly possess one of the most powerful ethnocentrisms in the experience of mankind. This is one of the reasons why the spread of Euroamerican culture over the world has given rise to so many examples of the social demoralization that develops when a more powerful group not only imposes its rule on another, but actively depreciates the things they hold to be of value. It is not generally recognized that one of the few times we experienced real psychological demoralization in the United States was in the late 1930's, when the Nazis were saying, "Our way is better then your way; dictatorship is better than democracy. If you don't like it, try and do something about it." Yet it was not until after the Japanese attack on Pearl Harbor, when we did do something about it, that the air cleared and our psychological equilibrium was restored.

In the case of our reaction to Nazi aggression, we were feeling nothing different from the frustrations of colonial peoples all over the world, for not only was the technology of those who conquered them proclaimed superior, and proved it, but the morals, the religious beliefs, the art, the music of their conquerors were similarly proclaimed to be better. Since it was discovered that gun powder could be used to kill people as well as to provide amusement, as it will be recalled was its original use in China, Europe had the power that made possible the expansion of the political controls which laid the basis for demands on other peoples for changes in their fundamental values. And those demands they were powerless to resist.

All this may seem removed from the actualities of day-to-day living. Yet if one probes beneath the surface, and really cares to know as individual human beings some of the people who have been the recipients in this process, one finds a heritage of bitterness against Europe and America that is to be traced back to the fact that Americans and Europeans have gone about the world saying, "There, there, what you are doing is all very well, but I really know how to do it better, and in any event you will do it my way, or else . . ."

What is one of the most severe handicaps under which the democracies struggle at the present time? It is the charge of colonialism. And what is colonialism? It is in the minds of most subject peoples, something that a white man does to a man of color. And since most colonial peoples are colored, this definition is accepted by practically all the inhabitants of the world who happen not to be white; but who, it must be stressed, make up most of the world's population.

Let us see how this works out, in terms of important issues of foreign relations. When England and France moved into the Suez Canal there was a tremendous outcry of "colonialism." A few months later, when Russia moved into Hungary, whereas some of the Asian powers had been quick to denounce England and France, Prime Minister Nehru of India, for example, did not comment on the Russian adventure until pressure had been brought on him. It so happened that there was at my University a visiting professor who knew India intimately. He was asked, "What will be the reaction of the Indians to Russian suppression of Hungarian aspirations? Will they not see that this is the same kind of thing that European colonial nations have done?" It was something of a shock when he pointed out that this attack would by no means be equated with colonialism, but that it would rather be held to be no more than a quarrel between European Nations.

Shortly afterwards, I was able to test this statement in talking to a student from Liberia. Liberia has been an independent country ever since it was established, so that the issue of colonialism enters minimally. This student, in New York, had stayed at the same hotel with the Liberian delegation to the United Nations just at the time when the vote was taken on a resolution condemning Russia for its assault on Hungary. In the vote, Liberia abstained. When I asked him if Liberia did not believe in rebuking imperialist aggression of this kind, the answer was, "But this was just an affair between white folks." In Africa, later, I took occasion to bring up this question, and the reactions of Africans were almost identical to those I have described. It is not unreasonable to hope that the Chinese conquest of Tibet and the later tensions between China and India may demonstrate that colonialism is not necessarily the monopoly of Europe—although we may be sure that it will be pointed out that the lesson learned by the Chinese and other non-European expansionists is one that had been taught them by Europe.

The point is that in addition to political control, colonialism imposed this much more insidious and demoralizing assumption of cultural superiority. Even today, it is difficult for us not to do what I term "thinking colonially," by applying to peoples whose ways of life differ from our own words like "primitive," or "childlike," or "savage," or any of the rest of the dreary vocabulary of inferiority that we have developed. It is understandable why these peoples resent such words deeply, and why the attitudes their use reflects and engenders lie at the base of one of the most serious problems of international relations with which we are faced at present.

One result of taking an anthropological, cross-cultural point of view has been a growing realization of the need to study the values of different peoples, so we can grasp those things that make life meaningful to them, and that give sanctions to their behavior. It is these values, we now realize, that are the basis not only of the moral and religious beliefs of all peoples, but of their technology, their economic system, and their political organization. Democracy, for instance, is in these terms more than a slogan. It is a value, a way of life, something for which a people will make even the ultimate sacrifice.

When we approach the problem of studying values cross-culturally, we find that narrative and poetic forms, particularly in societies where a written language was never developed, are of particularly great help, since in them the basic assumptions that underlie their values on the unconscious level are so clearly apparent. Some years ago, my wife and I collected a fairly large number of myths, tales, and narratives of various kinds in West Africa among the people of Dahomey. Later we analyzed them from a cross-cultural point of view, not as folklore, but as literature. There is nothing that a literary critic does in analyzing a story or a novel that cannot be done with these narratives—we can study plot construction, their imagery, the way in which a particular character typifies a certain situation or a certain response. Not only this, but the socially accepted motivations and drives that validate behavior can be seen with great clarity in them. Proverbs, too, offer particularly good materials for the analysis of value systems, because like a people's myths, tales and poetry, their proverbs reflect the things that are important for them. Those values are, of course, not usually stated as explicitly as the proverbs of Benjamin Franklin, though *Poor Richard's Almanac* does reveal the system of values that was maintained in early American society, such as the value of hard work, or of not being a spend-thrift.

This brings us to another important point. How does the individual come to know the values of his society? These are learned through a process that I have been forced, for want of a better word, to call enculturation. In its essence, this is the educational process, using the form in its widest meaning of socialized learning, to which all human beings are exposed. Most of the enculturative process is effortless; we learn our cultural lessons so well that our knowledge is internalized and comes to have a strong emotional as well as cognitive content. Why must one hold his fork properly? It is not only because "this is the way it is done," the simplest answer, and the one most commonly given. Beneath this lie a whole series of aesthetic responses, of considerations of social position, of implications of prestige, that rarely rise to the level of consciousness. Indeed, in most of our behavior, we do not think— we react. Most of our life is not lived through the use of the higher cortical centers but in accordance with impulses from the spinal cord. Our response to socially recognized cues is spontaneous. If we had to stop and question what we must do in each situation we face, we would literally never get anything done.

Perhaps most of the sanctions of our culture are learned by sensing the implications of the behavior of the other members of our society. Children are, of course, also explicitly taught those sanctions, and they are thereby passed from one generation to the other, this being one of the reasons why every culture is stable, as well as ever-changing. Music offers an excellent example of this process. If the ordinary person in our society, who happens not to be a professional musician, is asked to describe the modal structure of any given song, he would be hard put to it to find an answer. Yet most of us do sing, even though most of us are innocent of how our music is structured. Why, then, do we make, and like, our particular kind of music? Because this is the kind of music we have always heard; this is the music to which we have been enculturated. It is highly instructive to take someone fresh from China to a symphony concert, and watch his bewilderment. The basis of Chinese music is the single melodic line. The basis of European music is polyphony. Again, why does African music not seem strange to us? This is because Jazz, which we have adopted as one of our own musical forms, is a development out of African music. But there are kinds of African music which would be extremely strange to us, and for which an American would have to cultivate a taste.

Because we have been brought up on our own musical forms, we have learned to appreciate them; which is to say, to value them. The value-structure, insofar as the individuals who listen to the music are concerned, then, underlies the actual performance, or the perception of the sounds themselves. And in the same way, the values that sanction any kind of behavior are what make the behavior meaningful. It is just because they lie beneath the level of consciousness, that is, because they are *subliminal,* to use a technical term, that they hold such importance for the people who have them. And this is one of the reasons why, despite the contacts of the last four or five centuries between Europeans and Americans, on the one hand, and other peoples all over the world, on the other, the societies that have been subjected to domination have by no means given up the things that they have for generations felt to be good and proper.

Let us recapitulate the three aspects of the study of man we have considered. First of all, we discussed the cross-cultural point of view, which developed out of the anthropological objective of studying Man in the large, in the light of differences and similarities between societies, and in the ways by which different peoples must achieve these ends that all peoples must achieve if they are to survive and adjust to their natural and social environments. We then say how the factor of bias is inherent in all human societies; how it arises out of the very nature of human social life, making the individual devoted to his culture, and affording him the basis for his judgments of other bodies of custom. Finally, we assessed the significance of the fact that the values by which a people live underlie the whole structure of their culture.

From all this we draw a conclusion of enormous practical importance. An understanding of these phenomena is essential if we are going to live in a world where communications are shrinking distances, and where language study is making peoples able to speak to one another to a degree never possible before. We must recognize that the pluralistic nature of the value systems of the world's cultures, and that the ways of the many different peoples of the world cannot be judged on the basis of any single system. In the United Nations, in all kinds of international commissions, in all sorts of world cooperative movements, we now deal with persons from societies having the most diverse cultures. Unless we realize that perhaps we do not have the only answers to questions of common concern, and that our biases, though they seem natural enough to us, cannot be universally accepted, we will be in for some very difficult times.

rear-guard action*

Racism breeds counter-racism, and those of us who as scientists approach the problems raised by the differences between human beings fear the consequences when slogan and bald assertion take the place of controlled investigation and reasoned judgment. . . . We found that our patient efforts to define and comprehend the concept of "race" were being misinterpreted by those who would distort findings so as to . . . preserve inequalities, not of race, but of opportunity, reward, and social condition.

Perspectives in Biology and Medicine has as its purpose "to communicate new ideas and to stimulate original thought in the biological and medical sciences." It also presents "original essays" which advance "new hypotheses representing informed thinking," and "interpretive essays . . . which take stock of recent and current research and develop heuristic ideas not yet fully tested." It is in this journal that we find an essay by Henry E. Garrett, Emeritus Professor of Psychology at Columbia University and now at the University of Virginia, entitled "The Equalitarian Dogma." This article is an attack on those who hold that the assumption of the existence of inherent racial inequalities has not been established by scientific research. It

* A review of *Perspectives in Biology and Medicine,* Autumn, 1961 issue.

assails those who maintain that this fact lays the burden of proof on students who maintain that race is a significant factor in determining human behavior and differences in the cultures of different peoples.

The appearance of this paper, by a psychometrist who is professor in a school of education, published in a journal devoted to biological and medical research, is at best curious. That an editor of this journal, a physiologist, felt it necessary to write an editorial explaining why he "invited and accepted" Professor Garrett's paper is significant. His uneasiness is reflected in two statements. "There are reasons for thinking that racial differences . . . may be real," he writes, countering this by another sentence which reads, "Similarly, there are compelling reasons to claim that all evidence on racial differences is unsatisfactory."

The editor continues: "There are promising approaches to the problem which have not yet been used." What these methods may be are not indicated, but the assertion, again, leads to what would seem to be a prime instance of confusion resulting in a *non sequitur:* "Is science to continue as the free pursuit of knowledge or is it to become subordinate to social and political theories?"

One gathers, both from this editorial statement and from Professor Garrett's article, that there exists a conspiracy of silence, aimed at replacing the scientific study of race with scientism in racial psychology, so that anyone who investigates the problem of racial differences presumably comes under some kind of attack that imperils his freeedom of scientific research. Except for one work cited by Professor Garrett, which certain university presses refused to publish because its findings showed that American Negroes stood lower than American Whites in intelligence test scores, we are given no evidence that such a conspiracy exists.

It is tedious to read the repetitions in this article of shopworn arguments about "racial" differences in "intelligence," by which is meant differences in test scores between "Negroes"—a mixed African-European-American Indian population—and those of European descent. Perhaps what attracted the attention of the editor of *Perspectives* to Professor Garrett's article was the new interpretations it gives of the forces making for acceptance of the equalitarian point of view—in truth, about the only "new" hypothesis found in it. One reason given lies in the failure of the Nazi war effort; another the rise of African nationalism; still another the Supreme Court decision of 1954 ordering desegregation of public schools.

But apparently the crowning reason why, in recent years, ideas of racial equality have spread is the fact that "the Communists (and their supporters) have aided in the spread and acceptance of the equalitarian dogma, although the extent and method of their aid is difficult to assess." Their moves are presumably as subtle in this field as in others. "Direct action as well as subversion are both in the Communist creed. Communists have used equalitarian dogma as a device to gain converts among underprivileged people and also to foment trouble when possible. Many non-Communists hold the position that the free world must outdo the Communists in acceptance of this belief and must reject any further inquiry into its validity."

It is apparent that as a logician Professor Garrett is no more effective than the editor who gave his reasons for publishing this paper. The syllogism employed here is clear. "Communists and their sympathizers are against racism. Equalitarians are against racism. Hence equalitarians are Communists or Communist sympathizers." One need only substitute the word "measles" for "racism," and "capitalists" for "equalitarians," for the degree of validity of this argument to become clear.

Instead of echoing oft-repeated refutations of Professor Garrett's argument, let us rather look at some of the positive developments in the study of man which bear on the question raised in his article, developments of which he seems quite unaware. Critical here is why anthropologists, who study man as a physical type and a culture-building animal, and most psychologists, especially social and educational psychologists, are no longer much concerned with the problem.

The reason, in fact, does not lie in any conspiracy of silence. It lies in the scientific principle of economy, that rejects concepts which are too unwieldy to yield to intelligible definition and significant research effort. Definitions—and they were endless—fell of their own weight. At one time, race was defined as a major grouping of mankind marked by particular physical traits. Then it was established that there are far greater differences *within* any one of these groups in the very traits used to distinguish them than there are between such groupings. And so this definition was rejected on the count of what, in statistical terms, is called overlapping.

It fell on another point. Without getting into the controversy over the precise meaning of the word "species," the fact remains that all human groups are mutually fertile. This implies that mating between members of sub-groups has been going on since man became human. This in turn means that man provides no approximation, even, to the biological concept of "pure race." Inbreeding has occurred in isolated local groupings, such as the Eskimo, but this is scarcely on the level of race, however the word is defined. Man, indeed, is probably the most mongrelized animal in the entire biological series.

Nor was this all. As long as the end of the first World War, psychologists began to reject the validity of the concept of "racial intelligence" as measured by the tests. Together with cultural anthropologists, they came to perceive how greatly the factors of background, of opportunity, of training entered into the equation. One calls to mind a series of intelligence tests given to African children where the scores were so low that these subjects, described as normal and quite adequately equipped to meet the demands of their own ways of life, were in test terms below the level of survival requirements. The answer was clear—the test was culture-bound, and the questions were thus in large part meaningless. Nor did the psychologists solve their problem by devising tests which did not involve verbal factors—that is, answering questions. However they tried, differences in meaning, motivation, and value could not be avoided.

It is a long time since physical anthropologists have concerned themselves with the study of racial differences as such. What do they study? They seek to understand the genetic processes that are operative in the formation of population, to discover the influences that are in play shaping the growth and development of children, they investigate the evolution of the human form, the relation of *Homo sapiens* to other living anthropoids. Cultural anthropologists concerned with learned behavior have long ago learned that physical type is something that does not enter causally, except as a sociological factor, when studying the social setting in which human beings live their lives.

Even while the definition of race as applying to differences in physical type was an accepted scientific conception, it was being rethought in genetic terms. What came out was a revision of the idea of race which held these groupings to be aggregates of family lines marked by comparable physical characteristics. Here we had the beginnings of an approach to biological reality. For in effect, this revision held that the fact that two human beings have the same hair type, or nasal configuration, or skin color, is irrelevant unless their resemblances reflect common membership in a particular ancestral line. That you and I resemble one another in one of these characteristics, or any other, is of no significance unless we have inherited them from the same ancestors.

This brings us to the matter of intelligence. Unfortunately, no one has ever really told us what is meant by the word. But this does not matter. It is one of those concepts that means something we recognize when we come across it. We need not quibble over the point. Are there differences in this something? It needs no scientific research to tell us there are, and not only in "general" intelligence, whatever this may be, but in special kinds of ability. One person is "just naturally" musical, another tone-deaf. One has an aptitude for language or mathematics or is of a philosophical bent, another is sensitive to color, or is hard-headed, with a flair for practical matters that baffles those who do not have this particular ability.

The point here is that no scientifically valid evidence has ever been produced to show that these differences, either in general intelligence or particular aptitudes, are related to race. Rather, we find that to the extent they are inherited, they are inherited by individuals from their particular forebears. The dusty argument, produced once more by Professor Garrett, that "the black African has never constructed an alphabet, created a literature or a science, produced any great men, or built up a civilization" is only plausible for those who find such a statement in line with their preconceptions. It cannot be proved, but it can be, and is, dangerous for the peace of the world. Racism breeds counter-racism, and those of us who as scientists approach the problems raised by the differences between human beings fear the consequences when slogan and bald assertion take the place of controlled investigation and reasoned judgment.

It is the failure of these last to illumine our search for understanding that has caused us to give over the concept "race" as a useful scientific tool. We stopped referring to it because we became bored by it. More serious, we found that our patient unprofitable efforts to define and comprehend the concept "race" were being misinterpreted by those who would distort findings so as to apply them to preserve inequalities, not of race, but of opportunity, reward, and social condition. When a scientific concept becomes a political football, there are only two things for the scientist to do. The first, which concerns the scientist as scientist, is to change his terminology to escape the emotions aroused by terms that have become battle cries. The second, which concerns the scientist as citizen, is to fight the misuse of his scientific findings. The anthropologists, and many psychologists, did both of these, and did them with considerable success.

In the process many of the changes which I have noted and of which, we may recall, neither Professor Garrett nor the editor of *Perspectives,* who mentioned none of them, seems aware, occurred. There were others. Physical anthropologists came more and more to call themselves human biologists. No longer was an anthropologist to be defined as a man who went about the world measuring heads in order to classify peoples according to some system of racial affiliation. They began to ask the questions "why" man is as he is, rather than to describe the "what" of human differences. Recognizing the dynamics in all aspects of the world and of man, they came to frame their problems in terms of becoming rather than of being.

There was another, much more far-reaching change. Earlier physical anthropologists were heavily oriented toward anatomy. Some of them, indeed, felt that a medical degree was a prerequisite for their work. The facts of human life, however, began to force the realization that just as to classify men into types was an exercise in scientific sterility, so to leave out of account that which was learned in studying what was inherited led to the neglect of a factor of the highest significance in understanding why man is as he is. Thus, the force of tradition in defining what is desirable in a husband or wife will, and does, effectively influence the characteristics of the members of the society in which these ideas prevail. Where tradition dictates doing away with infants who have certain hereditary physical defects, this cannot but influence the extent to which these traits will be found in that society in later generations. Prestige, ideals of beauty, and endless other *cultural* factors invade and influence the course of human genetics and the formation of local types.

All this points up the scientific naïveté in the statement

by the editor of *Perspectives* when he says, "We are concerned here with a question in biology." The problem of
differences in racial intelligence is not a question in biology;
at most it is a question in *human* biology. Why the difference? Because while man is an animal in the sense of being
a member of the biological series, he has one trait that sets
him off from all other members of the animal world. This is
the ability to learn cumulatively; he is the only tool-using,
speaking animal, who not only gets ideas but through the
symbolisms of language transmits them as a base on which
future generations can build. It is a difference not of degree,
but of kind.

It is this that makes the biological approach to race so
unsatisfactory. This is not the place to try to explain the
temerity of biologists who, understanding the physical
mechanisms that dictate heredity in the infrahuman forms,
are so ready with their pronouncements about man, despite
their ignorance of the critical cultural factor. One need
only cite the unrealism in the position of the eugenists who
agitated for laws to force people to mate "properly" as a
means of curing social problems to make the case. What is
bewildering is why, as scientists, biologists have found it so
difficult to apply the basic principle of science to this problem, that all factors must be taken into account in investigating any question.

In the field of *human* biology the animal biologist is a
layman. His words would carry no weight did he not assume
the honorific role of "the scientist" in making his pronouncements. On the basis of his knowledge of the heredity of the
fruit fly, he concludes he can speak on the inheritance of
learned characteristics of man. Would he be as ready to
predict the heredity of the oyster or the butterfly or the dog
on the same basis?

As for Professor Garrett's argument, its significance lies
not in what it says, but what it really is. It represents a rear-
guard action of those who would base human relations on
the fact of race, in the face of world-wide scientific opinion

soundly grounded in numerous research findings. This kind of rear-guard action is nothing new in human experience. It is always to be expected in the face of change. On a far more significant level of the determination of human affairs, it represents a turning to the past that must be expected, certainly in the kind of dynamic world in which we live. It is identifiable with the racial terms of reference of the Faubuses of the American South, of the Verwoerds and Welenskys in Africa, or with the culturist, though not racist, terms of the essential anti-scientism of a Khrushchev, whose point of departure is a dogma of cultural evolution that dates from the nineteenth century.

Of themselves, Professor Garrett's repetitions of old arguments, the strictures of his editor, merit no reply. But insofar as they perpetuate findings which all the work of many scientific students of man have failed to substantiate when submitted to the test of scientific objectivity, their setting can profitably be recalled. It is the more important to do this because of the tensions in world relations and the consequent threat to world peace produced by the expression of comparable biases, a threat that continues to be fed by rear-guard actions of this sort.

three

economics and values: the modern world and tradition

the problem
of adapting societies
to new tasks[1]

The growing nationalisms in the far parts of the world,
in a very real sense, represent in no negligible measure
a reaction that has as its driving force the refusal to
accept evaluations of their traditional ways of life. . . .
The student of culture cannot escape the conclusion
that the movements called nativistic are highly keyed
reaffirmations of the values in the cultures we term
"backward."

In the rapidly growing vocab-
ulary of American social science a new term has come to be
heard with increasing frequency in recent years—one might
almost say in recent months. This is the term "manipulation." In this new use it applies where an individual or a
group, working with the tools research has provided, moves
into a social situation with the aim of altering patterns of
thought and action so as to achieve a given practical end. It
represents the logical working-out of those aims of physical
science, prediction *and* control, which for so many years
have been accepted by the students of human behavior and
human institutions as the ends toward which they, as scientists, should strive.

In a general, prescientific sense, the process of manip-
ulating human behavior and thus, to varied degrees, the

course of human history is nothing very new. The action of the democratic process itself, in terms of argumentation and persuasion, represents an attempt to manipulate behavior and thought for given ends. The rule of the manifold historical autocracies, or the ways of diplomacy, bring to mind countless examples of manipulation of peoples and their political and social destinies. Cross-culturally, colonization, commerce, the slave trade to the New World, the missionary activities of the eighteenth and nineteenth centuries—all served as conscious or fortuitous instruments of induced change in belief systems, social organization, and many other phases of the lives of those on whom these forces impinged.

What distinguishes the prescientific procedures in bringing about change from the methods which the disciplines that study man, whether as an individual or as a member of a society, employ today is the new dimension that has been given all programs of action, the dimension of scientific method. On its most ubiquitous level we have applied scientific method to the manipulation of preferences for one product as against another through advertising. It can be seen in such other varied aspects of our life as labor-management relations, town-planning, public administration, fund-raising campaigns, the development of new industries, and education and child welfare.

These random examples of the application of science to problems of directed ends have been drawn from our own society. Certainly in such areas of public concern as education, child welfare, or public administration, they represent attempts to solve problems of importance. Or, where manipulation of one group by another within the same population is undertaken, it is still a process which operates within the conventions of our society as a whole. Common cues to behavior, a common historical background, and common language are shared by both groups. The basic motivating drives can be taken for granted; the area of agreement as to the values that shape ends is large. To put the matter in technical terms, this is intracultural manipulation, in which only such differences as exist between subcultural groups need be taken into account.

When we approach the problem of influencing peoples other than ourselves, the matter becomes vastly complicated. The area of prediction is narrowed by factors that do not enter where concern is with one's own culture, where the task is to predict behavior on the basis of reactions that fall within a reasonably well-recognized framework of total response patterns. For to adapt another society to new ways of living involves the formidable process of reshaping basic habits that are manifest both in belief and in behavior. It calls for an induced shift in preestablished ends and a directed reorientation of value systems. It requires, consequently, an intensive analysis of the existing relationships among the various aspects of culture—technological, economic, social, educational, political, religious, and aesthetic —before any kind of prediction can be made of the results that will follow the disturbance of the balance between them.

Here, then, we come on a primary factor in the problem that has given rise to these discussions. "In the areas of technical aid to underdeveloped countries most attention has been paid so far to certain theoretical economic problems, whereas the relations between cultural changes and economic growth, as well as the aspects of the impact of the sociopolitical structure of underdeveloped countries on modernization, has received less attention." What kind of adjustments seem to be indicated when the technological and economic patterns of Europe and America are introduced into non-industrialized areas? What are the psychocultural mechanisms that cause peoples having different ways of life to hold tenaciously to their established modes of behavior, especially in terms of the sanctions which give these ways of life meaning and value?

Let us take a recurring situation under programs of economic development all over the world that has had to be faced by those in charge of operations calculated to bring the benefits of the technical proficiency of our industrialized economy to underdeveloped areas. This situation rarely, if ever, figures in discussions of those "theoretical economic problems" where considerations of large scope, such as basic resources, national income, labor pool, or location, determine the answers that set the goals for the operating missions. It concerns one of those elements in the total problem that has to do with the human factor in the equation, the element which, because of the operation of culturally prescribed motivations that lie outside the patterns of our own pecuniary economy, introduces unknowns that make for the gap between theoretically based prediction and actual achievement.

We here consider the problem of labor turnover. It is a commonplace that one of the greatest difficulties faced in the development of enterprises of any sort in underdeveloped areas, whether extractive, agricultural, or industrial, is that of holding workers to the job. Typically, what occurs is that men will take employment for a period of time and then, when money to meet certain specific wants is in hand, leave.

The problem of how to cope with this unstable labor market has had various answers. The imposition of taxes, payable only in currency, was attempted as an early solution. This method got roads built but could scarcely provide labor for large-scale, continuing undertakings. There has been wide recourse to contract labor, which permits the employer to compel a worker to stay on the job for a specified time. It is argued that the incentive of a larger wage would only increase the difficulty, since, the more the worker earned in a given time, the sooner he would attain his objective, and consequently the sooner he would leave his job. The encouragement of a wider range of wants, in terms of an induced goal of a higher standard of living, is another longer-range solution that has been suggested. Yet, in the final analysis, despite the many methods formulated of inducing change in economic attitudes and behavior on the part of the existing and potential labor supply, the factor of pre-established custom dominates the labor scene, and the problem remains essentially unsolved.

What, then, are some of the special aspects of tradition that, rarely taken into account, may be considered as operative in these situations, rendering it difficult to achieve what would, on the face of it, seem to be a simple task of utilizing available labor power for the development of underdeveloped areas? We may turn to Africa for some insight into this perplexing problem. This is not because the problem as such is in any way peculiar to Africa but because the examples to be drawn point the difficulties encountered here, as elsewhere, in the development of a rich continent, so dynamic in its present-day political and economic orientations.

The instance of an indigenous manufacturing system will give us something of the type of background against which proposals for economic development must be projected. It should be stressed that the instance is a regional example and is not to be taken as representative of Africa as a whole. No single instance could subsume the vast range of institutions, lying in all aspects of culture, that mark the many bodies of tradition found there. But if it is not to be taken as typical, neither is it to be thought of as atypical. It is useful, and it is here used because it highlights a problem.

Ironworking has, from very early times, been known throughout Negro Africa. Ironworkers are almost invariably members of a guild, membership in which is customarily based on family relationship, with the craft validated by supernatural sanctions. This is the pattern among the peoples of the Upper Volta River in French West Africa, where knives, hoes, and other iron implements are manufactured by members of such guilds. Yet because here, as in nonindustrial societies the world over, the lines of specialization are blurred, these men are not the full-time specialists they would be in our society. They are, as a matter of fact, primarily agriculturalists, earning their living only partially by the sale of their products and working their forges principally during that part of the year, the dry season, when the fields are not cultivated.

This is a significant fact, for it is plain that they would have no difficulty in supporting themselves entirely by the manufacture of iron implements. Their numbers in relation to the total group of which they form a part are small. In one series of districts enumerated some twenty-five years ago, there were 60 ironworkers in a population of about 20,000; in another series, there were 39 of these specialists out of some 18,000 inhabitants. It is apparent that this number of ironworkers cannot begin to supply the demand for the implements they produce. This is why, for generations, hoes and bush knives have been imported from other tribes and why, more recently, trading firms have stocked implements on the native model made in Europe.

One does not have to pursue the matter further to perceive that motivations quite different from those obtaining in the economies of Europe and America are operative here. The question that would occur to one conditioned to the patterns of business enterprise in the Western world would be why these ironworkers do not take advantage of the obvious market at hand. Why do they not supply it by complete, full-time specialization and the training of more apprentices to enlarge their operations so that, as entrepreneurs in the strict sense, they could then hire these trained workers to increase their production? And this is a fair question—fair, that is, for those who approach the problem in terms of current economic theory. All the conditions for the expansion of production are present, yet they are ignored. It is apparent that the answer lies outside the scope of economics as envisaged for our culture; that to reach a satisfactory explanation would require probing deep into what we know concerning the psychology of culture, as applicable to this particular situation. And since, in this case, we have nothing more to go on than the facts that have been provided us and are presented here, we can only have recourse to generalizations about the reasons why a people hold to such customary modes of behavior in the face of a patent economic opportunity—modes of behavior that seem logical, rational, and of self-evident worth to them, while to the outsider they seem so illogical and so irrational.

We shall return later to this point. For the moment the case we have cited will serve to illustrate how divergent from the conventions of societies with machine technologies and complex economies may be the systems of peoples living in underdeveloped areas. For we can ill afford to be unrealistic about the complexity of the problems of reconciliation involved in attempts to manipulate such peoples so as to achieve ends not envisaged by those whose ways of life are to be changed or not adaptable within the limits of possible variation of their culture.

If we examine the indigenous productive systems of the continent in more general terms—and much of what will be indicated is applicable to nonindustrialized societies outside Africa as well as to the peoples of that continent—we find that they present certain consistent characteristics that are highly relevant to the question we are considering. One of these has to do with the rhythm of work, a second with the way in which the available supply of labor is mobilized so that the economy can function, while a third concerns the motivations for labor, the factor of incentives. There are still other significant characteristics whose analysis must await more detailed presentation: the role of kinship groupings and sex division of labor in organizing and orienting the economics of production; the importance of supernatural sanctions governing ritual cycles for the service of deities or ancestors, when customary tasks are not performed; the influence of class stratification and native political structure on attempts to introduce new economic concepts and technical procedures.

Especially in the tropics the rhythm of work in indigenous

societies is the rhythm of the seasons. This does not mean that there are no daily rhythms, but these do not dictate changes in economic activity as do the longer fluctuations of seasonal change. Just what time of the day men and women go to the field, or on just what days they will work, will be determined by them in terms of the demands of the day. It is the total job, however, that is of primary concern. If a crop is successfully harvested, it is of little moment just how the time necessary to grow it was allotted. This is to be seen in the instance of the ironworkers among the Volta River peoples, where these men, primarily agriculturalists, divide their time seasonally between the two types of activities in which they engage. It is to be seen in other societies where housebuilding or house-repairing, or the making of mats or mortars or other utensils and the like is deferred until the dry season. It is likewise apparent when cycles of economic activity are compared with the ritual cycle. Except for emergencies, the latter coincides almost without exception to the dry season, since during the rains the demands of agriculture are too exacting to allow for the proper execution of forms of worship.

The daily rhythm that continues irrespective of seasonal change dictates the allocation of time during a given day to the tasks immediately at hand. The day may be thought of as broken into segments delimiting the hours between rising and retiring. The limits of these segments are set by the time of the day at which meals are eaten. In West Africa, and to a degree over all the continent south of the Sahara, the breaks come at about ten in the morning and at midafternoon. At times the large meal is eaten late in the day, often shortly before going to sleep. It must be recalled that night falls early. The day comes without a prolonged dawn. There is no time for the preparation of a large meal at waking. At night, cooking in the dark is not favored. Thus, arising with the dawn, the African takes but a bite before occupying himself with his other concerns; at the other end of the day, when the principal meal is consumed, he rests.

The contrast between this seasonal and daily work rhythm and the work pattern of the industrial laborer will be at once apparent. Except in the case of large-scale agricultural undertakings, the seasonal factor does not enter. The routine of work in extractive and industrial enterprises moves around the calendar with a schedule of operations fixed not by natural conditions but through decisions reached far from any contact the worker may experience and as much beyond his control as are the seasons. He is thus caught up in a system that goes contrary to his prior experience. The variety of economic activities in which he engages under his own economic system is, furthermore, entirely lacking. His task remains the same from one day to the next and his time is apportioned for him, so that he is not free to vary the monotony of his work by moving from one aspect of a job to another. This is a commonplace for the industrial worker in a mechanized society. But in our Western economy a rhythm of life has been developed to afford some outlet to compensate for this monotony. The African sees no adequate reward in forms of his system of values to make this acceptable to him.

There is some tendency to define the industrial routine as disciplined, in contrast to an assumed carefree round held to characterize "primitive" man. Yet it takes but cursory analysis of the economic organization of nonindustrialized societies to recognize that, if we approach this from a human point of view, what we are really contrasting is different types of discipline that derive their validation from differing sources. It soon becomes apparent that no question of the presence or absence of discipline, as such, enters in either type of economy. The discipline of the worker in nonindustrialized societies is self-imposed, while that of the industrial operative is imposed from outside. To the worker born in an industrial society, as well as to others who live in terms of the cultural orientations existing there, this outer source of discipline is taken for granted, as is any other culturally sanctioned mode of behavior. But to the worker who has been accustomed to different patterns, especially patterns under which the allocation of time and energy are self-determined, and who is newly brought into an industrial scene, the problem of reorientation necessitates a far-reaching process of adjustment. The degree of social no less than of personal disorganization that has resulted from many such attempts to make an adjustment of this sort needs only mention; when we consider how far-reaching it must be, we may take it as a measure of the plasticity of the human organism that the amount of demoralization is not greater.

Adjustment to the daily rhythm imposed by industrial work presents problems of an equivalent order of difficulty. Here it is not the question of a fixed as against a self-determined routine but of a difference in the cultural patterning of primary, biological drives. One of the most severe adjustments that is required here arises from the operation of a factor in the daily life of all of us, so taken for granted that it would be surprising if it entered in planning and executing technical aid programs. This factor concerns the schedule of mealtimes, whose importance in setting the daily rhythm of native labor has been indicated.

Habits associated with food consumption reflect some of the deepest conditionings of the human organism. It is a truism among social scientists that, while hunger is a basic universal human drive, the foods which satisfy the drive and the times when hunger is appeased are culturally determined variables. The applicability of this principle to the foods consumed is quite well recognized; but the importance of the fact that hunger, a biological phenomenon, operates on a cultural timetable is not. Therefore, where workers are furnished their native foodstuffs, as is almost always done today, only half the requirement for adaptation to the new situation is met. The time of eating is almost of equal importance and, when neglected, can entail acute discomfort for the worker and go far to shape his feeling-tone toward the new situation in which he finds himself. On the unconscious level many seeds of hostility and aggression are sown in the process of exacting this conformity to the new reorientation in the timing of meals.

This is true not only in industrial enterprises but also of projects in other fields with which programs of development are concerned, such as education. As has been pointed out, persons from the industrially developed countries, like all others, take their mealtimes for granted. Where the controls are in their hands, therefore, they tend quite automatically to set their own schedules for others to follow. That is why, when queried about the matter, Africans who were educated in mission schools have given as one of the most vivid recollections of their early school years the fact that they were constantly hungry because they could not eat at their accustomed times. Other Africans, employed by European industrial concerns, have stated that one of their principal adjustments was to adapt their time of eating to the schedule of hours set by their employers. One need only contrast a schedule of meals eaten before going to work, at midday, and early in the evening, with the indigenous pattern of midmorning and midafternoon meals to make the point that it is in such humble, taken-for-granted aspects of life that some of the most serious problems of adjustment are to be sought.

The second problem that we will consider arises out of the changes that occur in the manner in which the labor force is mobilized when indigenous societies are brought under the canons of employment prevailing in the industrial communities of Europe and America. While the generalization is not without exception, in the main it is true that the economy of the West differs strikingly from that of most other societies in that it is based on individual effort, whereas these other peoples are communally oriented. In terms of these canons, the worker in this country and in Europe acts as an individual, and, if he organizes trade-unions to protect his position, such organizations still remain aggregates of individuals. In the economies of nonindustrial societies, on the other hand, the individual acts primarily as the member of a group, whether this group is based on kinship or residence or both. In Africa the factor of cooperative effort well exemplifies this. The problem of cultivating considerable tracts of land in West Africa during the short period at the beginning of the rainy season is met quite effectively by group labor of this sort. The hoe, in the hands of one man, is not too efficient an instrument; but many hoes in the hands of many men will in a day ready a large field for planting. Or, again, in the eastern part of the continent and other cattle-keeping regions, where herds must be taken daily to pasture, it is the small boys of the village who together care for the animals belonging to all their elders.

Another aspect of this tradition of group labor has to do with the direction of work. Europeans and Americans who come to Africa soon discover how deeply the concept of the responsible leader lodges in the customary work patterns of the Africans. One who wishes a given task performed does not hire workers as individuals, or, if he is under the illusion that he does, he finds that he soon is negotiating the problems that arise with the head of the group, who may alone be held to account for the quality and amount of work done. To reprimand an individual worker invites difficulties; it is the responsible head alone who must see to it that those in his group do their work, and it is he alone who may call his men to task.

Again, far-reaching adjustment is plainly required when a person coming from a society where patterns of this sort prevail moves into contact with a system oriented in terms of individual effort. In a very real sense, such a person is likely to be lost in the new situation. The social support which he has been accustomed to expect and receive is entirely lacking. It is not chance that in the New World the descendants of Africans, like many indigenous American Indian groups, deprived of their aboriginal setting of a clan structure, took over the *compadre,* or godparent tradition, from some of the individualistically oriented cultures of Europe as a compensating device. The degree to which this tradition has been elaborated in various parts of Central and South America and the Caribbean region is an index of the urgency of the need for members of these groups for social support in their daily contacts.

Gang labor has been one response to the recognition of the tradition of cooperative work among workers in underdeveloped areas by those charged with the operation of large-scale projects in industry or agriculture or mining. Yet, again, the perception of this institution of cooperative effort as something that can be built on in effectively utilizing labor power has proved to be only a half-measure, owing to the superficial nature of the percept. For in the African pattern the accountability of the leader of a work group is only secondary to the employer and not as is the case in industry. His primary responsibility is to the members of the group he directs and of which he himself is a member. The system whereby a group of men working as individuals for a common employer is directed by a leader who is also hired as an individual by the same employer is the most casual of resemblances to the democratically controlled indigenous cooperative work group.

In short, then, the problem resolves itself into one in which the worker, who comes from a culture where the pattern is one of collective effort based on inner control, is to adapt himself to a system where individualism is the dominant motif. It is not too much to say that these differences in approach to the problem of mobilizing labor is at the base of much of the social disorganization and individual demoralization that has too often been the concomitant of even the best-planned schemes of development.

Some attention has already been given to the third point to be considered—that of labor incentives. Because it strikes to the very heart of the question of the impact of one economy on another, it is closely tied in with the two problems we have just sketched—the rhythm of work and the democratic pattern of cooperative labor—and can profitably be considered further.

One of the complaints most frequently heard, especially in Africa, is that when a native has become integrated into the system of Euro-American economic procedures, and his earnings, in terms of local standards become steady, his "family"—that is, the members of his wider kinship group —feel free to descend on him to share what he earns. In terms of accepted modes of conduct, he must care for them or in other ways make his contributions to their joint undertakings. This not only holds true for the wage-worker. The small native shopkeeper and the European-trained professional man are similarly called on to conform to these traditional patterns. In cultural terms such a man as an earner works in accordance with the patterns of an economy based on individual initiative, but his consumption patterns are dictated by the traditions of a collective system. The conflicts that arise from this, as regards both the earner and the group out of which he has come, can be serious. Equally pertinent is the fact that individual initiative, essential to any success in an economy of free enterprise, is scarcely encouraged by the necessity of continuously meeting such obligations, made the more imperative by the fact that they arise out of some of the deepest ties that an individual can experience.

The factor of seasonal rhythm also impinges on this matter of incentives. Here a reinterpretation of preindustrial patterns often operates to cause the worker to leave his job. In the indigenous economic systems the dry season was the time of travel. Men left their homes to trade or to engage in hunting or to pay visits to relatives. The ceremonial round likewise often took them away from home for considerable periods of time. These changes in the established routine were welcome, and they remain even more welcome to the native wage-worker in an industrial enterprise or in a mine or on a plantation. It would seem that, on the basis of past experience, thought could profitably be given to developmental projects, at least where agricultural development is concerned, wherein the cooperative principle can be applied to organizing the productive efforts of individual or group owners of land in which the routine would be close to the earlier organization of time given to the work to be done.

One of the most striking examples of an area that has brought this type of economic agriculture into the world economy, making its potential resources generally available and raising the standards of living of its inhabitants, is to be found in the history of the cacao-growing industry of the Gold Coast. Long antedating present-day developmental schemes, and initially quite without benefit of Western economic planning, it has in large measure achieved many of the ends envisaged in the technical aid programs of this and other countries and of the United Nations agencies concerned with these matters. In essence it represents the results of inner developments based on pre-existing patterns rather than development induced by the direct application of forces impinging from outside and cast in terms foreign to native practices.

Here there is no lack of incentive to expand production. Moreover, Africans, using the capital they accumulated through raising cacao, have moved into areas of commerce and minor industry with a minimum of dislocation of established institutions. There are no extremes of what has been termed "detribalization," but the claims of relatives have, in many cases, been resolved by opening opportunities rather than by merely sharing wages or profits with them. This is not unlike a situation found in eastern Nigeria, among the Ibo, where resources or large family groupings are being pooled to permit certain of their members to take advantage of opportunities that will accrue to the benefit of all. A promising young man is in this way aided to obtain the higher education that will allow him to function to the credit of his family unit in the changing economic and political scene. A good trader is helped to expand his operation and thus contribute to the resources of the group as a whole. This is an extension of pre-existing patterns to fit the new scene.

Admittedly, to move from this type of development, motivated from within, to planned programs brought from outside is not simple. Yet the African cultures, at least, are receptive to the modern scene, and, if the motivation exists, Africans show appreciable plasticity. In terms of existing orientations it is plain that it is less difficult to provide incentives in agricultural projects than in industrial developments. Developmental projects, it is plain, must build on ways that make sense to the people involved in them if incentives to active participation are to result in the effective attainment of stated ends.

Factors such as these, which come into play to further or impede the success of projects looking toward the economic development of underdeveloped areas, constitute only a part of the whole problem. We have still to consider how what is brought to a people is integrated into their ways of living, as against the manner in which their established patterns of behavior are adapted to the requirements of a new economic and technological system. Here we are confronted with the question of the meaning of a way of life for those who live in accordance with it. This, in turn, can be understood only in the light of the findings of that phase of psychoethnography that has to do with the mechanisms of learning and conditioning which shape the characteristic motor habits, reaction patterns, and accepted modes of thinking of a people.

It may be useful at this point briefly to recall the nature of culture and the manner in which it functions. By general consensus, culture is defined as the learned, socially sanctioned behavior of a people. As something learned, its dynamic quality derives from a continuous process of relearning that results from the constant readjustment of individuals to stimuli arising both from within the group and from outside it. Culture fulfills a twofold function. It provides those born into a society with means to adapt effectively to their human and natural setting by training them in the forms of behavior recognized as valid by their group. More than this, however, it provides a background against which the creative aspects of the total human response pattern can be projected, a base from which exploration into new orientations in living can move. From the point of view of human personality development, culture is thus the medium through which adjustment is achieved, a point of particular importance when the maladjustments that result from contacts between peoples with disparate cultures are taken into account.

As individuals, we learn our cultures by a process termed "enculturation." This is subtle and all-pervading and so thoroughly absorbed that for the most part we live our lives in terms of reactions that lodge below the level of our consciousness. Only when some alternative is presented to us do we become aware of the assumptions which otherwise we take as given or of the overt forms of behavior that we manifest so spontaneously. Then we must consider, judge, evaluate, choose.

It is in the area of values that enculturation strikes to its greatest depths. Here we learn the sanctions that give meaning to behavior, the rationale for living. Evaluations of this character, in the last analysis, maximize the satisfactions that culture affords man. Hence, when we put into force programs aimed at changing the modes of living of peoples so that they may enjoy satisfactions outside the purview of the system of values of their culture, we are saying, in effect, that the ends we envisage are so superior to those already in force that their desirability is beyond challenge. It is thus assumed that, when these new values are presented to peoples having other traditionally approved ends, they must ultimately displace the values to which these people were originally enculturated. But this is a proposition that calls for the closest testing in the light of our knowledge of cultural dynamics.

East Africa affords us an instance precisely in the field of those economic goals which are primarily under discussion here; that is, of the problems that arise when attempts to develop resources of underdeveloped areas involve the reconciliation of two different systems of evaluating ends. This instance has to do with the utilization of the rich possibilities presented by the high grassy plateaus of the area for the production of cattle for the world market. This region has long been noted for its excellence as pasture land. Here is where the great herds of wild animals roam, taking advantage of the same pasturage that has provided sustenance for the cattle owned by the natives.

One of the drawbacks to the utilization of this area for the purpose of producing beef for export has been the presence of the tsetse fly in various districts, since the sting of the tsetse is fatal to cattle. A few years ago the discovery of a vaccine against tsetse was announced. East Africa, it was stressed, now rid of its handicap, would become a new Argentina and would supply the meat-hungry parts of the world with beef. Potentially, all the favorable elements for development programs seemed to be present. An existing resource was to be utilized; an expansion of the pre-existing economy would raise indigenous standards of living by increasing cash income, while at the same time meeting a pressing world need; this could be accomplished without the evils consequent on detribalization and urbanization. Yet nothing seems to have happened.

We may leave to one side questions of a technical order that have been raised, such as the actual efficacy of the vaccine or whether the tsetse can be expected to breed a strain whose virulence will in effect nullify the immunization this new discovery was intended to provide. Here we will consider the problem of the value system of the indigenous peoples as it bears on the question of substituting new ends for those in existence. We may first describe the role of cattle in the indigenous cultures, in order to make clear the problems involved in attempts to utilize this resource as a profitable commercial venture.

In all East Africa wealth has traditionally taken the form of cattle. These animals, however, constitute a special kind of wealth, being essentially the depositaries of value in a system of prestige economics and not figuring appreciably in the subsistence economy, since only their milk is consumed. The subsistence economy, as a matter of fact, is simple. Each family is self-supporting to such a degree that, unlike many other parts of Africa, markets were found rarely, if at all, and, except for the ironworkers, there were no specialists. The subsistence economy, therefore, is taken for granted; it is an aspect of life to which a minimum of attention is paid.

Nothing could contrast more sharply to this than the attitude of these peoples toward cattle. Their herds literally give meaning and purpose to life. Ownership dictates social status; the passage of cattle alone validates marriage and gives children the stamp of legitimacy. Cattle, to the people of this area, have the sentimental value of our pets. They are thematic materials for poetry and songs. These animals are never slaughtered for food, so that beef is eaten only when a cow dies or when an ox is sacrificed at the funeral of the owner of a herd. Some of the languages of the area have fifty or more words which we can only translate by the term "cow" plus a qualifying phrase. By the use of this rich and specialized descriptive vocabulary, color, size, shape of horns, even temperamental characteristics, can be denoted by a single term.

An incident that occurred during the visit of the United Nations Trusteeship Council Mission to Ruanda-Urundi may be cited to illustrate the way in which cattle are conceived as having individual personalities. A native veterinary assistant, clad in a white laboratory coat, was injecting the cows in the herds of his district with a preventive serum. As he finished with each animal, he made a mark in his book, then turned to the next. One member of the mission, curious, asked him how he knew which cows had been injected, since no animal was branded or marked in any other way. The native assistant, puzzled by the question, showed the visitor his book. "See," he replied, "I just make a mark after the name of each animal every time I inject it."

It is significant to observe that one value introduced from outside these cultures by those who exercise control over cattle-owning peoples meets with no resistance—the value laid on improving the quality of the breed and preventing disease in the animals. This means longer-lived and better cattle and, as an end result, more cattle. This in turn increases the wealth of an individual and the prestige that accrues to him. The fact that this improvement has raised serious problems involving overgrazing the restricted reserve areas allotted to the natives, and thus has intensified soil erosion as the area of white settlement spread, is here aside from the point. What concerns us in our present discussion is that the resulting increase of cattle yielded no marketable surplus. The end of raising cattle in the native mind being to have more and more of them, any program which necessitated disposing of animals, in terms of the established patterns of value, induced social disutility.[1]

As far as can be determined, in one district only has any success attended efforts to persuade natives to sell their cattle. Here the political officers have instituted a campaign to convince the cattle owners that it is to their benefit, in the changed economy they now face, to dispose of a certain proportion of their animals in the market, so as to furnish meat for the various urban centers that have developed. They have painstakingly demonstrated that this can be done and still leave the owners enough cattle to permit pre-existing status patterns to be followed, to allow cattle to pass at marriage, and to continue the existing social orientations. There seems to be a growing response in the numbers of cattle offered for sale, but it is recognized by all

[1] This attitude has been modified in the past decade. Faced with the challenge of being administered by Western-educated tribal political officers, M.J.H. notes in his 1957 field notes being present when a delegation from an important cattle-keeping tribe came to inquire how many heads of cattle were needed for opening a school. —Ed.

concerned with promoting the project that this is a long process and must be developed at the local level on the basis of well-grounded personal relationships that engender mutual confidence.

Examples from Africa and the rest of the underdeveloped portions of the world could be multiplied to show how complex is the matrix of custom and sanction to be taken into account when the spread of technological knowledge and economic development to peoples living under differing conditions of life, and in terms of different goals, is contemplated. The fragmentation of knowledge in our society, as represented, for instance, by the specialized academic disciplines, has carried us so far that it is easy for us to forget that a culture is a functioning unit. We do not often take full cognizance of the fact that the aspects into which we divide custom for purposes of study are a fiction of science. By the same token, we overlook the principle that a change effected in any one of these aspects has repercussions over the total way of life on the culture as a whole.

This is as true for our own culture, despite its specialization, as for any other. Exclusive preoccupation with a single phase has been responsible for some of the more unrealistic approaches to various social, economic, and political programs that have been proposed in our society. The results of this overspecialization have become patent enough to give rise to the call for cross-disciplinary cooperation that is so marked a current in the intellectual stream of the present day. The introduction of new economic mechanisms based on technological innovations that increase production, even in our own society, has produced far-reaching changes in social organization, the functioning of religion, and accepted standards of aesthetic perception. This, be it noted, has taken place as the result of the operation of internal impulses, something that has permitted a reasonable adjustment of sanctions as changes have occurred in the forms of institutions and in our re-enculturation to new modes of behavior. But this is quite different from a situation where changes of a fundamental nature are abruptly introduced from outside a society, changes which envisage the attainment of ends differing from those that previously had motivated conduct. In such a situation change lacks the elements of gradualness and measured infiltration by which internally induced cultural innovations are worked into pre-existing patterns.

Because our know-how has raised our standard of living and by extending the frontiers of our knowledge has given us benefits that we prize, we assume it can be applied in other societies with equal profit. As we move into the area of technical aid programs, however, we discover that even the know-how on which we pride ourselves is not always transferable or even applicable. The knowledge possessed by indigenous peoples concerning the utilization of their land is not scientifically derived, but it is the result of a long process of adaptation to their natural setting, and much of it meets the pragmatic test. Large-scale planting by the use of mechanical agricultural implements has been introduced in many parts of the tropical world. In some instances, however, the land, unprotected by the forest growth, is exposed to the rains that leech out its chemical content and render it less productive than when worked in small patches with the hoe. Benefits anticipated on the basis of the returns these methods yield in temperate climates did not materialize.

This, however, is only one of the more obvious aspects of the matter. At the outset of this discussion note was taken of the acceptance by social scientists of the aims of the exact and natural disciplines, prediction, and control. As was indicated, the difficulty of predicting the outcome of a given social development, even in our own culture, is reasonably well recognized. The fact that controls, on the scientific no less than the practical level, when applied cross-culturally take us into questions of value and purpose of the most fundamental character is, however, a lesson that must still be learned. The manipulation of inert matter or of biological organisms that do not have recourse to the symbolisms of language is one thing. Man, however—and this must never be forgotten—is the only animal who can talk back. When attempts are made to manipulate his behavior, to say nothing of his thinking, important philosophical problems remain to be examined. Man alone, with his gift of projecting experience through the symbolisms of language, has developed culture and the wide range of institutions that mark human societies over the world. Because of the nature of the enculturative experience, the expressions of value that supply the motivations for the behavior of any given people provide the primary points of reference in any judgment that is drawn. The emotional loading given the institutions and values to which an individual has been enculturated makes conclusions that are obvious to one group anything but obvious to another.

When the industrialized people of the world bring their knowledge to those living in what we term "underdeveloped"—that is, nonindustrialized—areas, the assumption is made that our ways are those which hold the answers to problems which have, in actuality, been answered in many ways. The fact that we speak of these peoples as "primitive," the territories they inhabit as "backward," or our continuous use of the word "progress" as a general overall desideratum, when we really mean moving toward the attainment of goals we determine as good on the basis of our experience is an index of our attitude. This has not escaped the attention of the growing numbers of those who, enculturated to the ways of the native societies from which they derive, through Western education have come to know the deficiencies as well as the good points of our culture. They read what we write about them and with time and repetition come to resent the implications of the inferiority of their cultures so often expressed in what they read. The growing nationalisms in the far parts of the world, in a very real sense, represent in no negligible measure a reaction that has as its driving force the refusal to accept our evaluations of their traditional way of life. Indeed, the student of culture cannot escape the conclusion that the movements called nativistic are highly keyed reaffirmations of the values in the cultures we term "backward." If we but take the example of China and Africa, where the cultures are deeply rooted in traditions of the continuity of ancestral generations, it is not difficult to see how the derogation of established ways, even by implication, can arouse both latent and manifest hostilities.

In a world where increasing rapidity of communication makes for increasingly close contact between peoples, programs of any sort that cut across cultures must take into account the intangibles of established custom if there is to be any positive, lasting gain. It must be recognized, first of all, that there is no single answer to the problems that are faced by mankind. What we term technological and economic "progress" cannot be achieved without integrating the new into the old; moreover, this integration can only be suggested, not forced. The peoples to whom technical aid is brought will, in the final analysis, decide what they will accept and what they will reject. Even where they do not control their own political destinies, the force of cultural inertia prevents their being manipulated like pawns on a chessboard. We know today too well that they are imponderables in the world scene, not pawns.

This is why it must be understood, above all, that the diffusion of ideas, and even of technology, is more than a unilateral process. If we keep firmly in mind the force of our own enculturation, we will be able to understand how the ways of others are similarly valued by those who live in terms of them. We can learn as well as teach, and there is no more effective mode of convincing others of the worth of what we have to teach than by expressing a willingness to learn as well. Only when considerations of this nature enter into instituting and implementing technical aid programs can these projects unite rather than divide free men and women and leave the residue of friendship and cooperation that is their ultimate aim.

economic change and cultural dynamics

In studies of economic development . . . the historical component . . . of antecedent tradition in the receiving culture, and its functioning in the contact situation, are not fully taken into account. Models devised to guide studies . . . are, moreover, not only ahistorical, but where possible developments are calculated, the bases of analysis tend to be ethnocentric. . . . If we grant the power of established values to shape reactions of peoples undergoing contact, recognize the depth in time over which these values existed and allow for their continuing strength, we cannot but achieve a more realistic approach to the problem posed by the juxtaposition of tradition, value and socio-economic modernization.

The phenomenon of change, which encompasses all aspects of human social life, is at times more apparent than at others. Yet though the clock of change races or is retarded, it never stops, even where the student must seek out and test for movement if he is to perceive it at all.

This difference in the rate of change is not only apparent when we consider whole cultures, it is also to be discerned when we assess change in the several aspects into which every body of custom may be divided. Economic change can be accelerated, while religious conventions hold tenaciously to earlier usage. Or we can find instances where there is a flowering of concern with the supernatural, resulting in great expansion of religious beliefs and practices, in contrast to a concomitant conservatism in technology. The former condition, which characterizes the cultures of Western Europe and the United States as they have developed since the Industrial Revolution, may be contrasted to the many examples to the contrary that are to be found in the aboriginal societies of Central America and the Congo. And what is true of economics, or technology, or religion, is also true of social and political institutions, of art and music, of language and education, and of the systems of values that underlie all these and give them meaning and purport.

Whether rapid or retarded, change in any culture is consistent. This is the more noticeable where innovations arise from within a society than when they are introduced as a result of contact with groups having different ways. Even in these latter cases, however, no matter how great the pressures for change, continuities will be discernible. In every instance, innovations are found to have been projected against the background of pre-existing custom. If these new elements are incompatible with established beliefs and practices, and the recipients are free to determine acceptance or rejection, they will be rejected out of hand. Where a people have no freedom of choice, as under conquest or enslavement, innovations that are incompatible will be avoided as much as possible, to be replaced by earlier practices, residually continued, when pressures are released.

In cultural theory, this consistency of change, called cultural drift,[1] must be understood if we are to acquire an

[1] This concept is developed further in Melville J. Herskovits, *Man and His Work: The Science of Cultural Anthropology* (New York, 1948), pp. 580–88. It is an extension of the concept advanced by Sapir to explain regularities of change in linguistic habits. See E. Sapir, *Language: An Introduction to the Study of Speech* (New York, 1921), pp. 157–82.

adequate perspective on what is variously called economic development, or economic growth, or, in the case of the present volume, socio-economic development. In two important respects, the concept of drift epitomizes a somewhat different orientation from that customarily employed when problems lying in this field are studied. In the first place, the frame of reference here is cultural and holistic, rather than particularistic, as where exclusive emphasis is laid on the social and economic aspects of change. Secondly, in this approach the data are analyzed in terms of the methodology of the behavioral sciences, rather than that of the natural and exact disciplines.

It becomes apparent, in terms of this approach, that methodological considerations of primary importance arise when we introduce the concept of culture into the study of economic change. And because it becomes necessary to assess some of the differences that appear when the attack on these problems is mounted from the position of the sciences of human behavior rather than from that of the natural sciences, we must consider the perennial question of the nature and significance of the regularities in human experience as against the analysis of the unique historical event. Here we face the issue as to the most effective theoretical orientation for studying economic change, something that brings in the related question of the nature and utility, for this purpose, of those generalizations about human behavior and the institutions of society which we term scientific laws.

2

Let us, at the outset, differentiate the concepts of society and culture. A great many definitions of each have been given; for the latter, a compilation of over one hundred and sixty formulations has demonstrated the nuances of meaning that can be assigned to it.[2] For our purpose, we can

[2] A. L. Kroeber and C. Kluckhohn, "Culture, a Critical Review of Concepts and Definition," Peabody Museum of American Archaeology and Ethnology, *Papers,* XLVII, No. 1 (1952), 1–233.

most effectively conceptualize society as people, interacting in accordance with patterns of relationship that determine the position of the individual in the group to which he belongs. Culture, on the other hand, is to be thought of as *behavior,* in the psychologist's sense of the term, including idea as well as act. The former conceptualization leads to the analysis of social structures, studied at a given moment in the experience of a people. The latter centers on human beings as essential causal agents, and stresses dynamics as the primary object of study.

It must be made clear that to define culture in behavioral terms does not rule out consideration of social relationships, but rather extends their study by bringing sanction and meaning to the forefront. What the cultural approach provides is a way in which particular social phenomena can be set in the totality of a given traditional stream. It means that when we assess the nature and functioning of social relations within a group we also take into account interactions touching on all phases of the life of a people, provided only that these are not biological, but learned. These phases are what we technically term aspects of culture, and represent the universals of human need and satisfaction that can be inductively derived from comparative study of societies all over the world. Translated into our academic tradition, these universals represent the familiar division of labor into the several disciplines of the academic curriculum—economics, political science, language, literature, technology, sociology, art, religion, music, drama, education, to name but some of them.

We can approach the study of a given culture from either of the two positions we have indicated, the general or the specialized, depending on the kind of problem that is being studied. Here, however, another consideration enters, one that is especially critical where social and economic change in technologically underdeveloped societies is to be assessed. When an analysis of some particular aspect of our own life is made in terms of the concepts and methods of a specific discipline, we can to a considerable degree hold constant the total setting of the phenomenon we are investigating. We cannot do this, however, when our analysis moves to the comparative level, and we seek to generalize concerning human behavior as a whole or, more restrictedly, seek to understand changes in institutions and responses to these changes in another society, where the patterns of behavior and motivation are quite different from those in our own.

A classical example of how far this need to ascertain total setting in studying a problem in a culture not one's own can take one is to be found in the case of R. S. Rattray's work among the Ashanti of West Africa. Early in the 1920's, Rattray, a colonial officer, was assigned by the Gold Coast government to study the political implications of the sacred Golden Stool, which, it was known, was so important a symbol of Ashanti unity that rumors concerning its disposal had been the cause of the serious riots which followed its rediscovery in 1921. His directive lay essentially in the field of politics; but it was only eight years and three books later that he reached his goal and accomplished his mission. He found that he had to move through the fields of religion, ritual, and social organization before he was ready to write his monumental study of Ashanti law,[3] since only with this background knowledge could he grasp and communicate the political problem he was charged to study.

What Rattray came to realize, and what must always be realized in studying any problem that has cross-cultural reference, is that we are dealing with human beings reacting to situations they continuously project against the body of

[3] R. S. Rattray, *Ashanti Law and Constitution* (Oxford, 1929). The other volumes were *Ashanti* (Oxford, 1923), on the religion and social organization of this people, and *Religion and Art in Ashanti* (Oxford, 1927). It is also to be noted that Rattray's work likewise led him to publish his *Akan-Ashanti Folk-Tales* (Oxford, 1930).

tradition to which they have been enculturated from the moment of birth. Any approach that ignores this culturally apperceived mass of experience cannot but be inadequate for attaining significant and valid findings.

3

This brings us to a matter of some theoretical importance in the behavioral sciences, a controversy of long standing, customarily phrased in terms of whether the study of man is "science" or "history." It may perhaps be best approached by considering its methodological implications, as these apply to the study of phenomena arising out of the fact that culture is learned, in comparison with those employed in analyzing phenomena of the natural world. From this point of view, the difference between the claims of those who hold to the one or the other position becomes clear. This difference, essentially, has to do with the degree of variability found in any given element in the natural world, compared to the extent to which we find variation in behavioral patterns, whether encountered within a single human society or among mankind as a whole. Phrased in this way, it becomes immediately apparent that the former will be found to be incomparably less variable than the latter; in other words, variation in behavioral norms represents a vastly greater degree of plasticity than any non-behavioral phenomenon. In consequence, the degree of predictability that can be achieved in the natural sciences is far greater than in the sciences of man, particularly since in the natural sciences experimental controls can be applied so much more effectively than in the study of human institutions.

Phrasing this in different terms, we come to a more familiar expression when we state that the phenomena of the natural world show far more regularities than do social phenomena. A well-worn example, which loses none of its point or validity through the retelling, can be taken by referring to the basic unit of social organization, the family. This institution, we know, is not restricted to human societies; on the infrahuman level, it is present not only among mammalian forms, but in the lower orders as well. Yet if we analyze the total pattern of organization that controls mating and reproduction in any infrahuman society, the outstanding difference between it and that which obtains in human aggregates is found to lie in the degree of regularity and of predictability that obtains in the one when compared with the other.

If we take as an example the family among the Hamadryad baboons, so ably studied by Zuckerman, it becomes clear that a description of this institution in any given Hamadryad baboon society will portray a mating-reproductive cycle that can be duplicated in any other.[4] Not so with man. In human societies, the family may consist of one man and one woman, of one man and several women, of one woman and several men; the children may live with both their parents or one of them, or with a collateral relative of father or mother elsewhere; or they may be held by adoption. Extensions of the immediate family, lines of incest, and other institutionalized forms of counting and validating kinship and obligations that arise from relationships of this order introduce still other variables.

Prediction of what may be expected in a previously unknown human society is thus impossible, except in terms of a proposition that the social organization of any particular human group will be consistently structured, and will be followed with equal consistency by the members of that society. By extension, we can thus say that while regularities which invite scientific generalization are present in the ways of human groups, they are not regularities of the same order as those which characterize the phenomena studied by the exact and natural sciences. It follows, therefore, that the sciences of man must develop their own conceptual schemes and methodological tools, rather than ape those of these other disciplines.

[4] (Sir) S. Zuckerman, *The Social Life of Monkeys and Apes* (New York, 1922).

Two components are essential to any body of behavioral science theory. The first of these components is psychological. It derives from the nature of the conditioning process in man, which gives human learning the particular cumulative character that arises out of man's unique command of the instrumentality of speech. Because of this, the human being learns—or is conditioned to, or, as we say in technical terms, is enculturated to—the particular modes of behavior that, in their totality, make up the culture of the society into which he is born. The individual thereby comes to grasp the nature of his world, regulate his behavior, derive his motivations, and achieve his values in terms of the modes of perception, sanction, and control of his society.

All this he learns so thoroughly that, for most of his life, he need not call on conscious thought-processes to guide his behavior. In a far larger measure than is customarily understood, he reacts rather than thinks; and the immediacy of his reactions reflects the emotional loading given the behavior he accepts as right and proper.

We are coming to understand that for the individual the ultimate nature of reality must derive from his percepts, which, in turn, are screened by his culture. Insofar as the total group is concerned, the conventionalized realities accepted by the members of a society are consensuses of these individual percepts. What is of the greatest importance is that the resulting structure of thought and action is enculturated so early in life, and so thoroughly, that the responses to the socially sanctioned cues to behavior are subliminal, emerging into consciousness only when subjected to challenge. It is apparent that this is a critical point in any theoretical model that is to guide the scientific analysis of phenomena of cultural change. Since this category embraces the social and economic changes of the type with which the present volume is concerned, its relevance becomes immediately apparent.

The second component in the approach of the behavioral sciences to the study of man is historical. This takes its particular importance for our discussion from the fact that in most researches oriented toward the study of changing relations between social and economic institutions, the circumstances of their growth and adjustment resultant on contact tend to be relegated to a minor position, if not ignored, in favor of assessment of contemporary form and function. In studies of economic development, the bias thus introduced is compounded to the extent that the historical component represented by the nature of antecedent tradition in the receiving culture, and its functioning in the contact situation, are not fully taken into account. Models devised to guide studies of this kind are, moreover, not only ahistorical, but where possible developments are calculated, the bases of analysis tend to be ethnocentric. That is, these models take for granted the universality of psycho-social responses which, when comparatively and historically considered, are found to characterize the pecuniary societies of Europe and America to a degree not found outside these cultures, where they are more often than not entirely lacking.

A word may be said as to the meaning of the term "historical" as employed here. It derives from anthropological usage, and in essence implies recognition of the element of time in human experience. While it can comprehend the use of written documentary data where these exist, this is not essential. Perhaps it is best clarified if we consider it as a sense of historicity. Since the narrower meaning of the word "history" is held so widely, the need has arisen to draw a distinction between "historic" and "nonhistoric" peoples. Writing is aboriginally found in relatively few human societies, those of Europe, the Mediterranean basin and parts of Asia. It never penetrated the vast sweep of the Americas, except perhaps for the glyphs of Mexico and Central America. The peoples of Subsaharan Africa, of the islands of the Pacific, of aboriginal Australia, of the Circumpolar regions, never developed writing, and the same is true of innumerable societies of Indonesia, Southwest Asia, and many parts of India.

While in the restricted sense these people are not historical, anthropological conventions do not confuse written history with the total experience of a people or, more simply, with their past. Recognizing that the life of every group, in this sense, is historically developed, and that an unwritten past, no less than one which can be documented in writing, functions as a reality in the present, anthropologists have devised various techniques to recover as much of this as possible. The archaeological record is used to this end; comparisons of similarities and differences in the practices of peoples who can be assumed to have been in contact yield information; unwritten history—that is, oral tradition—when used with the proper methodological precautions, provides further leads.[5] It has been through the use of such techniques that the grand panorama of human history has been recovered, to tell us the ways in which the observed varieties of human culture existing at a given moment have developed, and thereby to provide a base for the long-term analysis of the dynamics of human civilization.

Because time is an ever-present factor in human experience, its neglect has invited serious distortion in findings of studies that concentrate too strongly on the present. Such neglect also increases the likelihood that conclusions of questionable validity will guide recommendations for programs of action. Of particular relevance to the present discussion is the tendency to dismiss earlier, indigenous technologies, which are the result of a long process of adaptation to the demands of the natural environment, when projects to introduce "improved" agricultural methods are under consideration.[6] Another manifestation of this same bias is seen in the failure to give sufficient weight to pre-existing patterns of economic motivation or marketing procedure where recommendations for aid are made.

[5] M. J. Herskovits, "Anthropology and Africa: A Wider Perspective," *Africa*, XXIX (1959), 225–38.

[6] See, for example, Pierre de Schlippe, *Shifting Cultivation in Africa* (London, 1956).

A further dimension to be taken into account, particularly in the study of economic growth, is that of ideology, from the point of view of cultural theory, may be thought of as comprehending those elements in the system of values of a people that can be abstracted from their attitudes and behavior, or is given overt expression in their myths, tales, and proverbs, and comprises the core concepts which justify and give meaning to their acts. We can thus say that an ideology is the socially sanctioned symbolization of accepted values. Obversely, any social institution may be considered the implementation of a particular segment of the total system of values. Because of the circularity of so much human reasoning, however, these values continuously function to reinforce the institutions that implement them. From the point of view of research, it should be clear that to neglect either the aspect of institution or of value, or to overemphasize either, will throw findings out of cultural perspective and to this extent further affect the validity of conclusions reached or recommendations drawn.

4

The analysis of economic and technical change falls under the heading of acculturation research, since we are here concerned with the results of contact between peoples whose ways of life are marked by a machine technology, a pecuniary economy, and what may be called the scientific approach to the solution of problems, and those who do not have these traditions. The societies which have been recipients of impulses emanating from representatives of the machine culture encompass a wide range of differences, one that is far greater than that among the Euroamerican donor aggregates, which by comparison are relatively homogeneous. As a result, we have a veritable laboratory situation, where advantage can be taken of the historic controls to be derived from the expansion of European and American influence over the world.

Like all human beings, those who carried the industrialized, pecuniary cultures of Europe and America accepted without question the validity of their own values. They held them to be the best of ways because they had been enculturated to believe them so. Yet there was a significant difference between the acceptance of established values in Euroamerican societies and the vast majority of others which came under the influence of the Western World. The donor groups possessed what can be called an evangelistic drive, in terms of which Euroamerican ways were not only held to be best, but in addition brought into play a principle new in human experience, that it was the duty of those whose ways were best to bring their benefits to others. The evangelical tradition, it must be made clear, went far beyond religious considerations which characterize proselytizing activities of other societies, such as Islam. This evangel was secular as well as religious, and was epitomized by such descriptive phrases as "the white man's burden," and the "civilizing mission," used to express the obligation to bring "civilization" to those who lived in accordance with different and therefore less desirable conventions.

This is not the place to analyze the ramifications in Euroamerican culture of this secular evangel. It represents part of a complex of concepts, such as the idea of progress associated with it, that strikes deep into the belief and motivational systems of Europe and American societies. It underlay moves to spread schooling and bring literacy to subject peoples. It is found in the insistence on the superiority of parliamentary democracy to other governmental forms, and gave the rationale for teaching these forms to the inhabitants of colonial possessions. It was behind the drive to bring the findings of scientific medicine to those who used other curing methods. And it has been manifest in the urge to spread to the rest of the world methods to raise standards of living through extending economic aid as a means of achieving technological growth.

If we analyze the complex question of why Euroamerican conventions were able to carry conviction to peoples whose customs were so different, we must first of all make explicit a factor which is not too often enunciated, but whose relevance becomes apparent as soon as it is identified. The success of this particular episode in the long history of the diffusion of culture, that is, arises from the fact that Europe, and later America, could achieve supremacy because they possessed the technical apparatus needed to attain dominance over the peoples with whom they came into contact. From the early days of the expansion of Europe, when the exploring conquerors enjoyed the advantages of superiority in their weapons, to the present time, when we find the great centers of development and dispersion of technical achievement in Europe and America, a situation has obtained in which claims to superiority could be backed by power deriving from demonstrable superiority in the only aspect of culture where superiority is demonstrable, that of technology.

The implications of this latter point, richly documented by the vast body of data accumulated in the comparative study of culture, must be explored further. This is particularly true as concerns our findings that though technological superiority can be objectively demonstrated, other aspects of a technologically superior culture cannot be accorded a concomitant qualitative differential. In the areas of social organization, or art, or religion, or political structure, that is, it has been found quite impossible to set up objective criteria of effectiveness or excellence that will hold under cross-cultural analysis. Here the question of standards that are erected as a basis of judgment, and of the ends that are achieved, make subjective factors so prominent that comparative evaluation having any degree of scientific validity is not possible.

All such evaluations, we find, are culture-bound, and conclusions drawn from them can therefore be meaningful only when accompanied by explicit statements of underlying assumptions. Even on the level of technology, moreover, questions of better or worse cannot be resolved unless we disregard all but purely technical considerations.

Acceptance of the values of Euroamerican culture, and

commitment to procedures developed as a result of intensive study and analysis of the economies of Europe and America have deeply influenced the findings of researches in this area. In cross-cultural perspective, we see that this is why the force of the traditional values of the indigenous peoples in situations of contact have been underestimated, and the institutions on which innovations have impinged neglected. The inevitability of what is being introduced has tended to be taken for granted, so that the responses of the population in a territory for which development is being planned have not figured.

The degree to which the concept of "human nature," so important in the thinking of the classical economists, enters here must not be overlooked. It is obvious that today it functions on the unconscious level of thought about economic planning since, like the idea of economic man, it has been largely given over in its original form. Yet to read the discussions of such a conference as that in which the question of the rise of a middle class in underdeveloped areas was discussed[7] cannot but raise serious questions as to the degree to which unsuspected, culture-bound assumptions of the inevitability of response arising out of the "nature" of man figure in approaches to the analysis of problems of economically and technologically underdeveloped countries. It is clear, for instance, that this particular discussion lay under the shadow of European social and economic history. Queries that might be raised as to whether the growth of a middle class in the areas discussed by the conference must be anticipated as inevitable did not arise. Nor was there speculation as to whether it is desirable or undesirable to have a middle class in all territories where Euroamerican technology is introduced into a nonmachine civilization.

If we grant the power of established values to shape re-

[7] International Institute of Differing Civilizations, *The Development of a Middle Class in Tropical and Sub-Tropical Countries*, report of the 21st session held in London, September, 1955 (Brussels, 1956).

actions of peoples undergoing contact, recognize the depth in time over which these values have existed and allow for their continuing strength, we cannot but achieve a more realistic approach to the problem posed by the juxtaposition of tradition, value, and socio-economic modernization than where any of those factors is overlooked. This phrasing, moreover, in placing such factors within the framework of cultural theory, makes it possible to attain a greater degree of objectivity than the hidden ethnocentrisms of a more restricted position permit, because of the emphasis cultural theory lays on the historical approach that requires the student to take into account all relevant elements in the cultures of both societies in contact. In these terms our particular problem may be set as follows: to determine how ideology, which by definition comprises the non-economic —that is, the nonrational—elements in the antecedent culture of a people, bears on the introduction of an economic system based on a technology that is an expression of the scientific tradition.

5

We may now consider in more specific terms how the student of economic growth can profit from the cross-cultural approach by taking certain aspects of the reactions to culture-contact observable in Africa as examples. In these instances, we can discern how insight and understanding are enlarged by taking into account pre-established patterns of belief, value, and behavior in the transfer of Euroamerican economic and technological conventions to African societies. We can at the same time see the gain that accrues from adding this dimension to the conventional analytic approach, which stresses innovation and tends to ignore the cultural background into which cultural theory teaches us innovations must be absorbed if they are to function in their new setting.

Attitudes toward time afford a good beginning. Instances lying in this field are particularly cogent in terms of the present discussion because of the differences typically manifested in these attitudes among industrialized and non-industrialized peoples, in Africa as elsewhere. This becomes clear when we consider the depth to which temporal regularities are imbedded in the ideology of industrialization which arises out of the fact that for industrial processes to be effective, it is essential that time be measured accurately and schedules adhered to with rigor. This has its semantic reflection, since in an industrial society such as our own, time is something we "make" or "save" or otherwise cherish. Hall has given us numerous illustrations, from all over the world, that demonstrate how unique this is.[8] His illustrations make it clear to what extent cultural shock may be heightened, on both sides of the acculturative experience, by varied orientations toward the meaning of and regard for time where there is contact between Euroamericans and non-industrialized peoples.

The difference between industrial and non-industrial societies has been phrased as a difference between groups who use "clock" time and those who live by "natural" or astrological time. It has also been expressed as the difference between time conceived as falling into carefully measured units, often of very small dimensions—seconds, minutes, and hours, as well as days, weeks, and years—and of seasonal time, where the limits of the units are blurred and imprecise, as they follow the uneven round dictated, for example, by the responses of agricultural peoples to the time of planting, cultivating, reaping and then the period when one awaits the turn of the year to begin the cycle again. The tendency to exactitude in measuring time may thus be regarded as an integral part of the technological complex. It derives its importance from the fact that the activities laid down in accordance with it, whether these be mechanical or behavioral, have made it essential that there be specific schedules maintained in all phases of life—a

[8] Edward T. Hall, *The Silent Language* (New York, 1959). See especially chaps, i and ix.

meeting with a friend, a church service, as well as a production line—if the daily round is to move smoothly.

From one point of view, then, technological change is to
be thought of as a process of adjustment between two time
systems, one exact and demanding, the other imprecise and
relaxed. Hence it would seem logical to assume that a primary requirement in bringing about economic and technological change, or "development" in the current sense of
the word, would be to effect an adjustment on the part of
the peoples who have a less demanding time-system to one
under which they must become continuously more aware of
the passage of time, and revise their habits accordingly.
How far-reaching a process this is can be realized, perhaps,
only by those who have watched it at first hand. For it
entails change in motivation, in goals, and in values that
becomes the more radical when living in accordance with
new patterns of conceiving and utilizing time is concomitant
with adjustment to many other innovations.

All this may be further complicated by the presence of
ideological elements that are political, or moral, or otherwise irrelevant to the particular kind of change we are concerned with here. Thus, for example, an attitude toward
time held by a non-self-governing people can symbolize a
newly won independence. Shortly after the Sudan gained
its freedom, one Sudanese, on being reproached by another
for being later than usual in keeping an appointment, protested, "Do you take me for an Englishman?" There are few
field-workers among indigenous African peoples, enculturated to the Euroamerican time complex, who have not
fumed as they waited for an informant or an interpreter to
come at an agreed time. One soon learns to expect a ceremony not to begin at the hour named. More often than not,
there will be a wait of long duration until everything has
been made ready, or on occasion, the rite will be well under
way at the time appointed for its commencement. Eventually the rite does begin, but experience teaches that it is
best to come prepared to sit pleasantly chatting until this

happens, profiting from whatever opportunities there may be to observe preliminaries. The student in the field also learns that his devotion to accuracy in timing is as incomprehensible to the people with whom he is working, and as irritating, as their disregard of his conventions are to him.

The indigenous tradition, and the attitudes and behavior it engenders, are not difficult to understand and work with once the setting out of which it arises is grasped. The curious thing is that despite its primary importance in shaping adjustment to technical and economic change, specific mention of it rarely enters into the literature. Yet it is not difficult to comprehend that the period a field can wait to be worked is much more flexible than is the case with a machine that depends on a steady flow of raw materials, which it must utilize at a fixed rate, on a fixed schedule. More than this, in a pecuniary economy which is based on a productive process where the concept of overhead is important, a plant that does not function according to plan, or an idle machine, means a diminution of return on investment.

One way in which the problem of adapting a non-industrial people to the demands of accurate timing of the individual process has been met in certain parts of Africa is by employing the compound system. Thus, in the Union of South Africa, steady application to work-schedules in the gold-mines has been insured by housing the workers at the mines. Here they remain for the entire period of their contracts, under close supervision, being allowed off the compounds at long intervals, and then only for a short time. They are therefore always at hand when a shift is called.

Under this system workers are recruited for periods of a year or two. They are brought to the mines from the districts of the Union set aside for Africans, called reserves, or from neighboring Portuguese and British territories, where they leave their families. A variant of this system, aiming at developing a labor supply that will be acculturated to the regularities of time and effort demanded by industrial production and at the same time attack some of the social problems that have arisen where workers are separated from their families under the South African system, is to be found in the Congo. Here workers bring their families to the mines and are settled there on a more or less permanent basis. The children who come with them or are born at the mines receive schooling where their fathers work. Moreover, in this setting they gain not only a measure of literacy, but learn to accept as normal the industrial round.

Whatever the degree to which this policy has over the years achieved its ends, the basic psycho-cultural considerations that the application of the theoretical principles outlined in our discussion rarely enter into analyses of its results. The employers of labor who worked out the system happened on it through pragmatic trial-and-error, hit-or-miss attempts to solve their problem of obtaining a labor supply whose proper response to demands for regularity of effort, and whose respect for industrial time, would be assured. The cases where certain of these approaches did not succeed—as, for example, the rejection of the South African system in the Congo—have, significantly enough, been ignored by students. Efforts seem rather to have been directed toward the study of ways and means by which, over the years, changes have successfully been brought about in the attitudes, motivations and values of the African workers that have made them more and more amenable to the demands of the disciplines essential to industrialization.

In terms of a scientific approach, the study of alternative means and results would seem to be called for. Since the human factor here is vital in studying acculturative adjustment, it would also seem advantageous that the problem be attacked on the cross-cultural level in terms of individual adaptation as well as in its institutional dimensions. In regions where the compound system was not used, we may ask, what were the procedures and stimuli that entered into achieving adjustment to the rhythm of industrial labor? To what extent, in this process, have the concepts of time that were current in the pre-industrial situation persisted, and how are these retentions reflected in the attitudes and performance of the African workers? Even more critical in this context would be the study of the cases where attempts to change earlier patterns had failed. Lacking such studies, the validity of any hypothesis, including the one advanced here, that adjustment to the requirements of an industrial effort entails concomitant adjustment to a new conception of the nature and importance of time, remains but an interesting suggestion. It is essential that the total range of alternatives be taken fully into account, since otherwise what may have begun as a question is likely to end as a stereotype.

It should be made clear that advancing a hypothesis such as this does not imply a simplistic approach to the problem. It requires no great acquaintance with situations of cultural contact to realize that the total acculturative process is very complex, the result of the play of many factors. It is essential to grasp the principle that the student is not necessarily committed to a deterministic position when he isolates one of these factors for analysis. The results of such contacts reach into all aspects of life; certainly this has been amply shown to be true as concerns the impact of Euroamerican culture on the indigenous socio-cultural systems of African peoples. The point being made here is that one of the fundamental and far-reaching adjustments in the process that has arisen out of the differing conceptions of time held in indigenous non-industrial groupings and in the impinging industrialized societies has gone unrecognized by those whose concern is to understand and direct economic development and technological change.

6

Let us consider another phase of contemporary Africa in terms of the theoretical frame of reference that has been discussed above. This has to do with the relationship between land tenure, patterns governing the ownership of property, and kinship structure, on the one hand, and economic development, on the other.

The importance of the land to Africans can scarcely be overestimated. In aboriginal convention, land is everywhere held through the sanction of some supernatural force. In some regions this force is an earth god, in others the ancestors, in still others both of these. The present-day place of the land is reflected in the fact that Africa is, and as far as we can tell will in the foreseeable future be, primarily a continent where agriculture dominates the economy. This is apparent from the statistics of exports, since despite its mineral wealth, fibers, nuts, berries, cereals, and fruits constitute a high proportion of its contribution to world markets. If to this is added the value of the food-stuffs grown for internal consumption, agricultural production becomes by far the largest sector of the total economic effort.

Typically, land is held in common. This takes its most characteristic form in family, clan, or local group ownership, title being vested in a king or family elder or local ruler. Tenure, for an individual member of a group, is valid only while use is actually made of ground that is occupied. Though control over and ownership of the products of labor are recognized, the obligation to make available what a man has grown to other members of his group who may be in need is everywhere present. In terms of this communal spirit, it can be said that no one goes hungry except when a crop failure or seasonal fluctuation in supply[9] causes all to hunger. Moreover, in the socially stratified societies of the continent, high rank requires that resources of a ruler be used for the benefit of the community. A king or chief may exact imposts on agricultural yield, or may levy a tax on trade, or may have a pre-emptive right to certain portions of the animals killed by members of his group, but the

[9] As, for example, is found among the Bemba of Northern Rhodesia. Cf. Audrey I. Richards, *Land, Labour and Diet in Northern Rhodesia: An Economic Study of the Bemba Tribe* (London, 1939).

principle of *noblesse oblige* holds strongly, and he must be ready to extend generous aid and hospitality to those who come to him.[10]

The application of Euroamerican conventions of private ownership of land to African societies necessitates even more far-reaching social adjustments than when non-industrial peoples have to adapt to the requirements of work in the industrial plant. This is not only because land is so essential to the functioning of African economies, but also because the powerful sanctions that govern the ownership of land and its use interpose substantial obstacles to change. Here another principle in the theory of cultural dynamics can be employed to advantage. This is the principle that, under acculturation, substitutive innovations require a greater degree of psychological reorientation than when innovations are additive. It follows that resistances to innovation tend to be greater in the former case than in the latter. In the instances we are considering here, industrialization is an additive innovation, like literacy or, in some parts of the continent, money. Agricultural reform, and changes in patterns of land tenure, however, are substitutive, and must be adjusted to preestablished patterns of response and behavior. Land-use, that is, has traditions associated with it that are deeply set in the aboriginal culture, while industrialization, which is something quite new, does not have to encounter comparable cultural imperatives and affective associations. The fact that the land is so important for the contemporary economy of Africa, plus the less well recognized factor of the substitutive character of innovation where land-tenure and land-use are involved, is why so much attention has had to be given problems centering

[10] Cf. R. S. Rattray, *Ashanti Law and Constitution,* pp. 107–119; M. J. Herskovits, *Dahomey, an Ancient West African Kingdom* (New York, 1938), I, 107–34; F. S. Nadel, *A Black Byzantium* (London, 1942), *passim;* John Roscoe, *The Baganda* (London, 1911), chap. viii; H. A. Stayt, *The Bavenda* (London, 1931), pp. 105, 217 ff.

about these aspects of African life, with strong measures frequently being necessary to assure compliance with changes that have been recommended.

Schemes for the reallocation of land which rest on the principle of individual ownership are numerous in the eastern and southern parts of the continent. The rationale of these schemes has perhaps best been expounded in the *Report* of the Royal Commission of 1953–1955,[11] which investigated, among other things, the question of the most effective use of the land in British East Africa. The problem is clearly posed:

> In whatever direction he turns, the African, whether he wishes to become a peasant farmer, a businessman, a wage-earner in the towns or a modern tenant on the land, is hampered by the requirements of his tribal society with its obligations and restraints. As a farmer, in many areas, he cannot buy or lease land or obtain a fully defensible title thereto. In consequence, he cannot easily specialize in particular forms of agricultural production for export or home markets. . . . The fact that the African who has land cannot readily sell it deters him from improving it, as in any case he is not certain that the increased value which he has imparted to it by his efforts or by his abstinence will accrue to himself or to his heirs.[12]

Later discussion carries further the reasoning that marks this approach to the problem. Thus we read: "In East Africa peasant agriculture is by and large not directed toward securing the greatest money-incomes, nor is it conducted with the aim or knowledge of how to achieve a net surplus after all the costs involved in production have been accurately taken into account."[13] Flexibility is urged in executing recommendations for land reform, to the end that

[11] *East Africa Royal Commission, 1953–1955 Report* (Cmd. 9475), 1955. (Hereinafter cited as *Report*.)

[12] *Report,* chap. v, p. 51, par. 9.

[13] *Ibid.,* chap. xxii, p. 291, par. 2.

"a rigid pattern of production which would inhibit changes which may later be found to be economically advantageous" can be avoided. The "acid test" that schemes for agricultural improvement or resettlement must meet is that these should yield "an increased net income to the producers, and to the economy as a whole, commensurate with the resources expended thereon."[14]

If we analyze this reasoning in terms of the realities of cultural change, and as revealed by application of the theory of cultural dynamics, it becomes apparent that despite the logic of its development out of the premises on which it is based, these premises have little ethnological validity. In this, the *Report* does not differ greatly from other studies of economic growth, particularly those that arise out of requests for technical aid or loans made by official agencies. Like them, it concerns itself almost entirely with economic considerations, ignoring the fact that the most fundamental problems of change with which it deals are essentially non-economic. This lack of realism in approaching the totality of the cultural scene is compounded by the fact that the economic principles that guide the study are strikingly culture-bound, in that they represent economic orientations of Europe and America and, as has been indicated, ignore the economic patterns of the indigenous peoples who are to change their ways.

Characteristically, as in the example used above, the remedies that are proposed cluster about assumptions that land-tenure and the use of land must be "rationalized" in accordance with the principle that only through private ownership can individual initiative be developed, and the best interests of the native peoples be served. Yet in Southern Rhodesia and the Union of South Africa, it has been necessary on occasion to employ force when implementing policies of land reallocation, particularly where these are parts of resettlement projects and mean displacement of

[14] *Ibid.*, chap. xxii, p. 293, par. 8.

Africans from land traditionally owned and used by them. Or, in the case of Ruanda, rejection of projects directed toward improving agricultural methods was so strong that it had to be countered by the imposition of penalties by agricultural officers for non-compliance, since attempts to institute changes of this sort by the use of persuasion tended to meet with polite but firm skepticism.

The approach to technical and economic change through the application of the theory of cultural dynamics reveals similar problems in still other aspects of the changing economies of African peoples. Aboriginally, the economics of Africa, as elsewhere, were geared to requirements of the total social systems of which they formed a part. Because of this, the communal principle went much beyond considerations of land tenure, and acted to strengthen the ties between members of groupings based on kinship or, to a lesser degree, on age or common interest. The aboriginal systems can thus be thought of as providing an economic infrastructure on which a network of rights and obligations could be reared, to bind the individual more closely to the group of which he is a member than could ever be achieved in societies whose economic systems are based on private ownership and individual initiative. The question that arises here, then, has to do with the adjustments that have to be made when an individual's wealth, traditionally at the disposal of members of his kinship or age group, has been acquired and can most advantageously be employed in accordance with the usages of the impinging economic system.

The resolution of this problem by Africans who have become acculturated to the ways of a free enterprise economy understandably entails many difficulties when they must also function as members of their native societies. The African who, by his own efforts and in accordance with principles that have brought Europeans success, has accumulated an economic surplus which he has used to set up as a small shop-keeper in his village affords a case in point.

The rewards of his enterprise and his effort, and hence his ability to continue to function in terms of the new system, cannot but be seriously diminished by the play of antecedent patterns which accord kin the right to take what they need from his stock.

A similar dilemma is faced by Africans who are members of the professions. Their obligations to their relatives, in the broad African sense of the term as applied to an extended kinship unit, require them to call on their resources to discharge the traditionally sanctioned demands that may be laid on them. This burden becomes the more onerous when such men, who for the most part live in urban centers, must care for kinfolk who have adapted themselves to city life less successfully than they. Still another difficulty that arises from this lack of congruence between the norms of the cultures that are in contact is to be found in the retention of these older obligations into the acculturated political scene. The inevitable result of the application of the rules governing obligations toward kinsmen to the new order is nepotism. This, however, means the negation of what, in Euroamerican conception, are the advantages to be derived from selecting civil servants impartially, on the basis of competence and merit alone.

These examples afford only a few of the many instances that could be given of the adjustments that come in the train of contact between cultures having institutions with differing ideological components, representing different means-and-end equations, and organized along different lines. New demands, and new responses to these demands, invade every phase of the culture undergoing change, as the members of a society move into an order of things different from that which prevailed in their pre-contact world. New kinds of motivation toward labor, different wants and means of satisfying them, previously unknown methods of exchange must all be, and are being, faced.[15]

[15] For various facets of this problem, see Wilbert E. Moore, *Industrialization and Labor* (New York, 1951); Walter Elkan,

This is to say that however complicated the adjustments and however difficult the problems they create, changes are occurring, even though they may not be proceeding according to plan, or in line with the models that shaped the original impulse. Acculturation, like any other phenomenon of cultural dynamics, is not reversible. Once begun, it develops in terms of the new directions taken by its drift, toward a logical working out of the historical impulses it has experienced. This is why efforts to achieve the return of a people to a "native" state cannot succeed. The difficulties encountered in the Union of South Africa stem in large measure from the unrealistic nature of the doctrine of separate development, called *apartheid,* which envisages returning the Africans to their precontact economic, political, and social modes of life. It goes contrary to all we know about the results of cultural contact; it attempts to turn back the clock of history. Change under cultural contact may be freely entered into, or may result from the application of force; it may be slow or rapid; it may be extensive or limited. But some change always results from contact, which has been one of the prime movers in the development of human civilization.

The key word in our formulation is "interaction"; the antecedent elements in the recipient culture mold what they are given, or take, from the donor. This is to be observed in the spread of Euroamerican culture over the world. Despite the evangelistic nature of this diffusion, the assumption of a superiority that could be validated by the control of power and the exercise of this power, the new institutions have

---

"Migrant Labor in Africa: An Economist's Approach," *American Economic Review,* XLIX (1959), 188–97; M. J. Herskovits, "The Problem of Adapting Societies to New Tasks," in B. Hoselitz, ed., *The Progress of Underdeveloped Areas* (Chicago, 1952), pp. 89–112; Herskovits, "Motivation and Culture-Pattern in Technological Change," *International Social Science Bulletin,* VI (1954), 388–400; Herskovits, "African Economic Development in Cross-Cultural Perspective," *American Economic Review,* XLVI (1956), 452–61.

not been taken over in their entirety, but have been reshaped so as to bring them into line with pre-existing custom. By the same token, it is well to remember that the behavior of those who belong to the donor group, when operating in this situation, is not what it would be in its own setting. To take an instance lying on a simple level of economic activity, it is apparent that European companies trading in Africa must adapt their methods to the African conventions of buying and selling or they will not be successful, whatever the usages of the home office.

It is thus apparent that our understanding of the processes underlying economic change profits by broadening our frame of reference to include the theories and methods of cultural dynamics. Approaches which attempt to take over the methodology of the natural sciences, and employ techniques and concepts developed for the study of phenomena having a far more restricted range of variation than those entering into the category of learned behavior, must be extensively revised if applied to this latter class of data. The use of models which, in the natural world, would be universally applicable, is restricted in the study of human behavior because of the ease of transmissibility and change of learned action and thought patterns. Because in most of the world economic development is an acculturative phenomenon, any theory that guides its study must take account of the theory of cultural dynamics; the methods used to test conclusions must include those of the cross-cultural approach. A fundamental proposition that must never be lost sight of is that institutions rest on sanctions and that these sanctions, in turn, dictate the behavior that is the essence of our study. From this it follows that the problem of economic development, like all problems of cultural change, is essentially one of discovering, assessing, and predicting responses of men and women to innovations that go beyond the bounds of antecedent convention.

the role of culture-pattern in the african acculturative experience*

Certainly at first glance, Africa at mid-century impresses the visitor, and has impressed many students,
with its degree of acceptance of European forms. One
sees Africans operating complex machinery in factories, on mines, in road-building, in agricultural projects. One meets Africans with University education,
entirely competent in the higher fields of learning and
technology. What could be more reasonable than to
assume that this represents the reality of Africa of today and tomorrow; that the African of yesterday is
doomed to extinction under the continuing force of
these forms? . . . It has taken time for the insights
provided by the work of anthropologists to attain a
truer evaluation of the real measure of the tenaciousness possessed by African cultures. . . . [But] it is
imperative to stress [also] the dynamic quality of the
African past. . . . The peoples of Africa have not been
unreceptive to innovation.

One of the most important
questions faced by students of cultural change in Africa

* A paper presented to the XXV International Congress of
Orientalists, Moscow, 9–16 August, 1960. . . . A reply to this paper
appeared in *Sovetskaya etnografia* No. 3, Moscow, May–June 1961,
by S. Artanovskiy, titled: "The Problem of Comparative Culture
Values and the Theory of Cultural Relativism."—Ed.

concerns the degree to which African peoples have responded to the stimuli resulting from contacts with ways of life different from their own. In most of the literature on Africa, it has been taken for granted that the image of Europe, projected against the African scene, would become permanently affixed to African cultures, and that given time, the Africans would in large measure follow the lead of those who ruled them. It has taken time for the insights provided by the work of anthropologists to spread in order to attain a truer evaluation of the real measure of tenaciousness possessed by African cultures.

Why the popular view persisted as long as it did is not difficult to understand. In the degree of their intensity, as well as in their extensiveness, the recent acculturative influences that have played on the peoples of Africa south of the Sahara have rarely been equaled. The intensity of this acculturation derived from the relatively short span of time over which the Africans were subjected to these influences, and the nature of the mechanisms that were operative in effecting their implementation. Their extensiveness is manifest in the ways in which they invaded all aspects of African culture—social, economic, political, religious and aesthetic —and their ubiquitousness over the Subsaharan continent as a whole. Given the ethnocentrism of those who exercised the controls, it was logical that attention should fix on the drama of change, and overlook the force of the antecedent indigenous ways which quietly continued to channel the modes of behavior of the vast majority of Africans.

In terms of the historic forces that have come into play in the acculturative picture, the factor of colonial control was of major importance. So important was it, indeed, that explanations of change in Africa have frequently been exclusively referred to it. Simplistic reasoning of this kind, however, cannot be countenanced in any scientific analysis of causation. Colonialism in Africa represented a late phase of the world-wide movement of European expansion. As the history of this expansion goes, however, its African phase was so short that the governing powers exerted their controls in the manner of the classical patterns of colonial exploitation for only a relatively brief period. This gives us a clue to the particular character of the African acculturative experience, especially to the reasons for the rapidity with which the changes that resulted from the contact of peoples there actually did take place.

It will be remembered that in most other parts of the world, colonial systems had been in operation, and in some continents, notably the Americas, had been already overthrown well before the spread of European domination over Subsaharan Africa, whatever the marginal contacts between Europe and Africa may have been along the coastal periphery, and whatever acculturative repercussions may have resulted from the trade in slaves to North Africa, Asia Minor, North and South America, and the Caribbean. We may date the beginnings of the African colonial system imposed by Europeans at about 1884, when the Treaty of Berlin was concluded. This instrument staked out the interests of the various Powers, and, in a general way, set the boundaries of territories that in the succeeding years were destined to encompass political entities which transcended the ethnic, geographical and economic realities that for the most part were ignored when these boundaries were drawn.

This later period of colonialism coincided with a time when there was great technological and industrial expansion in Europe and America, which resulted in the growth of a world economy such as had never before existed anywhere. It also coincided with developments in the field of communications which, in terms of distance translated into time, literally shrank the world and allowed the dissemination of ideas on a scale hitherto not possible. These ideas were also changing. It was not only the peoples of the colonial areas who, as they became more and more familiar with those who governed them, began to develop movements looking toward the transfer of power into their own hands. Concomitantly, the colonial system began to find critics among the peoples of the metropolitan powers. The cumulative force of all this was to encourage the development of nationalisms everywhere in the colonial world which, spurred on by an accelerating world-wide movement toward achieving—and granting—political independence, presaged the end of the colonial system and its culmination in Africa, the last of the great colonial areas.

What were some of the acculturative mechanisms that functioned in bringing new elements into African life? Some were institutional. Examples of those would be the organized missionary effort; the growth of governmental structures that demanded more and more African participation in the administrative process; educational systems that were developed to increase literacy and equip Africans to function in the situation of change; scientific medicine, and measures to prevent the spread of disease. Other of these acculturative mechanisms were, however, by-products of developments that arose out of the needs of the colonial system under impact of the world economy. One instance of this was urbanization that followed on the introduction of the industrial process. Another was the development of wage-labor, particularly important in view of the differing rhythm of work it demanded when compared to the schedules of the indigenous systems. Even less formal were the innovations that had to do with the ownership and use of property —reactions to such concepts as those of free-hold tenure in land, or of individual initiative and control of returns, and other activities.

This list, however, by no means comprises all the acculturative forces that functioned in the African scene. It includes but the most recent ones, and the most obvious. We tend to overlook those earlier, pre-European acculturations that, in Africa as elsewhere, have gone on wherever peoples of different cultures have come into contact. There were the relations between the peoples south of the desert and to the north of it—relations that were based primarily on trade, but which brought in their train a reciprocal interchange of cultural elements whose significance has scarcely begun to be analyzed, except in terms of the formula of Egyptian influence, an influence which, in the light of present archaeological and ethnographic knowledge, we know to have been far less important than was previously assumed.

In the eastern part of the continent, a similar process of contact and cultural exchange with Arabia and India and China went on for countless centuries. In recent times, too, Africa has seen the introduction of large numbers of Indians into the eastern part of the continent, and of an appreciable group of Lebanese and Syrians in the west, though the acculturative impact of these latter groups on African life has been relatively slight. Nor does this tell the whole tale of African response to contact, since the archaeological record, and what we can glean from the writings of the early travelers, demonstrate that Africa has known intertribal acculturation from earliest times.

What this means is that the acculturative experience is nothing new to Africa, and that what we have witnessed there during the past half-century is no more than the continuation of a process that in all likelihood has been going on as long as the continent has had human inhabitants. That this should be the case can scarcely be surprising. Cultural interchange between peoples in contact has long been recognized as a universal in human experience, and is a phenomenon implicit in the theory of cultural dynamics. It derives from the fact that culture, being learned, is transmitted from people to people with a degree of ease and of rapidity that is a function of historical and ecological factors entering into a particular case.

For those less conversant with cultural theory, it is imperative to stress the dynamic actuality of the African past, standing as this does in such sharp contrast to the stereotype of the continent as one existing in sluggish slumber, out of which it was only awakened by the circumstances of contact with Europe. The peoples of Africa, it is plain, have not been unreceptive to innovations, and have had no in-surmountable difficulty in adjusting their pre-existing habits to them. Their readiness to adopt many of the basic food-plants now widely spread in Subsaharan Africa—maize and cassava, for example—affords us one instance of this. So does the distribution of metal-working, which was intro-duced into Africa two or three thousand years ago, and gradually worked its way from people to people until the techniques of smelting iron-ore and bronze-casting had become diffused over almost the entire continent.

There is little question that the impact of the recent ac-culturative experience of the African has been far greater than those earlier ones, which entailed the introduction of innovations on a smaller scale and at a far more gentle pace. Yet the flexibility which marks the African approach to innovation, and certain elements in African cultures themselves, made the more recent experience far less diffi-cult for them than it was for non-industrialized peoples elsewhere, in North America, for instance, or in the South Seas. It is this element in the African past, and the psy-chological set toward innovation that it entailed, that makes the problems in the study of the dynamics of acculturative change in Africa so complex. For here three factors are inextricably intermingled—the cultural base, the innovative elements, and the established attitude toward change.

An example of how this attitude functioned in pre-Euro-pean times may be cited by referring to a pattern of inter-tribal acculturation found in Dahomey. The Dahomean monarchy, it will be recalled, from the seventeenth century onward, was undergoing a process of continuous expan-sion. From a small, typically West African local com-munity, the Aladahonu dynasty which ruled it steadily in-creased its power. With accelerated speed, it first conquered the villages in the vicinity, then in 1725 took Whydah to gain an outlet to the sea, after which it moved northward and eastward. Shortly before its overthrow by the French, it was warring with the Yoruba, aiming at the extension of its hegemony over Abeokuta.

As with most African peoples, successful exercise of power is linked in the thinking of the Dahomeans with supernatural support, and this was also the case with those whom they conquered. It was thus reasonable for those brought under Dahomean control to add the worship of victorious Dahomean deities to their own, a process which was facilitated by their polytheistic systems. But the matter went further than this. The borrowing of gods was not a one-way process; there was an interchange whereby the Dahomeans adopted the gods of those they conquered. The theory behind this is as revealing in terms of understanding the acculturative dynamics involved as it is significant for broader questions of the psychology of culture—a matter aside from the point here, and which I have already considered elsewhere. To the Dahomeans, all gods have power, which may be diminished, but is not nullified by defeat. Hence the gods of defeated as well as victorious peoples must be propitiated. In terms of cultural dynamics, this psychological resilience is a prime means of achieving adaptation to cultural change. And though in its particular form the response of the Dahomeans to the gods of peoples they conquered is only a single case, the total complex of response it represents exemplifies a kind of reaction that is to be observed in various situations elsewhere in Subsaharan Africa. It cannot be gainsaid that it must have stood the Africans in good stead in meeting the innovations resulting from European control as it did in pre-European times where there was intertribal acculturation.

In reality, in analyzing African acculturation, we are faced with a continuum of change, and not a dichotomy to which we can refer our instances, placing them in well-defined categories. The particular manifestations of African acculturation we study move imperceptibly along this continuum, ranging from the one pole, which is the complete acceptance of an innovation, through a theoretical midpoint at which innovation and indigenous custom are merged in a syncretic unity, to complete rejection. This is the theoretical frame; in actuality, it is impossible empirically to discover examples of either extreme, while even at the midpoint the combinations seem to retain enough of their earlier characteristics to enable us to identify the elements in them that come from the contributory cultural streams. In many cases, seeming contradictions between elements that enter are reconciled; thus, in East Africa, bride-wealth, or *lobola,* is translated into European currency which, however, cannot be accorded entire validity, since some cattle must pass; or in Ruanda, where a man will work for wages, use his money to buy cattle, which he then gives as bride-wealth to his prospective father-in-law in accordance with established custom.

Except for its polar extremities, the totality of our continuum has its theoretical base in a mechanism of cultural dynamics called cultural reinterpretation. Implicit in the concept is a recognition of the fact that every phenomenon in human behavior has two aspects—its form, and its meaning. In a society where there is a minimum of contact with other peoples, and a maximum of cultural integration, the two are so much a unit that it is difficult to distinguish between them. One of the reasons why it took so long, indeed, to do this was because earlier anthropologists were concerned almost exclusively with such stable societies; and it was only when we moved to the study of peoples undergoing acculturative change that we began to see that the elements with which we were concerned presented these two facets.

There is little question that under acculturation, form changes more readily than meaning. This brings us back to the concept of cultural reinterpretation, for as we study the phenomenon we see more and more clearly that peoples adopt new forms more readily than new meanings; that characteristically they assign old meanings to the new forms, thereby maintaining their pre-existing systems of values, and making the break with established custom minimal as far as their cognitive responses are concerned. On the emotional level, they retain the satisfactions derived from earlier ways, while profiting from adopting new forms that seem advantageous to them. Certainly in the study of acculturation in Africa, there is scarcely any aspect of the changing life of its peoples not illuminated by reference to this mechanism of cultural reinterpretation; it is essential that it be brought to the forefront of scientific thinking concerning cultural change in Africa if we are to analyze the phenomenon in realistic terms.

We must again refer to the ethnocentric component in Africanist studies in exploring further the reasons why perspective has been so distorted in the study of cultural change in Africa through the failure to recognize its reinterpretive component, and the consequent almost exclusive emphasis that has been laid on innovation. Certainly, at first glance, Africa at mid-century impresses the visitor, and has impressed many students, with its degree of acceptance of European forms. One sees Africans operating complex machinery in factories, or using tractors or bulldozers on the mines, or in road-building, or in agricultural projects; and doing these things efficiently and with a minimum of European direction. One meets Africans with University educations, entirely competent in the higher fields of learning and technology, who have fully mastered European culture. What could seem more reasonable than to assume that this represents the reality of Africa of today and tomorrow; that the Africa of yesterday is a picturesque vestige, doomed to extinction under the continuing force of these new forms?

An outstanding example of this kind of reasoning is to be had in the concept of detribalization, which has had considerable vogue among students of contemporary Africa. It was especially employed in analyzing African life in the new cities that came to dot the Subsaharan continent, especially in the Union of South Africa, where the twin forces of urbanization and industrialization have been more powerful than anywhere else. Again, in its formal aspect, modes of African city life seemed so different from indigenous patterns that it was *prima facie* impossible to continue antecedent conventions, and that adjustment in terms of earlier orientations was inconceivable.

It is significant that one of the first attempts to correct perspective was that of an African scholar, Z. K. Matthews;[1] writing some years before the concept of reinterpretation had been advanced, he clearly saw the power of aboriginal custom in shaping the life of the urban dweller in the Union. Anticipating by at least two decades the swing toward greater balance in the study of the urbanized African whereby the concept of "detribalization" came to be rejected, he stated: "It seems altogether unwise to attempt to drive a wedge between this urban group and the so-called purely tribal native by refusing to recognize what they have in common and the contribution which the former can make and are making to native life and thought by their synthesis of Western and Native conceptions wherever they are complementary and not contradictory."

A few instances may be taken from the rich documentation he offers in the critical field of social organization:

> Even the individual who feels that for him the old political organization of the tribe does not adequately meet his modern needs and will in any case not survive the white man's interference with it, still thinks that as far as his private married life is concerned the old code need not be entirely abandoned. The man who has accepted Christianity, for example, and belongs to a Church which prohibits the giving and taking of *lobola* is nevertheless not satisfied that the Christian wedding-ceremony alone gives sufficient validity and respectability to the marriage of his son or daughter. The husband who is willing and anxious to take his wife to a modern hospital for confinement still feels under obligation to observe at least some of the Bantu taboos connected with the pregnancy, confinement, and the nursing period of his wife. The educated man in seeking the hand of some girl in marriage still respects the prohibited degrees of marriage as laid down by his tribe in the

[1] Z. K. Matthews, "The Tribal Spirit among Educated Africans," *Man,* February, 1935, No. 26, pp. 26–27.

distant past, and does not often depart in any material point from the procedure prescribed for the marital negotiations of people of good class. . . . The publicity given to weddings, the slaughtering of beasts which provides the necessary spilling of blood, the attendance of certain prominent relatives or their representatives; the traditional gifts from one side to the other; the competitive dancing and singing which have replaced the bride on her departure for her new home . . . those features characterize the marriages of educated as well as uneducated Africans. The home life of educated Africans —evidences of Westernization such as the use of chairs, tables, pianos, etc. notwithstanding—conforms in the spirit to the old code. The relationships between husband and wife, parents and children, the position of the eldest male child in the family, that of the youngest child, the relations between brothers and sisters on examination will make us guard against the hasty generalization that there is nothing African about the house.

With the passage of time, and particularly as more Africans gained more knowledge of the cultures that had been brought to them, the persistence of earlier custom, often in reinterpreted form, began to be reinforced by rationalization in terms of explicit value being assigned to the old ways. The new came to be recognized as worthy of adoption, but selectively, and in the light of evaluation drawn from preexisting cultural convention. The values in the social support and assurance afforded by extended kinship units; the values in group holding of land as against free-hold tenure; the formation of African Christian churches or separatist Islamic sects where aboriginal sanctions come to the fore; the reinterpretation of new governmental forms so as to reconcile them with older political usages; the insistence on the importance of the values inherent in the ancestral cult—all exemplify the power of the antecedent cultures in the present acculturative situation, and permit the prediction of the continuing force that they can be expected to exert in the future.

As we penetrate beneath the surface of form to the under-lying reality of meaning by the use of the concept of rein-terpretation, we approach a deeper understanding of the current African situation. We can realistically assess the functional significance of such new ideas being advanced by African intellectuals as that of an African personality, or of *negritude*. In preceding decades, much effort has gone into demonstrating the fallacies in the idea of racism, by showing the scientific invalidity of assumptions of racial inferiority and superiority. It is important that, this accomplished, we not be beguiled by an equally fallacious concept of cultural inferiority and superiority, and thus replace racism by *culturism*. Certainly in Africa we are coming to know, and, as we learn, are coming to appreciate, the values in the cultures of the people of the continent. If we recognize that it is impossible, empirically, to establish an absolute scale of worth for different ways of life, we thereby arrive at a posi-tion of historical realism by acknowledging that the future cultures of Africa will develop in accord with the traditional values which guide African life, however much of the inno-vations to which they have been, and will continue to be exposed, they may adopt.

four

expressive arts: a cross-cultural perspective

art and value[1]

Almost by definition, the things a people hold beautiful go beyond physical needs of subsistence and the social needs of organization and control. Why, then, does the aesthetic drive, if it be one, or tradition, or response—however one may call it—lodge so deep in human need, and bring such manifest satisfactions to those who experience it? . . . a rationale for the cultural approach to art is not designed to supplant purely aesthetic analysis, but to provide a surer base for generalizations and insights from examining at first hand vast areas of creative expression . . . heretofore largely subject to speculative, impressionistic, subjective appraisal.

The incident I relate happened a little more than thirty years ago. It was during my first field trip, among the Bush Negroes who live in the interior of Dutch Guiana, in northern South America. I was getting into the dugout canoe that was to take me for a final run through the rapids that lay between the base camp and the railhead. My field kit, my notes, my collection of carvings and specimens were being stowed away. I was saying my goodbyes. At that moment, an old woman came up to me. In her hand she held a fine food-stirring paddle, which I had tried in vain to buy from her earlier.

"White man," she said, "take this. Ayobo made it for me
before I came to live with him in his village. Put it in the
big house, in your white man's country, where you told
me beautiful things are kept. And write on a piece of paper
that Ayobo made it."

I have seldom written or talked on art without that
picture at the waterfront in the Guiana Bush coming to me,
as do others of that first field experience among a people
who assign such high prestige to the creative process. For
in this group the fine carver, the gifted singer, or dancer or
story-teller is said, and said literally, to be favored by a
god, who has endowed him with special skills. Uprooted
from their ancestral Africa, composed of a mixture of stocks
ranging from Senegal to the Congo, welding a unified culture that yet retained elements of their ancestral provenience, these Bush Negroes have achieved a synthesis that
allots a prominent role in their everyday life to the artistic
embellishment of the objects they use—a winnowing tray,
a pounding board, a clothes beater, a food-stirrer, a paddle,
a canoe seat, a house-post, a comb, a fire-fan. Yet though
artistry is so highly lavished on the secular phases of their
life, sacred art is more casually handled. An ancestral shrine
will have the merest suggestion of a head incised on a
weathered post; a figure impregnated with magical prop-
erties for the protection of a village or of a shrine will be
no more than a roughly blocked human head atop a
squared off or rounded column.

These Bush Negroes were excellent teachers. From them
I got my first insights into the values of makers, and owners, and viewers of art objects. These insights came from
the piece I have mentioned, and many other pieces which
I acquired; from my talks with carvers at work, and those
who had carved pieces they would not part with for any
monetary inducement or other urging; even more from the
comment of the men and women who came to look at what
I had collected, their approval or disapproval of those who
had been willing to part with specially singled out pieces,

their talk among themselves about the qualities of what
they saw.

Speaking tonight under the auspices of a Great House
where beautiful things from all peoples are shown, I could
wish that you could have shared field experiences such as
I have had in Guiana and in diverse regions of Africa. For
then, I am sure, my task of raising doubts about some of
the formulations that have been made under the influence
of scholars who have written about the arts of nonliterate
peoples without a firsthand knowledge of those about whom
they generalized would be no task at all.

Let us start with the generalization supported by the
findings of many ethnologists, that the appeal of what a people consider surpassingly pleasing, beauty as an abstraction,
that is, broadly spread over the earth, and lies deep in
human experience—so wide, and so deep, that it is to be
classed as a cultural universal. It is simple to see why,
from the nature of the case, it was essential that man, like
any other animal, assure himself a food supply, obtain
adequate shelter, order the relations between one individual
and another. We can see how the physical structure of the
human organism rendered speech possible, and how
language became an essential vehicle for tradition. We
can understand why the need for psychic security could
have given rise to the many different religions which have
been recorded. But the universality of the aesthetic appeal
cannot be accounted for on any such grounds. Almost by
definition, the things that a people hold beautiful go beyond the physical needs of subsistence and the social needs
of organization and control. Why, then, does the aesthetic
drive, if it be one, or tradition, or response—however one
may call it—lodge so deeply in human need, and bring
such manifest satisfactions to those who experience it?
The experimental psychologists have thus far told us little
about the psychology of art; perhaps it is because this fragile
thing is not susceptible to manipulation by any techniques
that have thus far been devised, and hence has died under

the probe, leaving only a frame from which the essential quality has escaped. The psychoanalysts, out of their depth studies of the impulses that move from below the level of consciousness, have given us a sense of the power of these impulses to shape behavior, attitude, and value. The philosophers have given us suggestions and insights; they have raised many searching questions; but they, no more than the experimental psychologists or the psychoanalysts, have given us answers.

I should like to suggest that one of the reasons for this is that their studies of the aesthetic have lacked a cross-cultural dimension. For though these studies have historic depth, documentation has been drawn from the few cultural streams out of which the literate societies have developed. The existence of a museum such as the one under whose auspices we are gathered, devoted to the arts of peoples who never developed writing, demonstrates pointedly our need to widen the base of aesthetic theory, to break through its culture-bound limits. If the aesthetic response is a universal in human experience, it must be studied as such, everywhere it is found. The day is long past when humanity could be equated with the literate societies alone; when values found in the cultures of peoples having written languages could be placed on aesthetic and moral scales and weighed against those of peoples without writing.

Let us then proceed to examine some of the points that arise when we approach the aesthetic with full cross-cultural reference. We may first of all consider a matter I have already raised, that art is something that goes beyond the utilitarian demands of everyday living. What peoples over the world define as "art" has not been studied extensively, but we have some information to which we can turn, such as that given by Schneider, who has investigated the ideas of beauty held by the Pakot of Kenya, in East Africa. The wooden milkpot used by these people is evaluated as *karam,* a word translated as "good," but a projecting lip on the rim of the pot is *pachigh,* "beautiful," also translated as "pleasant to look at" or "unusual." Pakot visual art, says Schneider, is thus defined as "man-made embellishments with aesthetic appeal," and consists of the decoration of objects which of themselves do not have aesthetic qualities. Beautiful things, that is, "have only the function of pleasing the eye and only the function of enhancing non-aesthetic things."

I must make it clear that, in saying that art goes beyond the utilitarian, I am in no way suggesting that it is removed from life. One of the clearest conclusions to be drawn from the many studies of the art of nonliterate peoples is the intimacy of its relation to the daily round. This is what is meant when we say that art in these societies is in many cases more living, more meaningful than among ourselves; a statement, however, that depends pretty largely on how one defines art, for even the mass-produced objects we use in our day-to-day existence go beyond the requirements of efficient functioning. The shape of the fountain pen, the colors in which a water-tank is painted, the chrome on the automobile all represent this kind of non-functional embellishment. And it is the same in all cultures. A food stirrer need not have its carved human head, nor the incised design on its blade, to make it a more effective instrument with which to stir the food in the cooking-pot, any more than, on the simplest level of decoration, the brightly painted streamlined instrument we use in turning over the buckwheat cake on the griddle is necessary to produce a satisfactory breakfast dish.

On one point there is general agreement. To be classified as an object of art, a drawing, a painting, a piece of sculpture, no less than a musical composition or a narrative or a dramatic representation, must meet cultural criteria of form. More than this, the form which it takes must demonstrate control over the medium. However, technical competence is not enough. We all know the painter or sculptor—to confine ourselves to the graphic and plastic arts—who has competence but no creativity, whose work is derivative, who breaks no new paths. Such persons are found in every society, and in every age. What we see in our museums represents the work of the more gifted artists, works that at the same time demonstrate supreme control of the media of their choice.

Let me commend to you, if you do not know it, a visit to the Maritshuis Museum in The Hague. Every room is hung from floor to ceiling with paintings that date from the great periods of Flemish and Dutch art. In this mass are works of the highest quality—Vermeer landscapes, for example. Most of the paintings, however, represent a level of artistic effort that never reached greatness, and while they are competent, they are no more than this. What a visit to the Maritshuis teaches us is that even in one of the greatest periods of art history there were many mediocre painters; and if we take our lesson to other cultures, we find that in no society does artistic excellence lodge on a single level. When expressed in this way, we are perhaps stating the obvious, but in this case the obvious must be stated, because it is only obvious when applied to our own society and, indeed, to our own time. Certainly those who have studied the pieces from nonliterate cultures found in ethnological museums, or in a museum such as this, devoted to the art of such peoples, seem rarely to reflect that what they see represents selection and not the total range of aesthetic competence. To make the point bluntly, we may lay it down as a general principle that every people, in every age, has poor artists as well as good.

What distinguishes the appreciation of art among smaller, nonliterate societies and in a great, highly specialized aggregate such as our own is that their standards are not verbalized. There are few explicitly stated rules to guide appreciation. But the difference is one of degree, not of kind. Again, my Bush Negro friends taught me much about this. "This man wants carving, not lumber," was the way it was phrased when, on one occasion, I rejected a poorly carved piece, and praised a better one. The men who

stopped at the base camp to see what I had bought—for
news travels fast on the river along which these people live
—would differ in depth of feeling for the pieces, and in
reasoning that guided appreciation, much as among ourselves. But there was no Bush Negro who reserved his
judgment until experts in judging works of art gave their
decisions. Not everyone in this society, where artistic ability
is accorded high prestige, can carve. I was able to see this
at close range, in the crude attempts made by a young man
whom I came to know well. The fact that he was a poor
carver caused him continuously to compensate for what he
felt to be a serious deficiency, but his judgment of a piece
shown him was based soundly on the evaluations of the
culture, and he could apply them with sureness in forming
his aesthetic responses.

Perhaps we may phrase our point in this way. In recognizing the universality of artistic expression, we must understand that this applies to societies, not to individuals.
Every society, that is, numbers among its members some who
are more creative than others, some who are not creative
at all, and many who vary between those extremes in the
sensitivity of their responses. The extent to which creativity
and appreciation are specialized into distinct callings varies
from our own society at one extreme to certain nonliterate
groups at the other, especially those small, isolated ones
in Australia and Africa and the Americas that live on the
subsistence level. Specialization, however, does not of itself
increase nonconformity, and the concept of the "primitive"
as a man who lives in a kind of cultural strait jacket, who
follows custom and does not question it, is as invalid in the
field of art as it has been shown to be in other aspects of
culture. It is one of the interesting paradoxes of the reaction
of art critics and art historians to the work of nonliterate
peoples that they could so long accept the stereotype of the
"primitive" and yet show such insightful appreciation of
work that could only have been the creative expression of
individual artists who, because they were creative, must

have brought about transmutations as they expressed their own personalities as artists within limits set by tradition.

Until recently, the role of the individual artist in nonliterate societies was not explored, creativity somehow having been thought of as due to qualities inherent in the group as a whole, wherein the artist was but a kind of undifferentiated unit. The anonymity of the nonliterate artist when what he has created is removed from its social setting, or survives to another generation, has encouraged this point of view.

This fact of anonymity has had another, more far reaching effect. It reinforced the stereotype of the "primitive" artist as one impelled to follow the traditions of his ancestors blindly, unthinkingly. It has made the more convincing the assumption that has been so widely held that he but responds to the collective representations of his culture. In some instances, indeed, where the artists in certain nonliterate societies marked what they made with some indentifying sign, such as a particular geometric design on the base of the pedestal of a figurine, the presence of such signs, when noted at all, was buried in an ethnographic account, because it seemed so unlikely that a "primitive" artist could be this much of an individualist. It was several decades after the interest in exotic art became established that systematic attempts were made to reduce regional stylistic differences to local ones, and still later that differences were recognized within these local styles which arose out of the idiosyncrasies of individual artists.

Let us take a moment to consider this concept of the collective representation as it has been applied to the arts of nonliterate peoples, in order to assess its influence on art criticism, and its role in stifling inductive, cross-cultural testing of hypotheses. It derives, as you know, from the work of the French philosopher Lucien Lévy-Bruhl. From his wide reading in the literature, over many years, he became convinced that "primitive" mentality differed in kind from that of "civilized" peoples; that they reasoned from assumed rather than from actual, verifiable cause to effect; that their identifications with the souls and spirits of the dead, with animals, plants or other phenomena went so far that they did not differentiate themselves from them. Students of comparative art and literature took up the concept of primitive mentality because, seeing in carvings or paintings, or in tales or songs this quality of anonymity, and lacking first-hand field experience, they found it natural to reify traditions into causal entities of which the carver, the painter, the story-teller or the singer was the creature, not the master.

Today, fortunately, we need not prolong the discussion of this theory of "primitive" mentality. Its inadequacies were such that before his death in 1940, Lévy-Bruhl himself, as already noted, repudiated it, concluding that the kind of reasoning he ascribed to "primitive" man was human, not primitive; that its manifestations, found everywhere, depended on the circumstances of moment and tradition. The theory of Lévy-Bruhl, however, was not alone in providing psychological orientation for students of the art of nonliterate peoples. It was but a part of an intellectual current which assigned to the "primitive" a different mode of thought than that of literate, "civilized" man. The Jungian formulation of the collective unconscious is not, conceptually, very different from that of the collective representation, and both have mystical components that make objective proof of either equally impossible. There was also the Freudian approach, in which, as Firth puts it, "the . . . dogma of equating the savage with the child is taken as sufficient," and "the primitive is alleged to be free from the shackles which hampered civilized man, and to be capable of expressing directly in his art his instinctive impulses."

All these theories as they bore on "primitive" art had one point in common; it was students of art and literature, not those concerned with the scientific study of culture, who found them congenial, and used them to analyze exotic arts. Yet, we may ask, does not the portrait of the creative artist and writer of our own society, the man or woman who turns to his intuitions to guide his artistic reactions, who is sensate in his responses rather than cognitive, fit the specifications of the one who thinks prelogically, in terms of representations that are collective and unconscious quite as much, indeed, as does the "primitive" artist to whom these concepts are so often applied?

Perhaps the reason why art and literary critics rejected the conventional portrait of the artist in their own societies while applying the theories of prelogical thought to Africans and American Indians and Polynesians was the same as brought the ethnologists to reject those theories for the peoples they studied. The artists and writers whom the critics knew at first hand reasoned as well as felt; they argued from cause to effect about as much as most people, even while they were listening to their intuitions. In the same way, ethnologists who in nonliterate societies had come to know artists as individuals realized that they were not too different from persons of artistic bent in any other social group, including our own. Through first-hand acquaintance it came to be understood that the theories advanced about artists in exotic societies applied no more—and no less—to them than to creative painters and sculptors and writers working within the framework of our culture.

It seems inevitable that the artist, by the nature of his gifts, should in any society be to some degree the individualist. The very act of artistic creation makes it necessary to question in some measure what has gone before. The questioning itself may be in accord with socially recognized rules. Thus a dream may inspire a new design painted on a Pueblo Indian pot, or in the South Seas a realignment of a geometric motif on a tapa cloth may be accounted as as act of creativity. Yet creativity, I must emphasize, implies innovation. What we would like to know about is the kind of person the artist is in these nonliterate cultures. Is there any consistency of type that relates personality to creativity? Is it the inner make-up of the artist or cultural patterns that cause him to be the rebel in one society, the conformist in another? In a society such as that of the Bush Negroes, where art is highly valued, is it not reasonable to conclude that insofar as social response is involved, the artist will tend to confine his experimentation to his art? Some of the best artists I met among the Bush Negroes were, as a matter of fact, men of wealth and high position, and they reacted like those of comparable social standing in other societies.

It is difficult to generalize on this point, however, if only because while the art of nonliterate peoples has been given considerable study, the artists themselves have received no comparable attention. Thus I can contrast the artist among the Bush Negroes with what I found in a culture historically related to this South American one, that of Dahomey in West Africa. Here the wood-carver presents almost a one-to-one correspondence with the stereotype of the artist found in our own society. He is held to be a person immersed in his affairs; pleasant, but calmly concerned with his own ends. When I took a motion picture of one of these carvers at work, he could not have been less disturbed by the clicking camera, something he had never before seen, held close for a near view of his hands as they carved; he turned the piece he was making this way and that, judging its proportions as he held it at arm's-length, quite as though he were alone. A powerful chief had summoned him, but he took his own time in answering; the chief was annoyed at his dilatory response, but, as he put it, "What can I do? Punishment won't get me another artist, or the pieces I want."

In all probability, the Dahomeans or the Bush Negro artists represent types that any society may produce. This would be the point of view of the Anang, an Ibibio group in southeastern Nigeria. Here the wood-carvers, who have created some of the most distinctive and prized African art, are carefully taught, either by working with a father or uncle who is a carver, or serving a year's apprenticeship with a master, who receives a substantial fee for teaching the young man. According to Messenger, who has studied this group, "Once an individual commits himself to this occupation by paying a fee and participating in a religious ritual, he almost never fails to develop the skills which will enable him to enjoy success as a professional. It is simply taken for granted by all concerned that he will become an accomplished and creative artisan." The prestige of the artist is so great, the economic returns so worthwhile that, as Messenger puts it, "when we questioned the men in the village as to how many youths fail to develop sufficient carving skill, we created considerable bewilderment among them. They were unable to comprehend the 'sense' in such a question." Hence, while "the Anang do recognize that a very few carvers exhibit talents that are somewhat superior to their fellow craftsmen, they will not admit, as we tried so hard to get them to, that there are those who lack the requisite abilities."

With this range of variation, it would obviously be unjustified here to propose any sort of theory concerning the relation of the artist's personality to his early experiences, or to his traditional position in a given society, or to any other single set of influences that has impinged on him. I do not think, for example, that we know whether repression and frustration and rejection make of artistry a medium for dissent or whether a permissive childhood causes the artist to be a lesser innovator. Nor do we know whether the drive toward creativity is something innate or learned, though the best evidence in hand would suggest that it is a combination of endowment, motivation and opportunity. What is apparent, when we take the broad view of art as found in societies the world over, is that whatever the size of the group, it seems to be able to produce those who are gifted; that no matter what the social sanctions, at least some of those endowed with talent will express it. Perhaps the Anang have a formula whose implications are worth exploring, when, as Messenger phrases it, they hold that "talent implies the possession of certain capabilities that anyone can develop if he sets out to do so."

What a society does, through its approved patterns of art, is to channel the way in which talent is manifested. Here we have a lead to an understanding of the important aspect of art we call style; that intangible which, passed on from one generation to the next, marks the artistic products of a society, an epoch, just as it allows us to identify the work of a given artist. Ethnologists have made clear the consistency of stylistic conventions, and the fact that style sets the limits within which, at a given time, the artist carves or paints. The power of a style to channel the forms that a given society produces is impressive. So impressive is it, indeed, that it presents us with another paradox in the study of culture—how one of the least tangible elements in the experience of man can be one of the strongest.

We speak of the power of style to shape an art in its formal aspects; yet it does more than this, for it provides a system of artistic values which equally frames the appreciation of art. The late Robert Redfield gave us a vivid portrayal of this in describing the reaction of a visitor in the New York Museum of Primitive Art to a piece of African wood-carving. In the terms of our present discussion, the good lady of his example was experiencing a mild degree of cultural shock; she was reacting to an art object case in a frame with which she was not familiar. She was assured, because the piece was exhibited where it was, that it had value, but she could not see this attribute of it despite the word of the experts on whom she placed reliance. In art, familiarity breeds appreciation, which is to say that it takes time and experience to perceive, internalize and respond to the aesthetic values in the art of peoples whose culture differs from one's own.

Style may be thought of as something that gives an art cultural identity. It derives its psychological power from its subliminal character, for it flows below the level of consciousness, guiding taste and expression the more firmly just because most of those who appreciate, like those who create, are for the most part quite unconscious of its controls. As found in culture after culture, the consistency with which a given style is followed is arresting. This is why we can identify with sureness a piece of unknown provenience. There are, of course, certain limits to stylistic patterning, which can be imposed by the nature of the medium itself. Thus, basketry from the American Southwest and the African Guinea Coast will be found to bear certain resemblances, both in technique and decorative design. This is, however, merely to recognize that, try as one will, it is impossible to reproduce curved lines in weaving, just as, when a composition is on a flat surface, only perceptual conventions can allow an artist to give a two dimensional rendering of a three-dimensional composition.

This brings us to the important point of the role of perception in art. For though the question of the nature of realism and its relation to conventionalization has been much discussed, this middle term between artistic convention and the work of the artist has tended to be overlooked. The reason for this, perhaps, is that most students of aesthetics, who are not cross-culturally oriented, tend to take the natural world for granted. It is not so long ago in our history that art, almost by definition, was held to be representational in its aim, a point of view that has not altogether disappeared from discussions of art. Our fixation on pseudo-realism contained a hidden, culture-bound judgment wherein the values of our own society, based on our particular perceptual modes, were extended into universals and applied to art in general.

This fact helps us to understand why the aesthetic products of nonliterate peoples were traditionally displayed in ethnographic and natural history museums rather than in art museums; why there had to come into being museums of "modern" art to accommodate the canvases of those artists of the present century—some of whose works are already called "classical"—whose paintings and sculptures were so different from those which found a place in "art" museums that special arrangements for showing them had to be made. It is significant, for our present discussion, that the break with earlier tradition came as a result of the exposure of those now technically called "moderns" to the art of cultures outside their own, among which the wood carvings of Africa and the South Seas figured prominently. It is a great achievement of these men that they were able to divest themselves of the conventions of aesthetic perception of their day, and sense the artistic values in work that had heretofore never been admitted into the category of valid art objects.

This involved a shift in patterns of perception that has had far-reaching effects on aesthetic judgment. For the patterns of a culture frame the response of the creative artist to the world about him—frame them for him as they do for all the other members of his society. They are among the least conscious of our reactions to the world in which we live, and are thus the most difficult to change; it is because we turn to them so automatically in interpreting the "natural" world, that the stylistic component in art, as we have noted, is so stable. In actuality, the "natural" world is natural because we define it as such; because most of us, immersed in our own culture, have never experienced any other definition of reality than the one to which we have been accustomed all our lives. Let me take a simple example; the drawing of a rectangular table, with four legs. And this is what we "see" when we look at the drawing. But are we actually seeing what is on the paper, or are we interpreting lines in terms of a convention of representation taken for granted by artist and observer alike? Because when analyzed, the representation of the rectangular table top resolves itself into two acute and two obtuse angles; and the legs, which by measurement can be shown to be of equal length, are in the drawing represented by shorter and longer lines.

We do this, as we say, to attain perspective, which in turn we hold to be essential to realism. But should we show this realistic representation to a man or woman from another society, one who has never had contact with this kind of realism, the meaning we so readily ascribe to the drawing will be found to evaporate into lines of unequal length. I have had an experience of this kind, similar to that reported from many parts of the world by those who have had occasion to show photographs to persons who had never seen a photograph before. To those of us accustomed to the idiom of the realism of the photographic lens, the degree of conventionalization that inheres in even the clearest, most accurate photograph, is something of a shock. For, in truth, even the clearest photograph is a convention; a translation of a three-dimensional subject into two dimensions, with color transmuted into shades of black and white. In the instance to which I refer, a Bush Negro woman turned a photograph of her own son this way and that, in attempting to make sense out of the shadings of greys on the piece of paper she held. It was only when the details of the photograph were pointed out to her that she was able to perceive the subject. I have been told by anthropological friends who in more recent times have shown color photographs to people with whom they worked, that the addition of color facilitates perception; brings it, if you like, nearer "reality." And certainly stereoscopic viewing would complete the process, for here we would have a reproduction whose interpretation could be cast in terms of whatever conventions the society had set up to define the setting in which its members live.

This entire area of research, which holds the greatest importance for the cross-cultural analysis of aesthetics, has only begun to be explored. Many years ago, as observed earlier, W. H. R. Rivers, the British psychologist and ethnologist, recorded the responses of Melanesian Murray

Islanders to certain perceptual illusions that had been devised by the German psychologist, Müller-Lyer, and compared them with findings on English students of comparable age. Significant differences were found in the responses of the two groups; in one series of tests, the English were more subject to illusion than the Murray Islanders, in another, that has been less discussed in the literature, the latter were more subject to illusion than those tested in England. Recently, this line of research has been taken up anew by my colleague, Professor Donald Campbell, and myself. Tests of perceptual illusions, worked up by Dr. Marshall Segall, have been made available to psychologists and ethnologists doing research in various parts of the world. We are hoping that the resulting data will, for example, give us ideas about the acuteness of perception of angles by peoples whose experience has been with circular houses, circular enclosures for domesticated animals, knives with circular blades—peoples who live, as Campbell puts it, in a "non-carpentered world"—which we can then compare with the responses of other peoples, including ourselves, where the angular component dominates experience.

The interpretation of these results, understandably, will entail balancing a number of factors. I may give one example. Preliminary working up of results obtained by Dr. Jules Golden, who recently gave these tests in Dahomey, showed that in two of them for which the materials have been analyzed the Dahomean children varied in the same way, and to about the same degree, from those given children in Evanston, Illinois as did the Murray Islanders from the English subjects tested by Rivers. To what extent, we now ask, are the similarities in these differences due to the fact that the English and Evanstonians are in the same general perceptual tradition when compared to the Dahomeans and the Murray Islanders, who stand in no such apparent historical relationship? Certainly insofar as perception affects art styles, that the United States and England lie in one historic stream is a factor that cannot be left out of account. But can the fact that both Murray Islanders and Dahomeans inhabit a tropical environment be an effective determinant? Can it be considered significant that similarities between West African and Melanesian art styles are sufficiently close so that at least one serious author, whose works have received substantial recognition, was led to include a Melanesian statuette in a volume on African art?

That every art style is determined to some degree by the world about the artist is self-evident. The problem that the cross-cultural study of art poses is the degree to which differences are found in the interpretation of that world which, as I have said, rests so significantly on the perceptual configurations which the artist brings to his medium. Here one of the principal contributions of the ethnologist enters; and it is so simple that it is rarely mentioned. It arises from a tradition of research that only dates from the turn of the century, and follows the principle that if there is to be a science of culture, it must be based on data gathered at first hand. Field investigation, that is, must yield personal experience of the life of a people being studied, so that induction can confirm or negate theory. In practical terms, this has meant that the ethnologist has himself gone to see, instead of relying on the reports of others; and seeing has revealed many things that are not to be had at second hand.

Let us go on with some further implications of our line of reasoning. We have, in the first place, seen that the creative expression of an artist, in any society, is to be referred to a perceptual system that provides the mesh through which his world is screened. We have, further, seen that it is this world, the reality of which is sensed in consonance with his perceptions, to which he reacts. But it has been equally clear that this system does not exist by and of itself. It is deeply influenced, if not actually determined, by the patterns of the culture of which it is a part, to which the artist, like others in his society, responds. Thus, because there is this common tradition of how to approach experience, the system does more than set a framework for creativity; it also explains its social recognition. Our argument thus provides a rationale for the cultural approach to art; not as something designed to supplant purely aesthetic analysis, but to provide a surer base for generalizations and insights that can come from examining at first hand vast areas of creative expression that have heretofore been so largely subject to speculative, impressionistic, subjective appraisal.

There are still more implications in this approach. Once we accept the proposition that art is a cultural phenomenon, and that its appreciation is best gained through the broadest possible understanding of the cultural matrix out of which it comes, we can correct our perspective in other respects. Thus, for instance, the statement is repeatedly encountered that the arts of nonliterate peoples who have come into contact with the cultures of Europe and America can no longer flower as they did in precontact days. The reason customarily given for this is that these art forms are so intricately bound up with the religious life of the people that with the destruction of their aboriginal beliefs, and the concomitant impersonalization of the relations between members of the group incident on industrial development, the function of the artist is lost and his art must disappear.

The concept of the essentially sacred character of the societies of nonliterate peoples derives from the work of the French sociological school, and has done much to color critical comment on the arts of nonliterate peoples. Again we must take cognizance of the fact that it grew out of their analysis of the literature, rather than from field research. Lacking first-hand experience of such societies, and dominated by assumptions that the cultures out of which those arts arose were essentially oriented toward the sacred, they took if for granted that the pieces they analyzed were without question ritualistic in nature.

Now it is one thing to recognize that the culture of a small isolated society may be more tightly integrated than that of a larger agglomerate, and that in these societies art is therefore more closely related to the daily round than among ourselves; but is is quite another to go on to the position that holds art in these smaller societies to be exclusively ritualistic. There is, of course, a measure of validity in the position, for art is closely related to worldview; but this applies to all societies, since art everywhere affirms the manipulation of supernatural controls for the benefit of man. This relationship between art and religion lodges on a much deeper plane than that of sociological reference; one which, because it is more in accord with a universal in human experience, can be held more valid. The closeness of the relation between art and ritual, that is, is best referred to the emotional response which both the religious and the aesthetic experience call forth. This is not only true of the graphic and plastic arts, I should add, which everywhere are to be found in association with worship, but all other aesthetic manifestations as well—music, dance, drama, and narrative.

The association between religion and the aesthetic has been richly documented—so richly, indeed, that it has given rise to theories which relate the very origin of art to religious impulse and motivation. This is not the place to discuss such theories, except perhaps to observe that there is grave doubt as to our ability to establish the absolute origin of any element in culture. These theories, which were based on the assumption that we could recover the earliest modes of human living by reference to contemporary nonliterate societies, have been long rejected by anthropologists. This does not mean, however, that in certain instances, specific arts could not have arisen in response to religious belief.

One example of the actual introduction of an art form among a people, something rarely reported in the literature, has been given by Wolfe for the Ngombe of the Congo-Ubangi district of the Congo. The originator was a man named Bosokuma, a person "not deviant in other respects, who introduced figurine-carving into his own group, to whom the tradition was foreign." He was a "child of sorrow," because the death of his father and mother left him "without so much as a sister whose bride-wealth he might use to obtain for himself a wife." One night he was visited in his sleep by the spirit of his father, who "gave him a wooden figurine with the help of which he was to kill an animal the very next day." Later, other spirits—of his mother, and of his grandfathers—came to him in his dreams, and with their help he became a successful hunter and worker of magic. He was "taken" into the forest, where he remained for some time, learning among many things the art of making figurines. Wolfe assumes that he learned his technique of woodcarving from neighboring peoples, as well as some of the magic he uses. What is important for us is the fact that "while Bosokuma is the only carver of figurines in his society, it is not the aesthetic quality of the carving that has earned his renown, but rather the power of carvings and other medicines in making for successful hunting." In other words, he will presumably continue to earn his living as a practitioner of magic rather than as carver. The fact that he has chosen the carved form onto which to add magic powers is, of course, significant as the beginning of a tradition which, however he and the other members of his group see it, stems from contact with neighboring peoples who are carvers.

While instances of achieved relationships between art and religion are too numerous to permit the point to be argued, what is not so apparent is the association of art with other aspects of life. Yet here too, the evidence of close association of art with social status, with political position, and all manner of other activities of a secular nature, is overwhelming. Thus the secular character of clan organization has tended to be lost in the classification of totemism as a religious rather than a social phenomenon, but we have only to consider the societies of the Northwest Coast of North America, the region from which the word "totem" has come, to realize how great is the secular component in the social structures that have their position validated by the carvings that we know as "totem poles." In these same societies, also, a wealth of artistry in wood-carving and weaving is lavished on storage boxes, on house decorations, on special kinds of ceremonial blankets, none of which have any religious significance. The beautifully designed and hafted adzes of Mangaia, in the Cook Islands of south central Polynesia, are a mark of position, not an instrument of religious ritual; the paintings made by Plains Indians on buffalo hide were *aides-mémoire* to which a warrior referred in the ceremonial boasting of his feats of valor with which he validated his status; Congo carvings on cups, or of boxes to hold red ochre, or of stools, are appurtenances of men of position and not articles of religious rituals; the brass figurines and appliqué cloths of Dahomey are articles for chiefs to display as an indication of their wealth, made on order for those who can afford them; the Eskimo carvings of animals, according to Boas, "serve no practical purpose but . . . are made for the pleasure of artistic creation."

If these societies are secularly as well as religiously oriented, and if art has its non-religious aspects as well as its religious ones, it follows that the assumption does not hold that the arts of nonliterate peoples in contact with Euroamerican cultures are things of the past, as is so frequently maintained. The point usually at issue here, as I see it, is whether a people, whose art forms are presumably oriented toward the service of the supernatural, can adapt themselves to the secular character of the art of our day. Where art has an exclusively religious orientation, it is clear that the artist who loses the supernatural sanctions for his creativity will have difficulty in adjusting to a life based on secular values. Yet while difficulties in the adjustment of artists do arise, it is questionable if they are any more serious than those which other members of these same societies must make in adapting their rhythm of life to an urban setting, or to sustained hours of labor in an industrial plant or on a mechanized farm. Since many aspects of art in nonliterate groups are, however, not religious, we can thus raise the question whether the secular phase of the aesthetic tradition of these peoples does not provide them with a fulcrum for achieving the shift in cultural alignment required because of the circumstance of change.

Many instances, from all parts of the nonliterate world, can be called on to demonstrate that the question can be answered in the affirmative. The Eskimos, for example, as I am sure many of you who have been to Canada know, have continued to make their little animal figures in soapstone, just as they did in the past before their contacts with the white men. The difference is that they now make more of them, that with greater quantity the range in their quality is also greater. Moreover, and here is the significant fact, they make them for an impersonal market, rather than for themselves and the members of their own group. Some of these carvings, it is true, show signs of haste under increased production, but if one chooses with care, as one would when acquiring a canvas done by a painter of our own society, one can find a figure that in its artistry is quite the equal of anything that was achieved in earlier days. What has happened has been that a transfer has been effected, pieces earlier created for the artist's own group now being made for sale to persons unknown to the artist. Since the secular level of this carving has been maintained, no transfer or sanction has been involved, and the reinterpretation of objective has been carried through with little difficulty.

Adjustment to change in the field of art has perhaps gone furthest in Africa. Here it is the more striking because of the size of the market available to African carvers, this in turn resulting from the great prestige of African art, especially of African wood-carving, in European and American art circles. So great has been the response to the opportunity to acquire pieces carved by Africans, indeed, that carving has been taken up by peoples in the eastern and southern parts of the continent, where work in wood was secondary—peoples who have mastered the degree of skill required to produce works of sufficient appeal so that carving has become a significant element in their changed economic situation.

In western Africa and the western Congo, the regions from which the "classical" arts of Africa have been derived —"classical" that is, in the sense that their artistry was the first to be recognized by the critics of Europe and America—the economic component in the work of the artist in wood and metal has always been present. This is an aspect of the life of artists in nonliterate societies that has been little investigated, though its significance becomes almost self-evident as soon as stated. That it has not been studied more is surprising, unless one takes the somewhat romantic view that what these artists created was done because of a mystical force within them, during their leisure moments, without recompense except that obtained from the regard of their fellows. Certainly in these parts of Africa, this was far from the case. Woodcarvers and metal workers, to name only the two most outstanding categories of artists, made a considerable part of their living, in our sense of the phrase, from their art, just as do our own artists. Secret societies, cult groups, persons of high status ordered from artists the masks, statuettes, figurines they needed or desired, and these were in due course produced, delivered and paid for. An experience of mine, many years ago, that opened a whole new line of thought in this regard for me was when, in the Nigerian city of Abeokuta, a Yoruba woodcarver whom I was visiting brought out and later sold me a small model of a mask that, with several others, he would show his customers when they were placing orders with him— and sold me as well a full-sized, finished mask that had been made after this model.

It must not be concluded that the African artist, living in a society that from early times had known a considerable degree of division of labor, with an economic system based on the exchange of goods for money in stated markets, was any the less of an artist because his art provided his livelihood. Here, no less than in other societies, overall patterns of accepted form and content were followed, and innovations tended to consist of variations in detail and not the introduction of entirely new forms. For it is the mark of greatness in art that the artist, while working within the frame of a given style, puts his stamp on what he produces through his manipulation of accepted techniques and forms, adhering to stylistic conventions so that the locale and the period in which he painted or carved can be recognized as well as his own distinctive contribution. Some of the finest examples of African art have this characteristic; there is no mistaking a Yoruba *ibeji,* or twin figure, but to one who knows the varieties of this form, a pair of *ibeji* from Oyo cannot be confused as coming from Abeokuta.

This tradition of carving for a market has allowed the African to slip without psychological difficulty into the new situations that confront him. That there have been, and will be, changes in his art forms cannot be gainsaid, though even as regards this point, the degree of change or its direction cannot be predicted. One thing would seem to be reasonable; that the assertion so often made that the arts of Africa are a thing of the past, must be re-examined. It is quite true that much of this art was inspired by the needs of worship, and that the inroads of Christianity and Islam have diluted the function of the artist who supplied the needs of aboriginal religious groups. Yet not only the carvers, but their traditions are there, and masks and statuettes of high quality are being made as they were in the past. "I can make you the kind of mask you want," was a statement I heard again and again from woodcarvers, "if you give me time." And often, in his *atelier,* where he and his apprentices might be busy turning out replicas of figurines and masks for general sale, I would find a carver or one of his associates working on something that was destined for use in the traditional manner.

What seems to be happening is that tendencies latent in the art of the past have been brought to the forefront and accelerated. Let us take as an example the seat of one of the high arts of West Africa, Benin, whose bronzes have achieved world-wide renown, and which is the source of the ivory mask, one of the finest carvings that ever came out of Africa, that is in the New York Museum of Primitive Art. Today the classical media are still worked in Benin; the street of the brass workers hums with activity. That traditional patterns have by no means been given over was brought home to me when a chief whose treasures escaped the sack of the city because his compound was outside it had brought out a bronze piece dating probably from the fifteenth or sixteenth century, still in use in the worship of his ancestors, and with equal pride caused to be placed beside it two other pieces which, only a few years before, he had commissioned for the altar dedicated to the spirit of his own mother. The classical tradition is likewise being retained for work in wood. I was able to acquire an excellent example of this in an ebony carving, depicting a royal personage with his coral ornaments clearly indicated. What was not in the traditional manner was the inscription carved on the underside of the base: "Benin Native Authority Arts and Crafts School, 1953."

As in Africa, so elsewhere in the nonliterate world, men with artistic endowment and drive are continuing to respond to their environment and their learned experience. What they will produce will vary in quality as always; some are greater artists than others, and will react more sensitively to their new situation than those less generously endowed. But it is only in degree that they differ from what they did, not in kind. Let us remember that though the Dahomean metalworkers turn out their mass-produced ashtrays of female figurines balancing poles on their heads, to be hawked along the coast by Hausa traders, they are also modeling the traditional figures depicting ritual and secular aspects of the life of Dahomey much as they did in earlier years, and with traditional artistry. Let us not forget that the carver who makes masks and figures in quantity for sale to curio dealers can still lavish the same meticulous carc on a piccc that has bccn commissioned, whether by a member of his own group or an outsider, that marked his earlier work. Indeed, he is really doing nothing that is much different, in total allocation of his time, than he did in earlier days. For the same African artist who made the masterpieces we have learned to value also had to help support himself by hacking out articles of everyday use which, quite undecorated, were as far removed from art as, for example, the grain that was pounded by the women in the mortar and pestles he made for their use. Now, as then, and as is true everywhere, he needs only to be able to support himself by this art to continue to pursue that art.

The task of the ethnologist concerned with art, then, as I have tried to show, is to introduce the broadest based, and, in human terms, a many-faceted approach to the understanding of the aesthetic phases of human life. For whatever his object, the ethnologist brings to the student of art understanding that can be attained only through his cross-cultural approach. More than this, what he does is to give to all concerned with aesthetics a sense of differing values laid by different peoples on what they hold to be beautiful; the universality of the aesthetic response; and the plasticity in man's reaction to a perceptual world that receives new impulses from familiarity with a foreign mode of aesthetic expression. He can bring to the aesthetician who approaches the art of cultures other than his own a sense of the artist, not as an anonymous figure moved by mysterious forces, but as a living human being, whose work reflects his response to a culturally accepted pattern of aesthetic values that by no means remains static, but allows for the mutations, however discernible, of time and the personality of the artist. He thereby introduces a human component into this humanistic approach, bringing an added note of living reality to aesthetics that has too often been clouded by a romanticism which blurs rather than illuminates, a contribution which the broad cross-cultural approach to art, such as this Museum stands for, can make.

references

1. Harold Schneider. The interpretation of Pakot visual art. Man, 56, art. 108, 1956: 103–106.
2. Raymond Firth. Art and life in New Guinea. London, The Studio, 1936: 30.
3. John Messenger. Reflections on aesthetic talent. Basic College Quarterly, 4, 1958: 20–24.
4. Alvin W. Wolfe. Art and the supernatural in the Ubangi District. Man, 55, art. 76, 1955: 65–67.
5. Franz Boas. Primitive art. Oslo, H. Aschehoug & Co., 1927. (Instituttet for Sammenligende kulturforskning. Pub. ser. B: Skifter 8): 124.

a cross-cultural approach to myth[1]

If ritual is symbolic action, then symbolization is the essence of myth. . . . In the beginning, we may assume with Harrison, was the word, *not* the act. . . . A fundamental difficulty with all theories of myth . . . is that the nature, extent and significance of internal innovation is ignored. . . . The question why men make myths remains to challenge us to account for a universal human response in its most significant, because its most imaginative, expression. . . . Mythic symbolism, in any age, and at all levels of abstraction, is a cultural fact. Mythic themes are not emanations of images engraved on the unconscious in primordial times. As a cultural fact, myth is seen as deriving from human language skill, and man's fascination with symbolic continuities. We advance a pluralistic theory of myth, recognizing the demonstrated universal fact that men everywhere have felt impelled to symbolize metaphorically the relationship between man and his world.

the mystique of the archetype

It is necessary to examine here the influence on students of literature of the concept of the

* Excerpts from Introduction to *Dahomean Narrative,* pp. 95–98, 103–22. Melville J. and Frances S. Herskovits, Northwestern University Press, Evanston, 1958.

archetypal mythologem, a kind of living psychic fossil preserved in the collective representations of "primitive"
peoples, and the assumption in this context, that archetypes
are universal. Of special pertinence are certain of its
methodological implications.

Let us see how C. G. Jung, with whose name the concept
is primarily associated, himself defines the archetype. Moving from the base of his system of analytical psychology,
which revealed certain consistent themes that, he asserts,
are akin to mythic motifs, he says, "These products are . . .
mythological components which, because of their typical
nature, we can call 'motifs,' 'primordial images,' types or—
as I have named them—archetypes." These mythic manifestations in individual psychology are to be differentiated
from myth itself: "In the individual, the archetypes occur
as involuntary manifestations of unconscious processes
whose existence and meaning can only be inferred, whereas
the myth deals with traditional forms of incalculable age.
They hark back to a prehistoric world whose spiritual preconceptions and general conditions we can still observe today among existing primitives."[1]

It is unnecessary here to enlarge on Jung's definition and
point of view with further citations from his work; it is
more important to consider his ideas on the psychology of
the "primitive." From his discussion, we infer that he was
influenced by the concept of the *elementargedanken* of
Bastian, those fundamental ideas of all mankind that find
their specific manifestations in the *völkergedanken,* the
parallels that have been recorded from all peoples, and
which, thus early in the history of the scientific study of
man, posed the problem of origins with which Jung is concerned. Another influence that is discernible in his approach and phrasing is that of the French philosopher and
anthropologist Lucien Lévy-Bruhl.

[1] C. G. Jung and C. Kerenyi, *Essays on a Science of Mythology,*
New York, 1949, pp. 99–100. We use citations of the most recent
relevant publications to document the current Jungian position.

To those who have had first-hand experience with non-literate peoples (or, in the specific case of Dahomey, have gained an impression of how hard-headed, realistic, and logical Dahomeans can be), the passages we quote from Jung take on an air of fantasy. "Primitive mentality differs from the civilized chiefly in that the conscious mind is far less developed in extent and intensity," he says.[2] "Functions such as thinking, willing, etc., are not yet differentiated; they are pre-conscious, a fact which in the case of thinking, for instance, shows itself in the circumstance that the primitive does not think *consciously,* but that thoughts appear." From this it follows logically, in terms of Jung's frame of reference, that "primitive mentality does not invent *myths,* it *experiences* them." In other words, "Myths are original revelations of the pre-conscious psyche, involuntary statements about unconscious happenings, and anything but allegories of physical processes." Myths, indeed, "not merely . . . represent, they are the mental life of the primitive tribe, which immediately falls to pieces and decays when it loses its mythological heritage, like a man who has lost his soul." Finally, as regards the problem of the processes that are the causal factor in the creation of myth, we are told that "Many of these unconscious processes may be indirectly occasioned by consciousness, but never by conscious choice. Others appear to rise spontaneously, that is to say, from no discernible or demonstrable conscious cause."[3]

The breadth of these assumptions, with their assurance of universal validity, and the certainty that they provide an answer to one of the most complex questions faced by students of man, account in large measure for the conviction they have carried. Yet the fact remains that the "primitive" automaton, as pictured by Jung, ignores the most elementary lessons that have been taught us by the

[2] *Ibid.,* p. 100.
[3] *Ibid.,* pp. 100–2, *passim;* all italics are in the original.

scientific study of man. It is, indeed, sheer mysticism, and lies on a different plane, conceptually and methodologically, from those attempts to understand human beings everywhere which use the methods of induction. Any search for supporting facts from cultures that have been studied in the field becomes an exercise in frustration, for there is little with which to come to grips except in terms of bare assertion and denial.

There is no question but that the problem that gave rise to Jung's theory of the archetype is a real one. It has been recognized ever since there has been contact between peoples of differing ways of life. In essence, all these inquiries represent attempts to account for the resemblances found in the cultures of man which, though exhibiting wide variation, manifest unities that give them their common human base. There are two possible answers: One ascribes these similarities to the historic experience of humanity, holding that they represent the working out of inventions made in the early days of man's experience as a culture-building species, and the interchanges of contact since then. The other relates these similarities to tendencies inherent in man, and as in the instance we are considering, bases its formulation on some not very well defined idea of unilineal evolution, with an overtone of invidious comparison between the various "stages" of presumed development.

Bearing in mind this theoretical orientation we may quote again from Jung, giving his comments on a collection of American Indian trickster tales that date a decade and a half after the passages cited above were published. The figure of the trickster in mythology, we are here told, "is obviously a 'psychologem,' an archetypal psychic structure of extreme antiquity." This being the case, "When . . . a primitive or barbarous consciousness forms a picture of itself on a much earlier level of development and continues to do so for hundreds and even thousands of years, undeterred by the contamination of its archaic qualities with differentiated, highly developed mental products, then the causal explanation is that the older the archaic qualities are, the more conservative and pertinacious is their behavior." This "senseless appendage" as Jung calls it, in terms reminiscent of the nineteenth-century concept of the survival, "still 'functions' provided they have not been spoiled by civilization."[4]

Inherent in this thinking is an assumption of the conservatism of the "primitives" to a degree that goes beyond the postulates even of those who, as we shall see in later pages, hold that nonliterate peoples lack any of the curiosity that leads to innovation and creative expression. Yet the germ of validity in the approach remains, and in constructive terms this is what concerns us here. In this context, we return once again to the problem of universals.

The *mystique* of the archetype falls into that large body of theoretical formulations that explain universals in human behavior without the benefit of empirical proof; formulations that, as we have said, must be taken on faith or not at all. The "proofs" offered are those which fall within the framework of the theory; the exceptions, the complexities, the inexplicable elements are disregarded. The vitality of all such theories is due in part to the fact that they represent attempts to explain fundamental problems in human behavior and to account for recurrent themes in the creative efforts of man. But in part, also, they tend to be well received because they give simple answers to questions that remain to challenge those willing to face the complexities of objective inquiry.

functional and ritualistic approaches to myth

There remain three other approaches to the study of myth that have wide currency. Each of these has its particular emphasis, but they have so influenced one another that for

[4] C. G. Jung, "On the Psychology of the Trickster Figure," in Paul Radin, *The Trickster, a Study in American Indian Mythology,* New York, 1956, pp. 200–201.

purposes of discussion they can best be grouped together.

Despite individual orientations, all three share certain points of view. First of all, psychological considerations play a minor part in their analyses, so that the factor of individual creativity does not enter into their theories of the origin or development of mythic narrative. While the idea of the group mind is not a part of their conceptual apparatus, the myth is taken somehow as a kind of extra-individual "given," and tends to be reified in their discussions as a *ding an sich*. In the second place, they share a strong anti-euhemeristic position, being agreed that myth—and, by extension, any narration of events that has not been reduced to writing—must be refused any measure of historic credence. Finally, all of them are "anthropological" in the sense that the mythologies of nonliterate peoples, usually denoted in their works as "primitive" or "savage," figure importantly in their argument and documentation.

Chronologically, the first to appear was the group termed the Cambridge School, whose best-known representatives were Sir James Frazer and Jane Harrison. This group draws its data and its conclusions primarily from Greek mythology, and its members have made outstanding contributions to classical scholarship. More than any others, they have urged the ritual theory of myth, their basic assumption being that since myth explains ritual behavior, it can have come into being only after the rituals they explain were fully established. This view is most energetically espoused in the United States by the literary critic Stanley Edgar Hyman.

The functionalist explanation of myth, the second of these approaches, was advanced by Bronislaw Malinowski, who based his theory on the anthropological field research he carried on from 1915 until 1918 in the Melanesian Trobriand Islands. The influence of the Cambridge School on Malinowski's thinking came principally through Sir James Frazer's major work, *The Golden Bough*. This is stressed in the Preface to the essay in which Malinowski states his theoretical position on myth, the text of an address delivered at the University of Liverpool in 1925 in honor of Frazer.

The relationship between these two points of view is not as close as later students of literature have suggested. For Malinowski was, first and foremost, the fieldworker; he dealt with living people. He did not confine himself to texts either handed down from cultures no longer existent, or sent to his study by those in first-hand contact with "savages," as was the case with Frazer, who, like the other members of the Cambridge group, had no first-hand experience outside his own society. But resemblances, along the broad lines we have indicated, are present.

The third approach, while fully accepting the ritual theory of the origin of myth, lays its major emphasis on the unreliability of oral tradition as history. It was propounded by Lord Raglan, its exponent, in his work *The Hero,* first published in 1916, a book showing the influence of both the Cambridge School and of Malinowski. Raglan's interest in testing the historical adequacy of oral tradition seems to have arisen from his study of the degree of truth and untruth to be found in the stories about various heroes. To his shrewd assessment of how the play of fancy can distort any historic reality, he brings many arguments from the accounts of recent events, in literate cultures, that have moved into the realm of folklore. His conclusions reflect the influences of the currents of thought that have stimulated his thinking: ". . . that the folk-tale is never of popular origin, but is merely one form of the traditional narrative; that the traditional narrative has no basis either in history or in philosophical speculation, but is derived from the myth; and that the myth is a narrative connected with rite."[5] A biographical item that may be of relevance is that, unlike the Cambridge group, and like Malinowski, Raglan

[5] Lord Raglan, *The Hero, a Study in Tradition, Myth and Drama,* London, 1936, p. 144.

did have first-hand contact with "savages," as he consistently terms nonliterate peoples. What influence this may have had on his thinking is difficult to say, but to the anthropologist approaching his theory of myth, it seems relevant that this first-hand contact was with a nomadic herding people of the Sudan, where for a number of years he was an officer in the British colonial service.

Hyman, whose excellent summary of the development of the ritualistic approach to myth[6] may be drawn on here, speaks of 1912 as "the watershed year" in which this position was fully enunciated. This was in Jane Harrison's *Themis,* where, he tells us, these points were made: "that myth arises out of rite, rather than the reverse; that it is 'the spoken correlative of the acted rite, the thing done' . . . and that it is not anything else nor of any other origin." This was long before Malinowski's demonstration, for the Trobrianders, that myth is to be thought of as an essential component of ritual, and associated with it; that while "there is . . . no ritual without belief . . . ," the rites themselves "are regarded as the results of mythical events"; that they are the "statement of a primaeval, greater, and more relevant reality . . . the knowledge of which supplies man with the motive for ritual and moral sanctions, as well as with indications of how to perform them."[7]

Yet before this point of view was enunciated, Harrison had been rethinking her materials, especially in the light of the developing currents of psychological theory, to revise her position to a degree not customarily recognized when her contribution to the theory of myth is discussed. "Man, the psychologists tell us, is essentially an image-maker. He cannot perform the simplest operation without forming of it some sort of correlative idea." Then, moving to ritual, she remarks,

[6] Stanley Edgar Hyman, "The Ritual View of Myth and the Mythic," *Jour. of Amer. Folklore,* Vol. 68 (1955), p. 463.

[7] Malinowski, *Myth in Primitive Psychology,* New York, 1926, pp. 29–30.

A rite is not of course the same as a simple action. A rite is—it must never be forgotten—an action *re*done (commemorative) or *pre*done (anticipatory and magical). There is therefore always in a rite a certain tension either of remembrance or anticipation and this tension emphasizes the emotion and leads on to representation. . . . If we were a mass of well combined instincts, that is if the cycle of perception and action were instantly fulfilled, we should have no representation and hence no art and no theology. In fact in a word religious presentation, mythology or theology, as we like to call it, springs like ritual from arrested, unsatisfied desire. We figure to ourselves what we want, we create an image and that image is our god.[8]

This quotation from Harrison takes on added importance because, among many students of literature, the derivation of myth from ritual is unquestioned. Thus Hyman asserts that "the important relationship of art literature to folk literature lies, not in the surface texture of folk speech, but in the archetypal patterns of primitive ritual, the great myths."[9] Elsewhere, he states, "a ritual origin for the blues constitutes a fascinating problem, although not a critical issue (too much obviously convincing ritual interpretation has been produced for the theory to stand or fall on any single form)."[10]

Yet if we move away from dogma to the realism of empirical analysis, we realize, as we have seen before, that assumptions of this kind concerning absolute origins are no more amenable to objective proof than any others. The concept of the survival, in its classical sense, as against its later meaning of a socially reinterpreted act, has long been shown untenable. We know enough about the ease with which new forms are assigned old meanings, or old forms

[8] Jane Ellen Harrison, *Epilegomena to the Study of Greek Religion*, Cambridge, 1921, pp. 27–28.

[9] Stanley Edgar Hyman, *The Armed Vision*, New York, 1955 (revised edition), p. 122.

[10] *Journal of American Folklore, op. cit.*, p. 471.

given new ones, to refuse credence to the act that has no meaning, essential to the myth-from-ritual hypothesis. If ritual is symbolic action, then symbolism is the essence of myth. It is thus inconceivable that any rite should have been initiated without there having been some antecedent idea of what was intended to achieve, and what forces might be called on to bring this about.

Here, if anywhere, we must have a formulation of the precondition for understanding the relationship between myth and ritual. In the beginning, we may assume with Harrison, was the word, *not* the act. A myth, in these terms, is either a rhetorical form that represents an elaboration over time of a core concept, or is part of a myth-rite complex borrowed wholly from another people. But whether originating within a culture or introduced from outside it, what is added by way of elaboration and accretion to the first category of myths, and what is changed in the second, will be governed by its congruence with the cultural base where it is to have a functioning role.

The proposition that ritual is the basis of myth presupposes random, unthinking behavior by human groups, behavior that becomes standardized before it is translated into belief. And here we are faced by a fundamental inconsistency in the argument. For many of those who hold to the myth-from-ritual theory are also those who insist most vigorously that but few men are interested in explaining the world about them, a point to which we will return shortly.

As students of classical mythology, the Cambridge School could scarcely be expected to evaluate myth in the more specific terms of its living reality. Who narrated the Greek myths can only be conjectured—or why they were told, to say nothing of how they originated. Let us read a lesson from the Dahomean materials. On two occasions, at least, Dahomean kings are reported to have summoned the clan elders so that the myths of clan origin that sanction clan prerogatives, and the rituals of the clans, could be regularized. We have indicated something of the political exigencies that dictated this move, and have suggested that the popular and the official versions of these myths do not necessarily coincide.

If we refer to the introduction of the Fa divining cult, we see that political exigency also dictated this move. However, we are also told that the Fa system of divination came from the teachings of prophets who "came down from the sky." Another myth introduces us to Gbadu (a hermaphroditic child of Mawu, born after the twins who were to rule the sea), and we learn that Gbadu is also known as Fa. It is interesting, however, to note that the myths as told by the *vodun* priests make no mention of Gbadu as a child of the Creator. We may surmise that this was a revision to give status within the existing cosmogony to a newly introduced cult.

Or, if we take the role of Aido-Hwedo, we are told in one myth "Aido-Hwedo, the serpent, is a *vodun,* but is not of the family of the gods. They say he is not the son of the Great Mawu, because he existed before any of the children of Mawu, before Sogbo." It is clear that we are seeing a deity of an autochthonous group made subject to a pantheon that, again, if we may rely on oral tradition, tells us that Agadja was instrumental in bringing the worship of the Sky Pantheon to the plateau of Abomey, where was located the seat of the Dahomean kings after they had conquered their way north from Allada.

We have determined all this by going to the Dahomeans, recording variants, and finding out why they are countenanced. But how, in the case of the Greek myths, could this be done?

Thompson, in summarizing the currents in the stream of ideas regarding myths and myth-makers, phrases the point admirably: "At journey's end, we come to the ritual origin and observe something that no anthropologist has told us about—that all rituals in the world have a single pattern and a single purpose, and that the only way a story could be made up originally was in imitation of a ritual. But though they show some undoubted instances of this occurrence, none of these writers tell us how the ritual itself evolved and how the inventive process which moved from ritual into a story about the gods and heroes is any easier than any other form of invention."[11]

In entering our reservations, we of course do not reject the proposition that the retention in narrative form of specifications for a rite no longer performed does occur on occasion. But however valid this revised version of the theory may be, it cannot replace the more realistic principle that recognizes the *association* of myth and rite, without assigning priorities, or insisting on either one as the primary causal factor in shaping the other.[12]

If we turn to the discussion of myth by Malinowski, we see how first-hand contact with societies where myth has a functioning role makes for a more sober point of view. Focusing on the life of the Melanesians, Malinowski tells us at the outset of his little volume, "I propose to show how deeply the sacred tradition, the myth, enters into their pursuits, and how strongly it controls their moral and social behaviour. In other words, the thesis of the present work is that an intimate connection exists between the word, the mythos, the sacred tales of a tribe on the one hand, and their ritual acts, their social organization, and their practical activities on the other."[13] In this passage, he summarizes the experience of all who have studied myth in the field, at first-hand. Without laboring the point, it is precisely this that we have tried to sketch in the preceding pages where we have indicated how the various forms of narrative in Dahomey relate conduct to belief, and function as a powerful enculturative factor from the earliest days of childhood,

[11] Stith Thompson, "Myths and Folktales," *Jour. of Am. Folklore,* Vol. 68 (1955), p. 483.

[12] This point has been well made by C. Kluckhohn, "Myth and Rituals: A General Theory," *The Harvard Theological Review,* Vol. 35 (January, 1942), pp. 45–79.

[13] Malinowski, *op. cit.,* p. 11.

stabilizing social behavior, giving meaning to acts in every sphere of life, and stimulating self-expression in the spoken arts.

It was, indeed, Malinowski's essential contribution to sharpen and bring into focus this concept of the association between narrative and behavior, between myth and ritual. "Mythology," he says in another passage, "is . . . a powerful means of assisting primitive man, of allowing him to make the two ends of his cultural patrimony meet." Again and again he speaks of the "pragmatic" character of mythology among the people with whom he worked. And he reads a lesson which exponents of the myth-from-ritual school, whose enthusiasm for Malinowski's work exceeds their mastery of what he has written, might do well to ponder. For in placing myth in the total context of the culture, he shows that to think either of myth or ritual as entities outside this cultural whole leads to distortion. We may even remember that, in discussing one particular form of myth, he tells us that it "shapes the ritual," that it "vouches for the truth of the belief in supplying the pattern of the subsequent miraculous confirmation."[14]

Let us now examine certain other aspects of Malinowski's position on oral literature. If the Cambridge School draws its generalizations from Greek mythology, Malinowski is equally centered on the Trobriands. In his case, this is the more serious, since in his study of myth, as in all his works, he sets up general principles that he asserts are valid for "savage" or "primitive" society in general. Now, it was well recognized, even at the time Malinowski wrote, that the cultures of peoples without written languages are of such great variety that to group them as a unit in contrast to "civilized" cultures is to mask reality. Specifically, a principle that might apply to the Trobrianders would not necessarily be valid for the Dahomeans any more than it would for the Danes.

[14] *Ibid.*, p. 35.

This is evident when we reread certain of his statements, which he makes without qualification, regarding the nature of myth, and project them against the Dahomean materials as a test of their universality. For example, he writes, "As to any explanatory function of these myths, there is no problem which they cover, no curiosity which they satisfy, no theory which they contain."[15] The logical conclusion would seem to be that the theory holding myth to arise from a desire to explain natural phenomena, and which assumes a certain curiosity among "primitive" peoples concerning the world in which they live, is valid in no society. Now it is true that theories of myth that ascribe the derivation of all mythology from attempts to explain the movements of celestial bodies have long been refuted, but we do not resolve the difficulty by substituting one untenable generalization for another.

We have seen how Dahomean mythology not only incorporates explanatory elements, but how it also gives important roles to the Moon and to the Sun. It would not be impossible, with a degree of emphasis that ignored other elements of reference, to utilize the collection of narratives we give to bolster either the position that myths are essentially explanatory, or that they are essentially of the solar-lunar type. But our point is precisely that just because neither of these, as overall theories of myth, applies to the Dahomean narratives, this does not mean that the insights they give cannot illuminate some aspect of myth in Dahomean culture.

As a matter of fact, if Malinowski had not been so intent upon controverting certain of those extreme theories of myth that at the time were prevalent and accepted, he would have recognized how many of the examples he himself gives contradict the position he took. For he was too good a field-worker not to present his findings in cultural context, and it is here that he provides us many instances,

[15] *Ibid.,* p. 59.

even in the short abstracts he gives, that show how lively
is the interest of the Trobriand Islanders in accounting for
certain elements in their culture. On pages 61–62 of his
book we read their explanation of why human beings die;
on pages 65–66, how black magic came into being; on
page 70, "why the spirits are invisible"; on page 71, how
the seasonal feast called *milamala* was instituted. And while
Malinowski is entirely correct in asserting that these explanations do not explain the reason for these phenomena
to the student, that is to say, to Malinowski himself, he
overlooks the fact that, in the ethnographic sense of the
word "explanatory," they do explain them to the Trobri
anders.

These observations are also applicable to much of Raglan's position, valuable though his strictures are in revealing
the untenability of certain ideas that have been taken for
granted among too many students of myth. His attack on
euhemerism is an example of this, for much undisciplined
writing has been done on the assumption that the heroes of
tradition must have historic existence; that unwritten narrative can be employed to establish actual historical happenings. Yet, here again, a good argument is pushed much
too far. In principle, the point has been accepted for decades by students of nonliterate peoples; but one does not
go to the other extreme, as he does, in asserting, "When,
therefore, we attribute to the savage an interest in the past
comparable to our interest in the history of England, we
are attributing to him a taste which he could not possibly
possess, and which if he did possess he could not possibly
gratify."[16] In terms of Raglan's definition of history,[17] he is
entirely correct; but his definition bristles with ambiguities,
many of an ethnocentric nature which assure their inap-
plicability to peoples of a predominantly oral tradition.

If the narratives in our collection tell us anything, it is
that the Dahomeans, at least, who have no written lan-

[16] Raglan, *op. cit.*, p. 6.
[17] *Ibid.*, p. 2.

guage and therefore come into Raglan's category of "illiterates," show an interest in their past that, were there any possibility of drawing valid comparisons, might well be found to be "comparable to our interest in the history of England." Indeed, the portrayal Raglan draws of the attitude of "the savage" toward past events is little short of caricature. "He may remember," goes one passage, "that there was a war with the next village in his father's time, because it led to a blood-feud which has not yet been settled. But when all the participants have died, then the war is forgotten. There is no inducement to remember it, and no machinery by means of which its memory could be preserved."[18] However true this may have been for the Sudanese people Raglan knew, Dahomey had its royal "remembrancer," who recited the genealogy of the kings, a genealogy that compared very well in its unwritten form as given us in 1931 with the names of the Dahomean kings, and when they reigned, given by early travelers in West Africa—works to which our informants could not possibly have had access.

To say that tradition cannot be taken at face value, as Raglan in his excellent discussion of the tale of Troy shows certain classical scholars have done, does not justify the assertion that *no* tradition can have *any* basis in fact. The arbitrary figure of one hundred and fifty years as the maximum for which "an incident which is not recorded in writing can be remembered," is negated by the Dahomean materials, which in certain cases can be documented as having been carried by oral tradition for more than twice that time. Similarly, the ethnohistorical study by Fuller of the Gwambe of southeastern Africa[19] shows how,

[18] *Ibid.,* p. 7.
[19] Charles Edward Fuller, *An Ethnohistoric Study of Continuity and Change in Gwambe Culture,* Ph.D. Dissertation (Microfilm, 1955), Northwestern University. Bascom (*op. cit., Jour. of Am. Folklore,* 1957) in his critique of Raglan's theory, discusses Fuller's data.

in this case, at least, traditional accounts of the tribal past
have a far greater degree of verisimilitude than even those
whose position on the historical validity of myth is less
extreme than that of Raglan might think possible. Nor can
we disregard the lessons that are being learned from research in West Africa, where traditional and written historical accounts are being carefully analyzed and collated, and
where oral tribal histories are being utilized under effective
controls.

Another instance of beginning with a good critical point
and expanding it beyond tenable proportions is found in
Raglan's discussion of the absence of creativity in the
telling of tales. No statement could be more explicit than
his dictum: "No popular storyteller has ever been known
to invent anything"; nor be more in need of clarification
than his comment that "the exercise of the imagination
consists not in creating something out of nothing, but in
the transmutation of matter already present in the mind."[20]
If the first is valid, it is difficult to understand how, in those
earliest societies of man where there was no writing, any
story could ever have been told. As for the second statement, one cannot but wonder whether Raglan is doing
more than repeating the axiom that most invention consists
in reworking pre-existing cultural materials; that in any
particular case the new is far outbalanced by the reinterpreted old.

Now it is quite true that the role of the artist as innovator
has tended to be overstressed, and that, as Raglan is saying,
the innovator does not create *de novo*. Yet this evades the
essential fact of innovation, which is that any exercise of
the imagination that builds on past experience to produce
something that has not existed in this same form before
is an exercise of the creative faculty.

We have seen how the culture of Dahomey affords institutionalized channels for self-expression in the spoken arts,

[20] *Op. cit.*, p. 133.

provided first of all by the prerogative of new songs for the annual rites in the worship of the Earth Pantheon, and by the comparable prerogative exacted by the human rulers in the worship of the Royal Ancestors. The two types, one on religious themes, the second on secular, often draw on the proverb for opening statement and moral. Whether in praise of gods or men, a favored vehicle is social satire. The comment is by indirection, and the imagery is metaphorical. More pronounced still is the outlet for social satire afforded by the opportunity to improvise songs and recitatives in criticism of the reigning king—or at present a chief—during his celebration of the rites to his head, which is to say, to his own Destiny, and by extension the Destiny of the land. Again, social dances, held in rotation by competing groups, such as the Abomey *avogan* which is given successively by each quarter of the city, afford widest opportunity to young people to develop virtuosity in composing new words to songs.

On the enculturative level, there are the children's storytelling sessions which are presided over by a leader chosen by themselves from their own group, where riddling and story telling serve to entertain, but, according to the Dahomeans, also to train in expression and, later, self-expression through the medium of traditional lore. This is continued into maturity and throughout life by the use of myths and tales in divining, wherein the individual ponders the bearing on his own life of the parables he had heard. But the outstanding example of artistry in narration is experienced when the Dahomean participates, whether as narrator or listener, at wakes for the dead. These storytelling sessions are performances to please the connoisseur, the dead, whom it is important to regale with the best at hand. As mentioned, there are no digressions to moralize. It is, in fact, on these occasions that incidents of the most deft caricature, of the widest play of fantasy, of the most daring assault on the inhibited and the socially inexpedient are introduced and developed; this is when the narrator of creative bent has full cultural approbation to introduce variant themes and explanations.

The problem, then, is not whether the story teller "creates" something that is entirely new—"imagined," to use the word Raglan uses—in all of its elements, unlike anything heard before. The need is rather to balance and give full weight to the degree to which creative expression, as an exercise of the imagination, can be recognized in oral literature when at present our essential comparative materials from most world areas are so lacking in time depth. We can only collate variants, and compare synchronically what we find. In our own cultural stream, we are quick to recognize and react to change, but even a stylistic innovator like Joyce gave us recognizable Dublin in dress, in speech, in ritual observance, and in the tensions that well up from political and religious differences.

How daring was the narrator who, functioning within the framework of Dahomean culture, and the role assigned in it to the person and office of the king, told the tale where the poor stranger refuses all worldly bribes so that he might enjoy the beggar's satisfaction of commanding the king? According to the narrator who told us the story, the shift in the plot to place the king above morality and the execution of the beggar were the only acceptable resolutions. But we are nevertheless led to speculate both as to the creative act of the first teller of this tale and, if the "intentional fallacy" may be forgiven us, cannot but wonder what occasioned its telling. It might have been during the ritual to the king's head, or it may have been brought to Abomey by a professional *ahanjito,* who wandered through the land as entertainer, stopping at the gates of the great compounds to beg entrance, and once invited enjoyed immunity from recrimination for the songs he sang and the tales he told. For his reputation—and his rewards—depended not only on the felicity with which he rendered the familiar, but also on the appeal of the new that he brought.

If we say the Euroamerican tradition tends to lay emphasis on innovation and to underplay the unchanging elements, then the antithesis is not the stereotype of the static "primitive" culture that Raglan depicts. As we have come to understand, in a cross-cultural situation the attention of the outsider seizes on the most common forms, and fails to recognize the variations. For variant forms are masked by the semblance of uniformity to an eye not fixed on the delicate gradations in response that produce deviation, and result in new forms.

This is why, whereas the role of the artist and writer as nonconformist has been stressed in our own society, in the so-called "savage" cultures the artist-narrator is conceived as being held to fixed traditional forms, with neither the urge nor the latitude to experiment. It is to the credit of Raglan that, in extending this admittedly extreme point of view to his own culture—though only for the peasants— he has to that degree injected a note of realism into stereotype. But this does not alter the fact that the concept of the fixity of the "primitive" tale or myth, as in Raglan's thesis, does not hold. The Dahomeans, it will be recalled, distinguish between the singer-narrator of good memory, and the one of great understanding. In effect, once improvisation is not only culturally tolerated but assigned a prestige role, the factor of innovation becomes a cultural reality.

There are, to be sure, good reasons why the idea of "primitive" uninventiveness has seemed so plausible.[21] If we consider that among peoples without written languages the innovator is anonymous, the reasonableness of the proposition that there is no creative individual among these peoples is compounded. Here, in truth, we have the explanation why students of literature have been so beguiled by the mysticism of Jung's idea of the collective uncon-

---

[21] For a full discussion of this problem, especially in the field of technology but by no means this alone, see H. G. Barnett, *Innovation, the Basis of Cultural Change,* New York, 1953.

scious, or have so readily accepted such a concept as that of prelogical mentality advanced, but later rejected, by Lévy-Bruhl.[22]

A fundamental difficulty with all theories of myth, when judged in terms of the available data, is that the nature, extent and significance of internal innovation is ignored. Neither Raglan nor Malinowski give the study of variants any place in their discussions. Yet we know that in all societies, the literate ones of Europe, America, and the Near and Far East, as well as those that do not possess writing, variants constantly appear to tales orally told, and by this very fact reshape their form and, over time, their point and meaning.

This is not the place to repeat the conclusions of the many students of myth in nonliterate societies who have recorded and commented on the multiplicity of these variants and their significance, and have remarked how differences in personality, age, sex and status can influence the form of a given myth or tale. Serious students of myth who are steeped in the writings of humanistic scholarship and accept the doctrine of the uninventiveness of the "primitive" might well study the extended analysis of the myths of the Wintu Indians of California by Demetracopoulou and du Bois, to which an entire issue of a major periodical in the field, the *Journal of American Folklore,* was devoted in 1932.[23] In this "study of change and stability in Wintu mythology as it exists at the present day" to name only one of the many relevant points discussed in it, we find, for example, fifteen versions of the single tale of Coyote and Death. Yet neither this collection nor any discussion of its conclusions nor those of any other com-

[22] Cf. L. Lévy-Bruhl, *Les Carnets de Lucien Lévy-Bruhl,* Paris, 1949.

[23] D. Demetracopoulou and Cora du Bois, "A Study of Wintu Mythology," *Jour. of Amer. Folklore,* Vol. 45, No. 178, Oct.–Dec. 1932.

parable researches,[24] as far as we have been able to ascertain, has entered into the analyses of myth by scholars who have proposed broad overall formulations for a general theory of mythology.

toward a general theory of myth

We may briefly consider a point that has entered into our discussion a number of times, but whose significance has thus far not been analyzed. This has to do with the fact that Dahomey, like other societies of Africa, represents a particular manifestation of what we have termed the Old World Culture. In this vast region, the basic themes of narrative show a remarkable correspondence, a fact that has direct bearing on the theories of myth that have just been explored.

We turn, first of all, to a quotation from the Preface to the abridged edition of *The Golden Bough,* a work that has so impressively influenced thought on the nature and sources of myth: ". . . It is no longer possible to regard the rule of succession to the priesthood of Diana of Aricia as exceptional; it clearly exemplifies a widespread institution, of which the most numerous and the most similar cases have thus far been found in Africa."[25] It is of no consequence for our discussion here that, as the argument progresses, Frazer has recourse to the outmoded classical form of the comparative method, which consisted essentially of bringing

[24] Some examples of these are R. Benedict, *Zuñi Mythology, loc. cit.;* E. C. Parsons, *Folk-Lore of the Antilles, French and English,* Memoir XXVI, American Folklore Soc., New York, 1933–1943 (and other works by this author); E. Goldfrank, "Isleta Variants: a Study in Flexibility," *Jour. Amer. Folklore,* Vol. 29 (1926), pp. 70–78. In the study by Daniel J. Crowley, *Tradition and Individual Creativity in Bahamian Folktales,* Ph.D. Dissertation (Microfilm), Northwestern University, Ch. I, and folios L 279–289, this problem is considered at length.

[25] Sir James Frazer, *The Golden Bough* (Abridged edition), New York, 1942.

together phenomena from peoples over the world, which on the surface seem to be similar, but which have been torn from their cultural context and utilized without regard to the meaning which provides them their essential, and often quite different, cultural reality. What is important for us is that, of his comparisons, the "most numerous and most similar cases" to the ancient Greek rite he uses on which to base his argument have been found in Africa.

It is impossible to read the narratives that follow without recognizing the many themes which they have in common with Old World lore. The fact that parallel animal stories are found in all the Old World is only one general expression of this—the resemblances between numerous African tales and Reynard the Fox of Medieval Europe, the Aesop fables, the Panchatantra of India, and the Jataka tales of China have long been remarked. But beyond this, many motifs with human and non-human protagonists, found elsewhere in the Old World, are present in this Dahomean collection. These include variants on the Oedipus theme, the Prometheus theme, William Tell, Lohengrin, Cinderella (Orphan tales), Delilah and Salome, Ali-Baba and the Forty Thieves—all these, but in forms shaped by the configurations of Dahomean culture, which, when stripped away, reveal the underlying unities.

The significance of facts of this order for the various theories of myth that have been propounded cannot be overestimated. For it will be recalled that, in most of the cases we have cited—Rank and Jung, the Cambridge School and Raglan—the examples that have been called on to "prove" the position taken derive predominantly from Old World Cultures. This means that, once we recognize the historical interrelationships of the entire area, we discover that in accounting for the basic unities we are dealing with historical phenomena, and not with causalities that inhere *ipso facto* either in the nature of man, or in the nature of myth.

In a very real sense, these comments are a *caveat* against

the use of these Dahomean materials to "prove" any general theory of myth that calls primarily on Old World materials for its documentation. We agree with the position taken by Graves, when he says, "Let me emphasize that my theory is intended to cover only the area from which the myths I quote are drawn—not, for instance, China, Central America, or the Indus Valley—that any statement here made about Mediterranean religion or ritual before the appearance of written records must necessarily be conjectural; that I regard my intuition as by no means infallible; and that if anyone can make a guess that rings truer than mine I shall be the first to applaud it."[26]

The question why men make myths remains to challenge us to account for a universal human response in its most significant, because its most imaginative, expression. And related to this is why such different explanations of the myth-making phenomenon, each so reasonable to its proponents, have called forth so much disagreement among students of myth and why the various positions are so hotly debated.

We turn once again to certain patterns of thought, germane to our discussion, that are characteristic of Euroamerican culture. These may be subsumed in the tendency to dichotomize experience, a tendency which reflects one of the most deeply set constellations in the cultures of Europe and America. It is of great antiquity in this vast cultural stream. It was present in the functioning religions at the beginning of the historic period, when writing was first discovered. It was given philosophical formulation in classical Greece.

This mode of thought gives rise to what we may term the *all-or-none fallacy,* the operation of which is exemplified in Rank's formulation based on the Oedipus complex, or in Malinowski's exclusive stress on the sociological role of myth. It needs no great psychological sophistication to

[26] Robert Graves, *The Greek Myths,* London, 1955, Vol. I, p. 23.

recognize that responses of this order move on the unconscious level, especially where a given proposition is ordered under the rubric of scientific analysis. This is why, for example, the concept of variability, when advanced in the nineteenth century, brought on a revolution in scientific thought; why it is still a concept difficult to grasp for those in our culture unaccustomed to working with quantitative data.

Recognition of the fact that this tendency to dichotomize is culture-bound could not have come until the researches of anthropologists were available for comparative purposes. For to one trained in a system of thought based on polarities, the idea of a continuum which extends to unspecified terminal points on both sides of a norm represents a major and often a painful reorientation in point of view. The proved validity of this approach in the natural and exact sciences, together with the anthropological findings, that show the dichotomizing pattern to be only one of a number of possible means of structuring thought, has opened the way to the reordering of concepts that had come to be more or less taken for granted. In essence, this approach cuts under the all-or-none fallacy, permitting us to examine accepted positions in terms of possible complementary elaborations.

We suggest that this is precisely the approach to myth that will be most fruitful. For a valid general theory of myth cannot be developed except in terms of a general theory of human culture. In essence, this recognizes man's endowment as a culture-building animal, through his ability to manipulate the symbolisms of language, and extend his personal powers through the use of tools. It stresses the exploratory aptitudes in man which, while always finding expression within the limits of a given body of tradition, yet interact with these so as to bring on change in them. Of this process, myth is but a part. But as a part, it cannot go beyond the terms of reference set by the overall concept, and must be ordered within this frame.

In demurring at the generalizing nature of the various theories we have discussed, we grant each what measure of validity it holds. It is for this reason we have recognized that though the Oedipus theorem as at present formulated needs to be broadened, it is not to be denied its place as one important segment of mythic conceptualization. This is why, too, though we could not accept the *mystique* of the collective unconscious, we have pointed out that the universals in human *experience,* and the historic factors that have played on these, may be held to account for the presence of similar broad themes in the narratives of peoples living all over the world. In rejecting the thesis that myth arises out of ritual, we have in no wise denied the importance of the relationship between the two. As concerns the sociological theory of myth, we do not disavow for myth its sanctioning role in social organization; nor, in our attempt to isolate the factors that in Dahomey encourage creativity, have we overlooked the influence of preconditioning and cultural imperatives, even when the narrator, or singer-poet is most creative.

We recognize all of these; but we are led to conclude that none of them provides a full answer. There is no easy theory of myth. We repeat, myth is a manifestation of human culture and must be treated as such. This means that it does not exist of itself. Mythic symbolism, in any age, and at all levels of abstraction, is a cultural fact. Mythic themes are not emanations of images engraved on the unconscious in primordial times. As a cultural fact, myth is seen as deriving from human language skill, and man's fascination with symbolic continuities. But as a cultural fact, it also finds dynamic expression in the play between outer stimulus received by a people, and innovation from within.

We advance, in essence, as far as causation is concerned, a pluralistic theory of myth, recognizing the demonstrated universal fact that men everywhere have felt impelled to symbolize metaphorically the relationship between man and his world. The answer to questions about the genesis of myth and mythic themes is no simpler, or more difficult, than the question why in Dahomey, in the rites for the ancestors, the boasting pattern of song and invocation does not cause the family singer to list the number of wives and children and palm groves and, in earlier times, the number of its slaves. Instead, he disposes of the pretensions of a rival by singing:

> *The serpent does not measure its shadow*
> *against the rainbow,*

or

> *This river and that river,*
> *It is the Sea who is their king.*

As we see it, the most important elements in the scientific approach to myth—and the literary approach as well—are the cumulative reality of culture in human experience; the factor of borrowing, whether achieved or in process, and over time and in space; and the creative drive in man. The origin of the symbolic intangibles of an oral tradition cannot be illuminated by carbon dating, even though archaelogical findings have given us, and are giving us, important leads to relationships between peoples. Nor can one speculative system which attempts to explain genetic relations do more than another.

There remains the challenge to take concepts and hypotheses into the laboratory of the cross-cultural field, and test their generalizing value, or arrive at new generalizations. Perhaps "challenge" is too austere a word for our implicit meaning. In the tradition of humanistic scholarship, it is an invitation to discover for world literature and thought vast resources which will inform and delight us.

the humanism in anthropological science

It must well seem paradoxical to those whose thinking is dichotomous, that it was precisely through following the dictates of Science that we were led to Humanism; that we were enabled to proceed from the study of men to the study of Man. . . . The unicultural nature of humanistic scholarship has served to restrict the outlook of scholars precisely where the greatest breadth of vision is called for. With some feeling for the cross-cultural point of view, we would have been spared the ethnocentric distortions of a T. S. Eliot, whose concept of culture is limited by the horizon not only of his own way of life and of his time, but even of his particular sub-culture. We would be spared equally the ethnocentric pretentiousness of a Spengler or a Toynbee, whose views of history have been limited by their commitment to the values of their own historic stream.

The humanism in anthropology has been masked by the essentially scientific orientation of the discipline as a whole. It is time we recognize its importance in our research and our theory, and give it the place its potentialities demand. The question may be raised, however, whether in doing this, we do not face a dichotomy that poses insurmountable problems in developing and utilizing concepts and methods that derive from a dual commitment of this kind. Can the humanism in anthropology be brought into balance and adequately integrated with its scientific orientation? Let us consider some of the implications of this seeming contradiction, and see whether we cannot erect some guide-posts toward its clarification.

In the early days of our discipline, the study of culture was classified without question as one of the natural sciences, as it still is in some contexts of academic life. The classical evolutionists, in consonance with the currents of their time, and utilizing methods that were justified by the kinds of data to which they had access, worked out systems of cultural development that paralleled, even where they were not stimulated by, the evolutionary models developed by the biologists and the geologists. To be sure, with the growth of the tradition of field-work, and as we developed more skilled methods and thus could reach more meaningful insights, there came an awareness of alternate orientations. But we continued as heirs of a naturalistic tradition, with patterns of theory and methods whose intricacies, though discussed for more than a half-century, have by no means been completely traced.

How was it possible for the earliest anthropologists, the evolutionists, and so many of those who have come after them, to disregard what would seem to be the crucial, and at the same time the very obvious point that any study of man which does not originate in the study of men is a contradiction in scientific terms? Herein, indeed, lay the overriding significance of the development of field research, and the insistence that came to be laid on first-hand contact with the peoples we studied. This, at last, was Science, and in the best scientific tradition we shifted from a search for data which would support deduced postulates to seeking out relationships that could be empirically established. After the manner of science, too, we could proceed to test those postulates in our heritage that had been reached by processes of deduction, by holding them up to the light of our inductions. It must well seem paradoxical to those whose thinking is dichotomous, that it was precisely through following the dictates of Science that we were led to Humanism; that we were enabled to proceed from the study of men to the study of Man.

What are the precepts of field method that have marked the path for our discipline? They can be summarized in a simple formula: We gather our primary data at first hand, utilizing what others have reported for comparative purposes. There are, of course, many facets to this formula. The refinements we have introduced into our procedures, the ways in which we test the validity of the statements that are made to us or the relevance of the behavior we observe, and above all, the more incisive formulations of the problems we study, are only a few of these facets. Moreover, our commitment to the principles of scientific method, which underlies our insistence on field research, also demands a search for larger relationships. We continuously compare data; we should not be scientists if we were content with the description, or even the analysis, of discrete blocks of facts, without relating them to a larger whole. But the methods of comparing data we have developed—and we often fail to recognize how many of them there are—are as different from their classical precursors as are the questions we raise, or the research techniques we employ.

This point must be underscored, for in building on our heritage of method and theory we have all too frequently held to earlier terminology, while reinterpreting its meaning without a concomitant reappraisal of the degree of scientific imprecision or distortion that results when an established designation drifts to a new meaning. Parenthetically, it may be observed that in this, students of culture are themselves responsive to continuities which are fully in accord with some of the general principles of cultural dynamics, whereby with the passage of time, old forms are given new meanings which are in accord with the functional requisites of their day. Is it too much to ask, however, that as students of culture, we apply the principles of our science to our own special sub-culture; that we raise unconscious responses of this sort to the level of tendencies which we can recognize, name, and understand the more clearly, and control, by utilizing the resources of scholarship we command?

With this point in mind, let us return once again to the methods of our precursors, the classical evolutionists, and those who have followed in their methodological footsteps. The key to understanding their procedures is the comparative method, in the strict classical meaning of the phrase. In this sense, it entails comparing items without regard to their cultural context. According to the terms of reference of our present discussion, it is important to observe that only formal, describable elements of culture entered into these systems. This paralleled in some measure the situation in conventional physical anthropology, when conclusions were drawn on the basis of the analysis of achieved morphological traits of adults, while the genetic and developmental sequences were ignored.

In these early studies of culture, human beings, the creators of the technical, social and even the ideological instrumentalities that were being described were, at best, introduced as lay figures, perhaps called on from time to time to illustrate a point, but tangential to the primary focus of the argument. In effect, this was a reification of behavior into entities that were implicitly, and in some instances explicitly divorced from men. It is not chance, consequently, that so much of the argument of those who have held to this point of view has been based on analogies drawn from the theories and methods of the exact and natural sciences. Rather it is the appeal of the offspring to its parent for aid and guidance.

With the development of the tradition of field-work, however, anthropologists came face to face with people. Even in the earliest days of field research the ethnographer, sitting on the porch of the district officer's bungalow, or within the mission compound, interrogating those brought to his table to give him information on their customs and beliefs, established some degree of interaction with his informants.

Nor could he fail to observe for himself certain external manifestations of the life of the people he came to study; or see, if only by walking through a settlement from time to time, the rough outline of their existence; and sense, in however general terms, some of the problems which they, as individual human beings, must solve in order to survive. These early field-workers were primarily concerned with overall patterns of behavior, with consenses of conduct. In consequence, their findings took the form of stereotypes that blurred, masked, or consciously suppressed the individuals in the societies they studied. But even in these patterned descriptions, we can on occasion discern a man, a woman; and on occasion we can sense, however dimly, the presence of the living reality in the abstractions from behavior with which we are presented.

There were, however, those who did not sit on the porch of the district officer's bungalow, or summon informants to the mission compound. In some cases, because of the setting in which they had to work, in others by their own choice, they went to the peoples themselves. We think of Lewis Henry Morgan working among the Iroquois, Boas among the Eskimo, Haddon, Seligman and Rivers in the Torres Straits, Torday in the Congo, Bandelier and Stevens in the Pueblos of Southwestern United States, Nordenskiold in the Amazon basin. By their continuing first-hand contact with the peoples they studied, they were able to sort out behavior, and to discern individual distinctions in the patterns that, within the conventions of their period, they felt a primary obligation to report when they published the results of their field researches.

We have traveled far since the student days of Edward Sapir, who was later to be among the first anthropologists to stress the significance of taking the individual into full account when studying the life of a people, but who, at that time was startled to read in J. O. Dorsey's *Omaha Sociology* the comment, "Two Crows denies this." Phrased in terms of our present discussion, we can see that he was responding to the natural science tradition in anthropology when, as he put it, he felt that in admitting dissent on the part of an informant, Dorsey "had not met the challenge of assaying his source material and giving us the kind of data that we, as respectable anthropologists, could live on." It was only years later, with the results of more field research in hand and closer contact between field workers and the peoples they studied, that anthropologists began to bring culture back to man.

The theme sounded by the casual aside of J. O. Dorsey on an observed difference in the culture of a group from what was "standard" behavior, has become a major preoccupation of ethnological science. It has brought about a reformulation of the concept of culture that, even while frequently not given explicit statement, has forced us to temper earlier reifications by reference to the ultimate fact of observed behavior. We have had to reexamine the nature and the validity of our categories, and to rework our conceptions of the ways in which they are adapted to each other. We have found in culture—in the response of men to the tangible and intangible resources of their group—a degree of plasticity that in earlier times never entered our calculations. We have come to understand that to call a culture a way of life is merely to resort to a convenient short-hand symbol. It is, in reality, a series of limits within which the behavior and ideas of the members of a given society may exhibit approved differences. In the larger view, these differences are to be regarded as setting the boundaries of sanctioned variation.

For many years, a phrase frequently encountered in the literature of anthropology designated man as the "carrier" of his culture. The image was vivid; we could visualize a man, weighed down by a sack containing "culture," continuing to toss yet more bits and pieces of experience into it as he toiled his way through life. It was scarcely perceived that this image, by its very nature, forced a conceptual separation of man from the system of belief and behavior by which he lived. His culture, that is, was in those terms something apart from him, bound to him by ecological, biological, and psychological cords, something that, from outside himself, dictated his reactions, his thinking, his behavior.

The linguists have taught us better, by showing us how we objectify and internalize concepts and values through the medium of language. We have come to recognize that this objectification and internalization not only provides us with the intellectual commitments that are necessary for the establishment and continuation of custom, but that they also supply the emotional validation without which they could not be assimilated to the subliminal level of knowing, feeling and behaving. We now know that by internalizing conventions, we literally make them a part of ourselves. From psychological theories of learning we have derived our conceptions of how the enculturation of the individual is achieved, and particularly of how the enculturative experience causes the sanctions for accepted modes of behavior to lodge deep beneath the level of consciousness, making much of human conduct reactive rather than reasoned.

The question may fairly be put whether, in stating this, we are not reaffirming the need to view the science of custom as falling within the domain of the natural sciences. Here, of course, the point at issue is what our definition is of being scientific, a point that cannot be taken up here. Whatever the definition may be, and while it behooves us as scientists to utilize scientific procedures, we should recognize that the category of scientific method comprehends many different kinds of procedures. Just because man, as a member of the biological series, may be studied as any animal form is studied, by certain methods of the natural sciences, it by no means follows that these particular methods are the ones we must use in investigating all the characteristics of man.

It is scarcely necessary to detail the implications of the distinction we draw when, in recognizing that man is an animal, we state at the same time that he is the animal that has built cultures. We take it as an established fact that while all animals learn, only man learns cumulatively. We can continue in this vein indefinitely. All animals communicate, but only man communicates through the intricate and arbitrary forms that make up a language. There are many social animals, but only for man is it impossible to predict the structuring of interaction in a hitherto undescribed society. The precepts we have laid down as to relation between race and culture are particularly to the point here. For though, in congruence with the principle of holism that gives coherence to the many facets of anthropological science, we study both the physical form and the cultures of man, we have learned that we can only assign to these a causal relationship of so tenuous a nature as to lay a strong burden of proof on the validity of any findings that may flow from research based on this assumption.

The fact that our anthropological beginnings date from a period when science was defined in terms of the concepts and methods of the exact and, in our case, more especially the natural sciences, takes on added significance when it is pointed out that all other bodies of knowledge which were concerned with studying particular aspects of human experience—sociology, economics, political science—were held to fall within the purview of the philosophical disciplines. It was the genius of the earliest anthropologists that from the outset they saw the applicability of scientific methods to the study of human beings more clearly than any other body of scholars concerned with the affairs of man and with the institutions of human society. This, and the fact that one facet of anthropology deals with the study of man's physical form and its evolutionary processes, made it logical that our discipline be classed with the natural sciences.

This is also why so much of the theory on which we draw in phrasing our problems, and the proportion of the methodology that guides the execution of our researches, derive from this tradition. It was this orientation that caused our anthropological forebears, early recognizing that the cultural reality of human experience, when objectively considered, is in actuality strung along a continuum of time, to order this experience into aspects, or units of culture that could be isolated for study so as to determine their functioning and the relationships between them. It was in this tradition, also, that students of man turned away from the use of second-hand documentation to data they themselves could gather and, once workable categories had been established, moved from classification to dynamics. We can best summarize all this, and at the same time phrase the extent of our obligations to these pioneers when we say that they laid the groundwork for the anthropological tradition that, unlike these other disciplines which treat of man in society, has always stressed an empirical approach. It is this empiricism that, in the final analysis, has provided our theoretical structure of culture with its firmly documented foundation.

Yet granting all this, it remains a fact, often not realized, that when we move from the study of the physical forms of man to the study of behavioral phenomena, we are moving quite literally into a new universe of scientific discourse. The difference, if only in the degree of plasticity between those aspects of the human being that are biologically inherited and those that are learned is so great as to bring differences of degree well over the threshold where they become differences of kind. This is true of all aspects of behavior. To make the point, we need but contrast the variation we find in the skeletal or muscular structure of man, or even in his physiological processes, with that which we continuously record for kinship structures, or economic organization, or material culture, to take account of only those aspects of culture that lie close to man's bodily needs, and leaving to one side the even wider range of differences with which we must deal when we focus on religious ideas, or stylistic traditions in art. Or let us reverse the order, and consider the difference in degree of predictability we can command in the instance of the inheritance of physical form undercrossing between two populations, and in that of two groups whose interchanges are on the level of acculturation. We can predict in both instances, but the variables that must be taken into account will be much less, and the consequent degree of validity we can attain will be far greater where we are concerned with physical type than with culture.

With the passage of time, ethnology has tended to move —or to be moved—into the category of the social sciences. Yet by the nature of their data, most anthropologists have never felt entirely satisfied when they have been restricted to any single grouping of academic disciplines.

The study of social organization, or, as it is sometimes called, social anthropology, or ethnopolitics, or economic anthropology are, of course, social sciences in the full sense of the phrase. But it is equally clear that physical anthropology, and most of archaeology, are not. In ethnology itself, studies of music, of art, of systems of belief, which constitute important divisions of our discipline, are difficult to compress within the framework of social science, granting they are but manifestations of human experience and that man is a social animal.

For the anthropologist who responds to the scientific mandate of his discipline to follow his data wherever they may lead, and is imbued with its holistic tradition, the label "social science" can be no more firmly affixed to the total anthropological corpus than the earlier one which read "natural science." To meet this need for clearer distinction we have invented new terms. For the discipline as a whole, we have had recourse to the designation "the study of man." Comparative anthropological studies in economics have become economic anthropology. We have turned to the word ethnology, and have bred a whole school of "ethno-" derivatives for our sub-disciplines. We came to speak of ethnolinguistics, of ethnohistory, of ethnomusicol-

ogy, and of psychoethnography, to describe the researches
we were carrying out in these specialized fields and the
studies of how they were interrelated with the other aspects
of life in the societies in which we investigated them.

In all this, without actually phrasing it, we were asserting our conviction that our discipline, as the study of man,
must comprehend all the manifestations of human existence
and human experience. From another point of view, we are
seeking ways of expressing our holistic concerns as contrasted with disciplines of more restricted scope. In effect,
the position of anthropology in relation to all the principal
groupings of organized knowledge—the exact and natural
sciences, the social sciences, and the humanities—is that of
a circle which intersects three others. It is a part of all, but
its totality coincides with none. Of the three intersected
circles, the one whose interrelationship with anthropology
today holds greatest promise is that of the humanities, since
it is an historical fact that the potential contribution of
anthropology in the area of the humanistic disciplines has
received least attention from anthropologists.

We have observed the seeming paradox that it was only
when we adopted scientific methods and came face to face
with our data that we reached an understanding of the importance of the humanistic component of our discipline. It
is equally striking that, for some of our most precise data,
we must turn to these humanistic aspects of science, a fact
that has gone almost unrecognized.

Let us, first of all, consider the structural approach to the
study of various aspects of culture. This interest in structure, it should be remarked, is by no means unique to anthropology. Even the examples we shall take from within
our science arose quite independently out of a more general
intellectual current that expressed a recognition of the fact
that understanding of function is largely determined by the
degree of refinement in our knowledge of structure. Within
our discipline, this stress on structure has been laid out-

standingly on the study of social organization and in linguistics.

In both instances, concentration on the analysis of structure has resulted in a more precise delimitation of concepts, and particularly in a more careful use of terminology. Considerable advance has been made in the field of social organization with respect to such matters as kinship relations, marriage forms, the role of the lineage and social stratification along lines of age, or rank, or economic resources. In linguistics, too, the differentiation of significant from non-significant variants in sound, and the delimitation of units of meaning and of morphological categories has resulted from the preoccupation of linguistics with structural forms. Yet it would be unrealistic to assume that the degree of precision which has been attained in the study of social structure is comparable to the fineness with which critical elements in the structure of language have been delimited and described by the humanistic sub-discipline of linguistics.

We do not find it germane to our present discussion to analyze the reasons for this difference, but there is one point of particular significance for us. This has to do with the level of agreement to be found in each of the two sub-disciplines with respect to its terminology. This is not pedantry; the standardization of nomenclature is closely related to the degree of communication between scholars working in the same field, and the comparability of the results of independent investigation of the problems common to their discipline.

In this respect, there is a great difference between the two sub-disciplines. Linguistic terms such as "phoneme" or "morpheme," or concepts like "bound" or "free" forms, are clearly defined and consistently employed. We need but contrast this acceptance of usage by the linguists with the disputes over terminology that have marked the history of the study of social organization from its inception. Where do we find general agreement on what constitutes a "lineage"? What consensus is there as to the relation of the lineage to the social units variously called "clan" or "gens" or "sib"? What clear-cut difference, concurred in by all, can we find to distinguish an "age-grade" from an "age-set"? Is "bride-wealth" to be the standard term, or "bride-price," or "dowry"? To what extent can it be held that there are regularities in "rules" of residence? When is a clan totemic?

The contrast between the standardization of usage in our humanistic sub-discipline and the variant and often ambiguous usages in its social science fellow cannot be ascribed to differences in the span of time during which the respective phenomena have been studied. If anything, the study of social organization, in the anthropological sense of the term, can be said to be older than the systematic study of unwritten languages. The grammarians were certainly functioning in the time of the Greeks, but there also were those who concerned themselves with man in society. Scientific investigation of social organization, particularly the study of kinship, can be traced to the time of Lewis Henry Morgan, whose *Systems of Consanguinity and Affinity of the Human Family* was published in 1871. Boas' linguistic studies, which may be thought of as having laid the groundwork for later investigations into the problems of structural linguistics, were begun almost three decades later. It is quite true that the biological and exact sciences have long held to well-defined rules governing their systems of nomenclature. But in the two instances we are discussing, it is clear that the time-factor cannot be regarded as critical.

What, then, is the reason for the difference between the two? Here a factor enters that has by no means been given the attention it deserves. This bears on the extent to which the materials of concern to the social and linguistic structuralist lie on the subliminal level of response to the total cultural setting. It is commonplace that the structure of a language, once it has so to speak been dissected out of an unwritten mode of speech, stands out more clearly than the structure of any society that has thus far been described.

By the same token, the consistency in usage is greater in the instance of grammatical forms than of social conventions. Almost anyone in a society can give an inquiring observer the terms of reference and address he uses for his kin and his neighbors. He can do this because they are the tools that he must have in hand if he is to maintain himself as a functioning unit of his social system. He can never relinquish a conscious command of them, since human relations, of whatever nature, are never entirely to be taken for granted. The ever-changing situations they call into being, through the impact of one personality or another, must be continuously reappraised in the light of the many factors that enter into the relation of one person to another. The same individual who provides the student with a kinship terminology, however, will not be able as readily to explain when and why he uses a particular word in his vocabulary to designate a particular act, or a particular object.

If we acknowledge, however, that kinship structure lies much closer to the level of consciousness than vocabulary, can we say that the grammar of kinship is less deeply imbedded in our thought processes than the grammar of language? In terms of systematic treatment, and particularly when it comes to generalizing on the basis of comparisons drawn between systems, linguistic morphology differs little from social structures. But it would be difficult to maintain the position that the level on which the student quarries a lineage system out of his inductions from social and political behavior plumbs subliminal depths to the degree to which the linguist must probe in working out grammatical categories from the texts he has taken down.

We must not overstress this psychological explanation, but we cannot permit ourselves to overlook it. We are in possession of extensive documentation from the study of cultures which demonstrates that those elements most taken for granted are the most resistant to change. This is the rationale for the principle of cultural reinterpretation, and for differentiating the dynamics of change in form from change in meaning. We have learned that it comes more easily to a people to fit an old meaning, or an antecedent value into a new form than it is for them to invest a pre-existing form with a new meaning. In a certain sense, this can be regarded as an expression of what has been called the pattern phenomenon which, from another perspective is seen to be a type of cultural structuring.

Let us take our reasoning one step further, and postulate that just as form changes more readily than meaning, and individual manifestations of a mode of behavior vary in terms of a recognizable pattern, so the more a cultural phenomenon is taken for granted, the deeper will its structural roots lie beneath the surface of behavior. Now, whatever the historical or psychological basis for the classification, it so happens that it is just these elements in behavior that are included in the category of the humanities. This holds particularly for the aspects of life wherein the play of creativity is most apparent—in the graphic, plastic and verbal arts, and in music—and whose structural forms are lodged the most deeply.

What we have observed regarding cultural structures is similarly to be discerned in cultural dynamics, toward which, indeed, we have already been moved in this discussion by the logic of our argument. This phase of anthropological interest comprises one of our major concentrations of effort over the past two or three decades, as we can see if we do no more than consider the sheer bulk of the acculturation studies that have been carried on during this period. In a very real sense, this represents a metaphysic that emphasizes "becoming" as against the stress on "being" of the pure structural approach.

Nevertheless, we must not fail to recognize that despite recent emphases, the study both of structure and of process represents currents of anthropological interest that are as old as our discipline. The two complement each other, as they must in any field. The "what" must be there to illuminate the "how," and the action is reciprocal; taken together, they lead to increased understanding of the "why." In earlier days, discussion of this was almost entirely confined to the question of whether anthropology was to be thought of as a historical or a scientific discipline, a debate that has by no means ended. The introduction of the question here, insofar as it is involved in our present analysis, turns on its appropriateness to the point we are considering, the relative degree of precision which we can attain by utilizing certain data from the humanistic aspects of our science, as compared to what we can expect from studying those facets of culture which have been our more common focus of interest. We have seen that in the study of structure, a more precise, standardized terminology has been achieved by the linguists than by the students of social organization. Let us see how this question is met in the study of dynamics.

For this, we may take as our examples political organization and music. We are here moving into areas of research where concepts and methods are much less sharply delineated than in the instances we have given, and where the number of studies are less numerous. Kinship structure, that is, has been given far more attention than political organization, and language much more than music. Yet resources in both fields are adequate to enable us to compare the two as far as the precision with which on the level of methodology they can respectively attack their data.

We raise again, as a significant criterion, the question of the clarity and unambiguity of definition of the analytic units with which each deals. In the study of political organization, the units, whether large or small, have proved to be extremely difficult to delimit. We hear much of change from tribal systems to nationhood, but there is vast disagreement as to what constitutes a tribe, and when and under what conditions tribal groupings may be accorded the status of a nation. One of the questions that has come to be much debated has to do with the way in which the democratic tradition of Europe and America is being incorporated into, and modified by the differing types of aboriginal political orientation of newly independent nations, all of which experienced contact with the political systems of their rulers during colonial times.

The concept "tribe," however defined, like the concept "nation," is a blunt instrument for the analysis of process. The concept "democracy," too, is diffuse. At times it is conceived as an ideology, at other times as a parliamentary system, working through the maneuvering of political parties. There is no question that the scientific problems of cultural dynamics, brought forth by the facts of political change, constitute a challenge on the first order for anthropological students of politics. Those problems merit the increasing flow of resources being devoted to their study. It is an area of research which, by its very nature, presents the anthropologists with a veritable laboratory situation, giving him the controls for an analysis in depth of the historical processes in play. Thus far, we find the anecdotal component in the published studies of political change to be appreciable, the documentation to refer to a single time plane, and sparse, with conclusions but rarely based on data that have been subjected to scientific controls.

It is obvious that the degree of attainable objectivity, a prime desideratum in scientific analysis, is clearly related to the kind of conceptual tools with which the student must work. The nature of those tools is perhaps one reason why the subjective element in studies of political change has been pronounced, not in normative evaluation, but in terms of unconscious commitments to a segment of culture which, in the nature of the case, is high in affective content, and carries implications for almost every phase of everyday living in a world of change.

In the case of music, the situation, certainly in this respect, is quite different. The basic categories relate so closely to the physical phenomena of tone and tempo that they can be controlled by the use of mechanical or electronic devices which give us an objective definition of them.

A song can be repeatedly recorded so as to show the relation of variation to distance as one moves from the place where the initial recording of it was made, a fundamental question in the study of cultural dynamics. An instrument can be studied in terms of the intervals to which it is tuned, and compared with others from the same area, or from distant regions. Moreover, the factor of commitment on the part of the student is minimal. Even where the precise nature of a contact involved in a comparison is not ascertainable, the complexity with which clearly differentiated elements are combined is such that, for example, when we find a Yoruba song in Brazil and Cuba, the problem of ascription is undebatable, and we are free to develop our hypotheses concerning cultural tenacity and cultural change over time and distance in the light of observed data that, according to the best criteria, are trustworthy.

Another point enters here, which has particular application to the case of music. We need not go so far as to define scientific method in terms of quantification to recognize the value of using the techniques of mathematical analysis that are available to us. Their relevance for musicology is self-evident, and they have begun to be utilized in this field with considerable effectiveness. A song can be recorded, its elements can be translated into numerical terms in the laboratory, and these data can then be manipulated in the same way as any other kind of quantitative materials. The same can be done with rhythm, or interval patterns, or modal structures. Degrees of deviance can be mathematically expressed, and the statistical principles governing the significance of differences applied with a minimum of difficulty arising from the nature of the units that are employed in the computations.

We should not lose sight of the fact in this connection, that this same kind of methodology can be employed in studying several other humanistic aspects of anthropology. These same recording and computing devices can be used in the study of narrative. Measurement to a high degree of accuracy is also possible in many manifestations of the graphic and plastic arts. In all these fields, treatment of the data in these precise ways gives promise of insights on some of the basic questions of cultural dynamics not otherwise subject to documentation, both as regards the processes of cultural innovation, whether internal or external, and of cultural change.

Attempts have of course been made to apply quantitative methods in the anthropological study of political organization, as, for example, where questions of political affiliation in situations of cultural contact have been under investigation. These are like comparable attempts in several of the other social science aspects of anthropological interest, such as the analysis of kinship, where statistical techniques have been applied to various problems of cross-cultural and intra-cultural relationships. In all such attempts, however, the difficulty of defining the unit to be counted has complicated the analysis, and because of this has tended to leave the findings open to serious question. In too many instances, indeed, findings from procedures that have the appearance of rigid methodological controls have proved to be significant only until one has gone behind the mathematical statement and has examined the nature of the data themselves. Even in the study of demography, counts of population are notoriously unreliable, however convincing the statistical results may seem when assembled in published form.

Just as in the case of structure, the extent to which the underlying organization of the data is carried subliminally is important in achieving clear-cut lines of form and clear delimitation of content, so in the study of dynamics, the more effectively a phenomenon under study can be isolated from its interaction with man, the more precisely can we investigate the processes of inception and change that apply to it. Man as an organism, in the sense that he is studied by physical anthropologists, falls into this category. So does the study of material culture. But once we are called on to move to the area of behavioral phenomena, particularly in terms of those cultural constructs that have no physical form or cannot be reduced to physical expression, we face the problem of less precision in definition, and the use of constructs that lend themselves to more impressionistic modes of analysis.

It is striking that, despite all the emphasis that has been laid on the application of scientific method in anthropology, many of its aspects in which scientific methods can be most effectively employed, as in the case of those we have named —the graphic, plastic, musical and verbal arts—have been given the least attention. Here the formal elements which provide the basis for a controlled scientific approach can be treated with perhaps more objectivity than any of the other phenomena we study. They can be most rigorously defined, and most penetratingly analyzed. It is not without irony that, because they carry the label "humanistic," and are not comprehended within the categories of data treated either by the natural or social sciences, we have thus far put them to one side, failing to perceive that their study offers us the best opportunity of reaching and understanding many fundamental questions posed by our science.

Such questions, moreover, go beyond those we have here been discussing. They move across the spectrum of the disciplines to reach normative affirmations of human life, as when they consider the nature and functioning of value-systems. They have the widest implications for such philosophical problems as the relation of man to the universe, and to the forces that control it. Most difficult, and perhaps most germane of all, is the challenge of understanding the uniquely human trait of creativity, indicated in our discussion above as the basis of the dynamic factor in culture, particularly as it is shaped and directed by the patterns of the tradition in which it manifests itself.

Here the cross-cultural point of view, the primary methodological contribution of anthropology to scholarship, comes into play. The unicultural nature of humanistic scholarship has served to restrict the outlook of scholars precisely where the greatest breadth of vision is called for. With some feeling for cross-cultural point of view, we would have been spared the ethnocentric distortions of a T. S. Eliot, whose concept of culture is limited by the horizon not only of his own way of life and of his time, but even of his particular sub-culture. We would be spared the equally ethnocentric pretentiousness of a Spengler or a Toynbee, whose views of history have been limited by their commitment to the values of their own historic stream. Or, with some comprehension of the cross-cultural factor, and some receptivity to ways other than his own, it would have been unlikely that a thinker like Isaiah Berlin would have written of historical inevitabilities with biases which clearly arise out of his limited view of the range of human culture.

For these, and for the innumerable lesser alluring generalizations drawn from culturally truncated data we, as anthropologists, have but ourselves to blame. We have sought out the peoples of the world, near and far, and have come to realize how varied is the experience of man, and how broad the range of human potentialities. We have been able to do this because we have projected ourselves into the lives of the peoples we have studied, have learned how powerful are the symbols of value and sanction in the lives of the members of every society. We have come to perceive the difficulties we face in drawing overall judgments between one system and another. In this, though often without such ends in mind, we have been reaching toward the clarification not only of our own problems of the nature of culture and its functioning, but also of some of the questions most often raised by the humanists. Our unique contribution to humanistic studies comes from the fact that we have been studying these problems by the use of scientific techniques. The generalizations we have drawn have thus compounded the insights of humanism by utilizing the controls of science.

This contribution has thus far been little recognized, its

potentiality little exploited. Having been beguiled by analogy, we have relegated the humanistic aspects of our discipline to a minor place in the repertory of our interests and our activities. We have been reluctant to accept categorically the fact that the study of learned behavior does not lie in the same plane as biological or natural phenomena, and have all too frequently been content to take over concepts and methods, rather than to strike out on conceptual and methodological paths of our own making.

In our search for "laws," after the manner of natural science, we have neglected to look at man. It is time we redressed the balance; that we study him in his totality, profiting from our scientific orientation so as to illuminate what are at once the most delicate, and yet the most powerful determinants that shape the human adventure.

rediscovery and integration:

The facts about African responses to culture contact make it difficult to understand how the idea of the African as a passive recipient of European culture could have gained such wide currency. It provided the ideological base for the nineteenth century concepts of the white-man's burden and the *mission civilizatrice*. To an unrecognized extent, it was implicit in the interpretation of the Marxist doctrine of social progress. . . . The need to re-establish the position of African culture by affirming its particular values was most vigorously expressed in the concepts of *Négritude* and of "the African Personality."

Even where African societies were under greatest pressure, traditional ways persisted in forms and to a degree that went largely unrecognized. The sources of this strength derived from the nature of the cultures themselves, especially their institutionalized mechanisms of psychological resistance . . . they allowed a person to retain self-respect even when subjected to indignities, for in his own household, the slave was master.

In the changed setting of African life, the search for values can be said to have gained effective momentum only with the attainment of self-government. During most of the time Africans were under foreign control, aboriginal African values, and attempts to balance them against what the Europeans had brought to Africa were rarely discussed. For one thing, the educational system was not calculated to encourage critical analyses of this kind; it was geared to inculcate the positive values in the metropolitan cultures. The cultures out of which the pupils had come were viewed as in process of being superseded by the higher cultures of Europe. There were few Africans prepared to raise questions of comparative worth; and where they did, their audience was minute.

Moreover, as the drive for independence became more intense, all effort was directed toward achieving self-government. Non-political discussion was for the most part confined to criticism of the existing social and economic order, and was therefore essentially negative. African revolutionists were no different from revolutionists elsewhere. They were much too preoccupied with immediate issues to speculate about underlying forces. They were so occupied with the next step, indeed, that it was difficult for them to give much thought even to the practical problems of government that would have to be resolved once they reached their goal. The planning of strategy for the political offensive, designed to end colonial rule and expand the areas of African power, left no time to contemplate the relative values of African and non-African cultures, or to raise the questions that were later to be raised. No African political leader or intellectual could remain outside the struggle, to enjoy the luxury of contemplative objectivity while it was going on.

When these questions moved into the foreground of African thought, the answers frequently took polemic form, as reactions to statements about African racial and cultural inferiority. As one African scholar wrote, they were,

a denial, an angry protest against the inferior and infantile role in which the West had cast the African on the stage of world history and culture. . . . Before the African could come into his own, he had to break out of the shell in which others had sought to contain him; he had to destroy the stereotyped idea of himself as an inferior being.[1]

Theories about the nature of race differences and racial worth that had lost scientific standing continued to be debated as though they had scientific support, and long-discredited ideas had to be disproved all over again.

Understandably, for the great mass of the African people, the question of values arose primarily as they bore on day-to-day life, and only rarely in their broader compass. Local issues were preeminent; in matters of wider scope they were willing to follow the lead of others. The discussion from which the preceding quotation was taken recognized this: "Protest has been most articulate not among the ordinary people whose lives have been relatively less disturbed by western contacts," but was carried on by "the intellectuals who had been made into second class citizens. . . ." The importance of the attention given by these intellectuals to the problem of values in African culture lay in the fact that, as in all societies, it was they who were to give direction to popular thought. With the paramount political issue resolved, some of them could turn to the philosophical and ethical problems raised by the historic forces of colonialism, and the implications of these problems for the system under which, as free agents, they now lived.

Even formerly, Africans who had remained abroad for extended periods, as students or in other capacities, and had accepted Western values, continued to be Africans. There were two compelling reasons for this. The first, a universal in human experience, was the force of their early cultural conditioning which assured the retention of various deep-seated African patterns of behavior and thought, despite the most intensive exposure to other ways. The other

[1] Ayo Ogunsheye: "The African Personality: Ideology and Utopia" (a paper presented to the International Symposium on African Culture, Ibadan, Nigeria, mimeographed, December, 1960), p. 1.

was the factor of physical type, which inevitably entered, even where there was no question of prejudice or of discrimination. What has been termed a high degree of sociological visibility was as inescapable for the African in countries outside Africa as it is for Europeans or Asians in Africa itself.

Being thus set apart, Africans could not fail to be critical of the foreign setting in which they found themselves. An example, (earlier alluded to), perhaps unique in the literature, is to the point:

> The African visitor is sometimes shocked at the behaviour of the English. In conversation, children do not hesitate to contradict the views of their elders.

As for the English women, they feel they

> must make conversation when they have visitors, and so they talk about all sorts of things, which may sometimes prove a bit boring or irritating to a stranger. But that is the way they are, and they feel that they are doing the right thing. We must learn to bear with these differences and recognize that certain of our ways may appear strange to them, too.

The men, to the African,

> appear even more mysterious. It may seem to us that they really play the role of children in the house. They are looked after very carefully and told what they are supposed to like, to eat, and to wear, and to do. They hardly ever talk. . . . Perhaps it is correct to say that the Englishman's home is a castle in which his wife offers him shelter.

Other culture differences were pointed out; how people in England are always in a hurry, how readily the word "nonsense" is used without meaning.

> But, perhaps, what may seem strangest to us, who respect age, is the English peoples' fear of age. Young women cease

to add to their years after a certain age. The old ladies . . . do all sorts of things to make themselves look young. The men are afraid of being considered old. In this culture, age, which ought to be a sign of maturity, and to qualify people for leadership in communal and national affairs, is thought of in terms of senility.

In drawing evaluations of this kind, which in the appropriate terms would describe African reactions to customary behavior in any non-African society, whether in Europe, Asia or America, a reciprocal viewpoint concerning African cultures was bound to emerge in the thinking of Africans. This evaluation of English culture had its parallel in views of African ways.

. . . These generalizations are similar to some of the statements often made by Englishmen about the African. It is very easy for an Englishman driving through an African village to conclude that women do all the work, and the men sit around all day. We know such an interpretation is not accurate, and so we shouldn't attach too much importance to our first general impressions.

And with prescience, it was stated that:

Culture contact . . . will, in our lifetime, become the normal state of existence between peoples of all parts of the world. . . . We, who have always been ready to welcome strangers and to learn from them, must now realize the need for a concerted effort directed towards the creation of decent and peaceful human relations.[2]

It was but a step from this line of thought about a non-African society to applying the lessons thus learned to African societies themselves. The assumption by adminis-

[2] Robert Gardiner: "Going to England," in *Other People Other Ways,* by Sir Alan Burns and Robert Gardiner (London, 1951), pp. 17–19.

trators, teachers, missionaries, and writers, repeated over
the years, that African ways had at best secondary value,
had had their effect. No matter how vigorously Africans
denied this, they found the argument, usually drawn from
a comparison of African and European technological and
economic attainment, difficult to refute. Beyond the emotional negative reaction lay a recognition, even among the
most vigorous critics of Euroamerican ways, that the historic processes which had been set in motion could not be
halted. When this was acknowledged, it became logical that
the old as well as the new had to be freshly viewed, in
order that what was desirable in both could be retained.

Gradually a formula to guide reintegration in these selective terms began to be perceptible, even though it was
nowhere verbalized as such. Three sources contributed to
it. These were, first of all, the aboriginal cultures whose
strength proved incontestably greater than had been
credited. Then came the impulses emanating from the
colonial experience. These derived primarily from western
Europe and, secondarily, because of the language factor
and the opportunities Africans had realized in the United
States and Canada for higher education, from North
America. Finally, and last in chronological sequence, came
the more heterogeneous series of influences that were derived from Communist eastern Europe and China, and
from the Near East and India.

Though we risk oversimplification of the complexities of
the integrative process, the influence of each of these three
historic forces can be generalized to aid us in our understanding of what was taking place. By and large, it came
to be accepted that the major values in African cultures that
would be important in shaping the new African nations lay
in the fields of human relations and the creative arts. In a
sense, this implied a refusal to define "progress" as a matter
of technological skills and economic resources alone. It
had been on the basis of this definition that the evolutionary theories of the Victorian era had laid claim to Euro-

pean superiority, expressing a point of view that was continued into the postcolonial period in the form of the Marxist doctrine of economic stages.

From western Europe and from North America, as a second influence, came technological development and vistas of improved standards of living; the drive to extend literacy and broaden the base of a schooled citizenry, and to make use of the resources of scientific medicine. The contributions were, however, by no means all material, for ideals of democratic participation on the political level, and new interpretations of the concepts of human rights and human dignity were also derived from this same source.

The third stream brought reorientations that were essentially political, though economic factors also entered. From Russia came the blueprints for the controlled, single-party state, with the Marxian economic philosophy seen as a prime instrument for mobilizing resources and for maximizing scarce means to attain socially desired ends. Its built-in mechanisms for holding power could not but render it attractive to African leaders. From China came techniques for intensive channeling of the energies of the people into planned production. The experience of Israel in solving ecological and other problems confronting the new African nations was also influential. India had been in touch with eastern and southern Africa for centuries, but in the present context, India contributed primarily the concepts of passive resistance and later, on the level of international relations, of neutrality in the cold war. From the Arab countries of North Africa came the impetus to extend the political implications of Pan-Africanism by bringing it in line with the idea of Africa as a totality, an invaluable instrument for maneuvering on the world stages.

These were the materials which the Africans had at hand as colonial controls disappeared. Given the eclecticism that lies deep in African patterns of thought, the process became one of selection. In this process, the question of values was critical. In the remaining pages of this book, we will therefore move to examine some of the values that guided the rediscovery of traditional forms and meanings which came to be the integrative element binding the old and the new.

The historic sense lies deep in the human psyche. The existence of writing has validated this sense as could no other form of communication. Documentation in the form of a scroll, a parchment, an inscription, a book, is independent of the vagaries of memory and, because it is a more trustworthy instrument of transmission than word of mouth, we have tended to neglect the contributions of oral tradition. In a world where knowledge of the past, based on written records, is given a place of high importance in the system of values, the fact that African peoples had not developed writing and were thus, in the restricted sense of the term, unhistorical, came to be of some moment. Psychologically, it meant that Africans were unable to call on a documented past to provide them with identifications of those who had written histories; legally, they could not support territorial claims by reference to contemporaneous records of their own which, for example, in South Africa, would have resolved many disputed claims and counter claims or original tenure.

For a long time, African history was regarded by historians, and by no means exclusively European historians, as the history of the expansion of Europe into Africa. In writing this history, narrowly defined in terms of archival and documentary research, African happenings were incidental to the tale of European occupation and the establishment of the colonial system. What was taking place inside Africa, and to Africans, entered only when there was armed resistance to expansion and control, or where, in the determination of policy, it was necessary to take African reactions into account. African history was thus an extension of the history of Europe. Before the First World War, it has been said, Africa was the safety valve of Europe, in that European tensions were often resolved by a readjustment in the boundaries of African holdings of the colonial powers, which were party to a dispute. Matters of this kind dominated the histories of Africa. Given the assumptions about African cultures that were current, the existence of a recoverable African past, antedating contact with Europe, was dismissed. And though some studies were made of the history of the Islamic northern portion of Subsaharan Africa, these, too, were oriented toward analyzing the impinging rather than the internal forces.

The swing of the pendulum to the other extreme was an understandable African reaction. In earlier pages, we have seen the fixation on the idea that in the process of cultural borrowing incident on contact between African and non-African peoples, Africa was essentially a recipient, and not a donor. With an intellectual climate of interest in origins, and an increasing scholarly and lay interest in Egypt, it followed logically that its role in influencing Subsaharan African developments should seem conclusive. In consequence, if linguistic or cultural resemblances, often farfetched and distorted to fit the theory, could even dimly be discerned, it was taken for granted that all such items must have originated in Egypt.

Initially, contemporary African response to this reading of its past was to rest the pyramid of probability on its apex. Egypt, and by extension the Near East, continued to be the essential point of reference, but whereas in the earlier writings it had been the source of cultural advance, these countries were now declared to have been recipients of this cultural ferment. A powerful variant of this developed from the Pan-African conception of the African future. In this, the fact that Egypt was a part of the continent of Africa, and that its achievements were therefore the achievements of Africans, became a principal tenet, though this was scarcely accepted in Egypt itself. The contributions of Egypt to the human adventure, that is, were not questioned, but rather credited to Africa as a whole. So appealing was this that one African writer charged that the documents which would have demonstrated the validity of this assumption had been suppressed by European scholars, because of the fear that a knowledge of their contents would undermine colonial controls by revealing the true historic role of Africa.

This, however, was but a short episode in the development of the field of African history. The most important factor in this development was the realization that, despite the absence of indigenous systems of writing, there was not only a tale that must be told, but one that could be recovered, once the problem of developing the requisite methods of attack was solved. The motivation of Africans, given the traditional attitude toward knowledge of the past and in particular the past of the world in which they now moved, was plain. Disciplined by training in the techniques of critical scholarship, they began to produce studies of significance. It must be noted, as well, that the drive to develop a new approach to African history, one that did not make of it an appendage of the history of Europe, was not confined to Africa. It was, in fact, an international scholarly effort, in response to a growing conviction that lack of knowledge of the historical development of African civilizations made for a serious gap in world history.

Gradually a new note began to be heard. Documents that had been available, but had gone unused, telling of events and personalities inside Africa, were re-examined. It was discovered that, even in terms of conventional historical research, far more data were to be had than the community of historians had recognized. From the moldy files of District Offices, from early Gazettes, came information about the beginnings of the colonial period, which students could employ to focus on internal developments in Africa itself, studying problems no longer held to be peripheral. Archival materials in the metropolitan countries began to be more effectively examined and analyzed. Not only were official sources tapped, but also the records of commercial houses and missionary bodies, which were found to have a wealth of data. The search went farther afield; the archives of American missions that from the first days of contact had operated in various parts of the Subsaharan continent, were found to contain documents that threw considerable light on developments there. Studies to which we have had occasion to refer, such as those of Diké on the commerce of the Niger Delta region during the middle five decades of the nineteenth century, or of Shepperson and Price on the Chilembwe movement of Nyasaland, or M. G. Smith on the government of the Hausa State of Zazzau, or Vansina on the early political organization of the Bakuba of the Congo, are good examples of the kind of new history that was being written.

Precolonial history also began to be documented more and more by the use of Arabic and other non-European sources. The existence of these materials was known, as is evidenced by the publication, in 1932, in Cairo, of a multivolumed work which reproduced large numbers of early Arabic documents on Egypt and Africa in French translation.[3] Documents of this kind began to be reworked, with a focus on events in Africa rather than on the political and military history of Arabic and Moslem invasions. New collections of these were published.[4] Sources in Persian and Chinese bearing on Africa were similarly scrutinized. And

[3] Youssef Kamal: *Monumenta Cartogeographica Africae et Aegypti,* 5 Vols. (Cairo and Leyden, 1932).

[4] D. Olderogge: *Zapadnyi Sudan v XV–XIX vv* (Trudy Instituta Etnografii, Novaia seriia, t. LIII, Akademiia Nauk SSSR), *The Western Sudan in the XV–XIX Centuries* (Contributions of the Institute of Ethnography, n.s., Vol. LIII, USSR Academy of Sciences, Moscow and Leningrad, 1960); L. E. Kubbel and V. V. Matveev: *Drevnie i Srednevekovye Istochniki po Etnografii i Istorii Narodov Afriki Iuzhnee Sakhary—Arabskie Istochniki VII–X Vekov* (*Ancient and Mediaeval Sources for the Ethnography and History of the African Peoples South of the Sahara; Arab Sources, VII–X Centuries*) (Moscow and Leningrad, 1960).

for the later history of the Islamic belt south of the Sahara, the work of African scholars began to fill in the picture, principally such as the collaborative studies by Hampata Ba on the Fulani Empire of Macina, or the biography of Tierno Bokar, who from the center of Bandiagara influenced so deeply the development of African Islam during the latter part of the nineteenth century.

The new approach to African history also recognized the need to use all possible materials and techniques in recovering the unwritten past of Subsaharan Africa. To do this it was necessary to supplement and extend the conventional methods of historical study. Oral tradition and archaeological findings began to be given serious attention. Comparative studies of the distribution of particular aspects of the aboriginal cultures; of such stable physical characteristics as blood types; and of historical linguistics, were called on to trace possible relationships between peoples. The contents of the *Journal of African History* reflected this breadth of approach; its contributions included papers of a kind not common to other historical journals. Thus, in a single number appeared a discussion of the economic prehistory of Africa, a study of the Somali conquest of the East Horn from the twelfth century onward, and an analysis of the archaeology of Ife, Nigeria, to name but three. To this approach the name of ethnohistory was given.

This was not achieved without extended discussions of the problems of method. Historians have long recognized documentary materials are of uneven reliability, and have developed criteria for determining the value of a given document as a historic source. But where writing was absent, the questions that arose had to do with the value of different kinds of materials whose testing involved new criteria—those of the archaeologist, of the ethnologist, of the student of myth and oral tradition. The problem was a knotty one. It involved the need for specialists to step outside their speciality, and collaborate with other specialists in utilizing and, where necessary, devising techniques of investigation bearing on a common problem. Above all, it meant adjusting to a new concept of historical probability when research was extended beyond the scope of "hard" documentary materials and archaeological artifacts.[5]

One of the most controversial aspects of the movement to recover the African past had to do with the value of oral tradition. "Euhemerism," as the attribution of historical validity to unwritten accounts is called, after the Greek philosopher Euhemerus who accepted myth as an explanation of historical events, had in its crude form been rejected. Defining history as "the recital in chronological sequences of events that are known to have occurred," Raglan and others flatly denied the ability of any nonliterate people to give a credible account of any happening farther removed than one hundred and fifty years from the time it was recounted. "Forms of knowledge which depend, even in part, upon written record, can have for the savage no existence at all." The events in his past, "are, in fact, completely lost."[6] Yet such an ethnohistorical study as that made among the Gwambe of Mozambique, in which traditional statements of migration, given orally, were found to be in accord with those in sixteenth century Portuguese documents,[7] demonstrated how dangerous it is to deny categorically any validity to unwritten history.

However, it was not only problems of method that had to be resolved. As Africans became conscious of the importance of recovering their historic past, and alert to the political uses to which it could be put, they came to lay stress

[5] Cf. Melville J. Herskovits: "Anthropology and Africa—a Wider Perspective," *Africa,* Vol. 29 (1959), *passim.*

[6] Lord F. R. S. Raglan: *The Hero, a Study in Tradition, Myth and Drama* (London, 1936), pp. 2, 6.

[7] Edward Fuller: "Ethnohistory in the Study of Culture Change in Southwest Africa," in *Continuity and Change in African Culture* (W. R. Bascom and M. J. Herskovits, editors, Chicago, 1959), *passim.*

on the traditions of that past which, in the period before
writing was introduced, was accepted as history by the members of each particular group. A body of oral tradition thus
became "official" history. This posed a particularly vexing
problem for Africans who, trained in historiography, were
expected to shape their accounts in accordance with sanctioned versions of the past.

Departure from recognized scholarly procedures in preparing histories of African societies, a practice by no means
confined to Africans, became less the exception as the
impact of the newer forms of historical research became
felt. There was a countervailing factor involved, as well.
With the general recognition of the African historical past,
and of the importance of knowing that past, the new ethno-
historians no longer had to combat the denial of African
history. Africans were thus freed, psychologically, to approach the study of their own history with the objectivity
of any trained historian, and to collaborate with their fellow
scholars in related disciplines, and outside of Africa, in the
full tradition of international scholarship.

The establishment of the field of African history as part
of world history was a major transitional factor in the reshaping and reintegration of the developing system of values
in Africa under change.

Though no attempt was made to define specifically the
indigenous values it had become important to retain, they
can be deduced from expressions of African opinion
throughout the Subsaharan continent. These values lay
essentially in the field of human relations. African intellectuals fully recognized that their indigenous economic systems and their technology would not permit them or their
children a full participation in the world economy. Acceptance of the fact that African technologies and modes of
production and exchange were insufficient did not give rise
to the negative reactions that spring from challenge. They
were not marked by the emotional "loading" called forth by

foreign evaluation of the intangibles of these cultures, such as their systems of kinship or morality.

There is another point to be considered here. Technological and economic change, or "development" as it came to be called, could be put to objective tests of comparative accomplishment. In the instance of technology, it was self-evident that, as the Africans had seen repeatedly demonstrated, a machine could accomplish much more, with the expenditure of far less energy, than could mere man power. Electricity provided better and, in the long run, cheaper light than oil lamps. Scientific medicine, whether curative or preventive, and a knowledge of nutrition, could prolong life and prevent suffering, ease child birth and lower the rate of infant mortality. Economic development, defined in terms of increased production and more effective distribution, could be measured statistically; and Africans, drawn into a system of thought where statistical data are given high value, were as susceptible as any others to their appeal.

In the nontechnical, noneconomic aspects of their new life, however, there were no such criteria. Africans, as they came to be better acquainted with the cultures of those who ruled them, and as they fanned out over the rest of the world, began to sense the variety of values among different peoples, and the many ways in which these values could be expressed. They began to ask why their own traditional values were being placed on a lower level than these others. And once the question had been raised, it answered itself. One machine can be compared to another because the end toward which both are employed—the value in each—is measurable. If one of them is faster, or produces a better finished product at a lower cost, it is the better machine. But to compare family systems, or ethical principles, or political organizations, or art, or music in this manner, is impossible, because we are here dealing with intangible values and ends about which there is no cross-cultural consensus.

This was at once a source of strength and of doubt to

Africans. It was a source of strength because affirmation of these intangible values could not be challenged except on the grounds of their difference from other systems. If the validity of criteria necessarily drawn from the cultural conditioning of those who advanced them was not admitted, any presumably objective proofs fell to the ground. The arguments advanced for or against plural marriage, pouring libations, or an ancestral cult, are all in this category.

Doubts arose, on the other hand, as a result of the long years during which, under colonial rule, criteria of worth set in European capitals had been inculcated in the Africans, and their aboriginal values belittled by arguments that carried conviction because of the technological and economic strength of those who advanced them. Political leaders, thoroughly schooled in non-African ideologies and techniques of organization, had keyed their objectives to economic and technological advancement in terms of the twentieth century industrialized state. Consequently, ambivalences arose from the variance between these aims and many of the values toward which early orientation and the need for cultural self-esteem propelled them. The result, as one African put it, was that

> We see the peoples of independent African states for the most part tormented by a basic cultural discomfort: they have not . . . recovered the spiritual basis for re-establishing their unsettled societies, they have not recovered their cultural independence.[9]

Values in aboriginal African society must be inferred from African behavior, African social institutions, African beliefs. These values are never systematically formulated.

[9] Harris Memel Foté: *Rapport sur la Civilisation Animiste* (a paper presented to the Colloquium on "The Contributions of Animism, Islam and Christianity to the Cultural Expression of the African Personality" (Abidjan, Ivory Coast, April 5–12, 1961) mimeographed, p. 2.

They are most explicit in the proverbs and moralizing tales, which reveal a system of ethical principles, once the hidden meaning of all aphorisms, and the patterns of their use, are analyzed in cultural context. In some societies the values found in these forms have a high degree of complexity, and cover approved behavior in many different kinds of situations. An instance of this is found in the concept of *ubgenge* of the Barundi of Ruanda-Urundi. It is described as "a variation on the idea of intelligence," and represents the value laid on ability to think clearly and argue cogently— to be astute, to be able "to get oneself out of a bad situation," or, in the conjugal setting, to be a woman who "knows how to escape the anger of her husband."[10]

Certain African values began to be repeatedly formulated in the discussions of Africans concerned with developing a cultural ideology for the new African nations. Two of these could be heard, or read, more often than others. One referred to the traditional interdependence of members of a kinship grouping, and the rights and obligations involved— a pattern of relationships that provided security for the individual, and a stable base for society. The other was respect for one's elders, who had knowledge based on experience. Grouped with these we find the value of cooperative effort.

Another aspect of African behavior, implicit in traditional narrative and reinforced by the experience of conquest, colonial or indigenous, was the principle of circumspection in dealing with all strangers and superiors. It was important to listen with passive deference, to disclose as little as possible when questioned, to reach decisions through discussion and consultation with one's own people, to manifest an outer docility while biding one's time for the moment of redress—all that which goes into the making of psychological resilience. The new esteem the educated Africans came to hold for aboriginal graphic and plastic arts, music,

[10] Ethel M. Albert: "Une Étude de Valeurs en Ruandi," *Cahiers d'Études Africaines,* Vol. II (1960), p. 158.

and the dance, and the new regard for aspects of African religion, such as respect for the elders, institutionalized as the ancestral cult, has already been discussed. All these must be viewed as affirmations of a basic metaphysic, of which the fundamental principle is the continuity of experience, under which the past, the present, and the future are conceived to be a unified whole.

Some of the values derived from contact with the outer world conflicted with these. The new values placed on a pecuniary economy, on practically all aspects of technological change, on many kinds of non-African material goods, were rarely challenged. Indeed, one of the induced values that came to be accepted almost without dissent in these sectors of culture was change as an end in itself. Roads, bridges, motor cars, multistoried buildings, power dams, were its more dramatic manifestations. In the same category was the value laid on literacy. The value of recognition as free and independent nations in international dealings was similarly accepted.

Of new values in conflict with the old, we find, not unexpectedly, a good many in the area of internal political organization. African leaders, faced with the challenge of economic growth and the need to establish higher living standards, began to re-examine traditional communal patterns with the objective of shaping them to fit the requirements of a new economic order. This re-examination occurred both where patterns of individual effort had become established, and where socialistically oriented plans sought to use traditional communalism as an instrument to make the new system function. The values laid on age and hereditary status came into conflict with systems of political democracy no less than those of strict one-party control. Indeed, herein lay the crux of the argument over the nature of "African democracy." Related to this was the debate over the question of tribalism and the role of the chief, a debate that arose out of the values ascribed to traditional prerogatives and defined lines of authority, as against the concept of the centrally governed state; a debate, that on a regional or continental scale, had as its major theme the various forms of Pan-Africanism.

The need to re-establish the position of African culture by affirming its particular values was most vigorously expressed in the concepts of *négritude* and of "the African personality." Following independence, these concepts were transmuted from a rallying cry for African independence to a symbol of African worth. They marshaled the forces toward the integrations that came to be a dominant objective of African thought.

To understand the importance of this aspect of the search for new values, especially as it concerns the concept of *négritude,* we must again turn to the pre-independence period. Its most precise expressions were to be found in statements of the *Présence Africaine* group and of the Society for African Culture, which was formed following the First Conference of Negro Writers and Artists in 1956. One statement of their objectives read:

> Since 1941, in Paris, Africans, Madgascans and West Indians have been preoccupied with affirming the "presence" or ethos of the black communities of the world, of defending the originality of their way of life and the dignity of their cultures. . . . They knew that the problem was not only that of assuring between black and white the theoretical equality of individuals. . . . They knew it concerned a fundamental recasting of the structures of European civilization and African life, and the links which bind us should spring from the cultural level. In short, it involved an emergence of an African personality from the accretion of Western culture, which colonization has thrown into disequilibrium and servitude.[11]

A further expression of *négritude* appeared in the call issued for the Second Conference of Negro Writers and Artists, held in Rome in 1959, explaining the aims of its organizing body, the Society of African Culture. "This asso-

[11] John A. Davis (editor): *Africa Seen by American Negroes* (Paris, 1958), p. 1 of *Supplement* at end of volume.

ciation comprises men of the Negro world," it stated, "and its mission is to organize our culture [*sic:* relations, activities?] in such a way that a) our culture patterns be first interpreted by ourselves, b) that they express both our inner life and the universal vocation of our cultures." The idea that "there can be a nation without a culture of its own" was rejected, and as for its task, the agenda of the Conference was to study "1) the foundation of our culture and its chances of achieving unity and solidarity, 2) the tasks and responsibilities of each discipline and art."[12]

One of the founders of the doctrine, the poet Léopold Sedar Senghor, who became President of the Republic of Senegal, defined the concept as a "positive affirmation of the values in African culture."[13] Students of African affairs, however, were disquieted by the overtones in the idea of *négritude,* that there is a quality of creativity and response peculiar to the Negro *race.* They found it difficult to forget the racisms of Europe, with their ascription of cultural superiority and unique cultural aptitudes, which culminated in the mystical Nazi doctrines of the *Herrenvolk.* Proponents of *négritude* rejected the analogy. They asserted that the racial factor, though present, carried no implication of superiority, but only laid stress on the validity of the cultural contribution of Negro peoples, that had for so long not only gone without appreciation, but had been actively disparaged by the rest of the world. Again, according to Senghor, the concept was not racist, but represented insistence on recognition of values that "must be accepted if Europe is to retain the good will of Africans."

The psychological reasons for this reaction were not difficult to understand, but a shift from compensatory emphasis on the positive values in African cultures to claims based on racial endowment seemed disturbingly easy to make. This was perhaps why those who defined the term "racism" as European attitudes toward non-Europeans saw

---

[12] *Ibid.,* final two pages of *Supplement.*
[13] Melville J. Herskovits: *Notes on African Field Research,* p. 60/D20.

négritude as "counter-racism." There was some danger of its developing into a rejection of all that was not African, though as far as those who originally espoused it were concerned, there was little likelihood of their drifting into a position which was the more repugnant to them because of what they had suffered from it.

In its political aspects, *négritude* could be related to the concept of "the African personality," favored by those who had shared the experiences of the Pan-African Congresses. As far as can be determined, the phrase "African personality" originated with President Kwame Nkrumah, of Ghana, but it was never defined by its originator to the degree that has made it possible for us to study the meaning of the concept *négritude*. Both had broad applicability, but the concept of an African personality applied to African states was developed after Ghana had attained self-government, and thus did not function in the development of nationalism in British West Africa. In contrast, *négritude* embraced all who were of African descent, wherever they might live, and its political implications were but a part of its overall humanistic approach.

In retrospect, it is easy to see how, under the pressure of the need to re-establish the validity of African cultures, and of integrating the old with the new, the two concepts should have come together. By 1961, Alioune Diop, in discussing the relation between them, was stressing the fact that *négritude* was a term devised in Paris by those who wished to re-establish the dignity of African culture; that "the African personality" emphasized the validity of the African position in the international scene. Both, he felt, were attempts to seek recognition for the universal values in African cultures, to stress the "originality and dignity" of what African peoples had achieved. In the same discussion, a Ghanaian expressed his conception of the "African personality" as "a symbol of the new and highly significant fact that the Africans have come into their own at home and have emerged as a factor to be reckoned with on the world stage." To

have "more than a symbolic content," certain broad lines
of implementing the concept must be found. And in this
"the values of traditional African societies" could figure, as
this image of the African was more widely projected.[14]

In our analysis of the various aspects of contemporary
Africa, the balance of our discussion has swung between
continuity and change. The simultaneous presence of the
two, never in equilibrium, we found to be nothing new in
the African experience. Africa had had a consistent history
of adjustment to elements introduced from outside. African
societies had been neither as static prior to European contact as they were thought to have been, nor as hospitable
to the cultures of their colonial rulers as at one time they
were assumed to be.

The application of the methods and concepts of the scientific analysis of cultural dynamics to the problem of
change in Subsaharan Africa revealed complexities of an
order not often recognized. This is not to say that certain
kinds of complexities had gone unobserved. Differences in
indigenous African cultures were pointed out by early
travelers, and their observations were confirmed by later
intensive and disciplined study. Similarly inescapable were
the complexities in the vast range of linguistic expression.
Students of colonial policy and administration were obliged
to deal with problems arising out of differences in the contact situation. Almost without exception, research findings
showed how dissimilarities in the policies of the colonial
powers, as well as the aboriginal linguistic and cultural
differences, distinctively shaped the impact of each power
on the peoples it ruled.

[14] C. G. Baeta: "Les Fondements Éthiques et Spirituels de
l'Humanisme Animiste" (a paper read at the Colloquium on "The
Contributions of Animism, Islam and Christianity to the Cultural
Expression of the African Personality," Abidjan, Ivory Coast, April
5–12, 1961) mimeographed, p. 7.

There was little overview, however, to compensate for the particularist findings that came to mark analysis of African affairs. Common features that were clearly discernible, once one moved across political boundaries and considered Africa in terms of its own cultural and historical realities, were held in the background or ignored. Similarities in the aboriginal cultures could be perceived on various levels—in terms of cultural areas, or of the twofold division of the African subcontinent on the basis of ecological setting and economic organization, or of resemblances throughout the subcontinent. Despite the differences in types of innovation from the several European cultures brought to Africa, and variations in colonial policy, certain identities in African response are distinguishable. These ranged from the accelerating African acceptance of the wholly additive elements not in conflict with antecedent custom, such as the introduction and spread of literacy, or scientific medicine, through substitutive adjustments in the new political structures or in the systems of belief, to deep-rooted attitudes making for the retention of basic food patterns, or aspects of the social structures, or indigenous values.

African cultures, in other words, were fed by inner resources which enabled them to maintain their strength under the constraints of colonial control and under domination by a permanently resident ethnic minority. Even where African societies were under greatest pressure, traditional ways persisted in forms and to a degree that went largely unrecognized. The sources of this strength derived from the nature of the cultures themselves, especially their institutionalized mechanisms of psychological resilience. The studied deference toward elders and officialdom was basic in ordering behavior on all levels. Whether in personal relations or politics, indirection in stating and holding to objectives, the high value placed on discretion in act and on diplomatic phrasing in statement, the use of aphorism and oblique reference to make a point in an argument were but a few of the more widespread methods for cultural self-preservation.

This complex of values had stood the Africans in good stead as they adjusted to the internal or external innovations to which they had been exposed through the centuries. Under the forced draft of change in the colonial period, such methods were invaluable for accommodation to the imposed alien institutions and for functioning under the new controls. More than this, they allowed a person to retain his self-respect even when subjected to indignities, for in his own household, the slave was master, and with a turn of the wheel of fortune he might take over a role of initiative and command. Roles, that is, were fluid and flexible; no situation was incapable of change.

One of the unities which marked the dynamics of the colonial period was the mode of African reaction to European culture and, by extension, to Europeans. This falls into three fairly well-defined stages that—though overlapping at any given moment in Subsaharan Africa as a whole—represent a consistent pattern for any specific group or any single territory.

The first stage followed on initial contact, and continued well into the time when Europeans assumed full political control, whether by the conclusion of treaties between native rulers and the representatives of the incoming power, or through the imposition of rule by force. Resistance was frequently encountered, and in some instances was prolonged, but except in the populous kingdoms with centralized governments and organized armies, there was no intensive fighting. Non-cooperation was resorted to instead. Thus, in the case of the Tiv of Nigeria, plans made about 1900 to run a telegraph line through their country had to be altered because they "were 'recalcitrant,' refused to 'submit' and supply labour, and because they stole the wire to make jewelry." It was ten years before they were brought under British control.[15]

[15] Paul and Laura Bohannan: *Three Source Notebooks in Tiv Ethnography* (Human Relations Area Files, New Haven, Connecticut, 1956), p. 26.

In this first stage, the European was looked upon as a being who controlled unfathomed power, remote from those whose destinies he ruled. He was to be listened to carefully, studied, and emulated insofar as comprehension of his ways, and ability to tap his resources, permitted. Any doubts the Africans might have had about his ways were well concealed. These were the days of the isolated district officer, the remote mission station. The strangers were counselors, judges and, where friendship could cross the deep gulf of status and cultural differences, friends. Where possible, good relations with these strangers were assiduously cultivated, for it was they who dealt with the forces of the new world that had come to the African.

With continued contact, and the close observation under which the European lived—unaware as he seemed of it— he was found to have frailties Africans recognized among themselves, and some which were new to them. Africans learned early of the rivalries and jealousies among Europeans, and of wars between European nations, in which Africans were called on to aid. The doctrines of those who came to preach a new truth were not always in harmony, and they made manifest their rivalries in contesting for the allegiance of the Africans they sought to convert. Africans learned about the machines that aided the Europeans in conquering time and distance. They discovered that they, too, could operate and repair these machines. The new skills of reading and writing widened their horizons, and as opportunities to travel brought them firsthand experience with the outer world, they learned that what had happened to them was not unique. Questions began to be raised concerning their present position and their future status.[16]

Thus far the path trod by all African peoples is clearly to be seen. But from here several paths lay open before

[16] Melville J. Herskovits: "Some Contemporary Developments in Subsaharan Africa," in *Africa in the Modern World* (Calvin W. Stillman, editor, Chicago, 1955), pp. 277–82.

them. It was at this later point of better acquaintance with the culture of the rulers that evaluation, and later, action, entered. Evaluation, positive or negative, was accelerated by the increasing freedom of choice which accompanied successive moves toward self-government. The elements of the alien cultures that were accepted, or the degree to which they were continued as reinterpretations, differed with time and place, depending on the extent to which the Africans had access to the culture of the rulers, the kind of relations between rulers and ruled, and the degree of identification with the rulers.

There was almost nowhere a complete retention of earlier custom, not even in remote outposts. Even where rejection took the form of violence, as in the Mau Mau of Kenya, the aboriginal practices that were presumably reinstated deviated greatly from the actuality of earlier days. At the other extreme, it was equally rare to find complete acceptance of what had been introduced. Invariably, probing beneath the surface, one would find some aspect of an innovation, whether in its form, its use, its meaning, or its value, which differentiated it from the form in which it had come from abroad.

Read has outlined the similar course of the educational aspect of African-European contact. The first stage "was marked by conservatism among the Africans toward this new form of education." Next came "a gradual acceptance . . . of some of the new ideas and new ways of living to which they were introduced through the schools." Following this was "the rejection . . . of certain traditional ideas and former ways of living." It was in this third stage that, as one Christian chief put it, "The white teachers taught us to despise our past." In time, educational opportunities came to be "fully accepted by the Africans." This achieved, there was "a partial reinstatement" in the curriculum "of certain elements in the traditional cultures," and this set the stage for the final development, when use was made "of the new selection by Africans of elements . . . which they wished to incorporate in their educational system."[17]

To be sure, the process is highly complex, and we should not underrate the difficulties in seeking to understand it. Considerations of personality and position enter, and we must recognize that even within a small community, considerable variation in degree of adjustment can be found. Epstein, in his study of the dialect called *CiCopperbelti* in the urban centers of Northern Rhodesia, stressed the role of "evaluations in terms of prestige" in its formation. Though prestige was assigned on the basis of "the European way of life," this was defined by "a very complex process of selection." The concept would have to include,

the behavior of Europeans living on the Copperbelt as it is perceived by Africans, patterns of behavior as they are observed in Hollywood films . . . , and even aspects of the life of American Negroes as it is transmitted through popular African magazines published in South Africa.

Given prestige as a value, a variety of factors, in conferring prestige, promoted "a continuous and unremitting struggle in which different and increasingly refined criteria" could be "variously invoked to advance one's claim to status," and led to "a bewildering assortment of rivalries, allegiances, and cross-cutting ties both within and between groups."[18]

The facts about African response to culture contact make it difficult to understand how the idea of the African as a passive recipient of European culture could have gained such wide currency. Yet, as we have seen, this point of view was held almost as an article of faith by perhaps a majority of non-Africans who lived and worked in Africa, and was

[17] Margaret Read: "Cultural Contacts in Education," *Proceedings, British Association for the Advancement of Science*, Edinburgh meetings (1951), pp. 366–68.

[18] A. L. Epstein: "Linguistic Innovation and Culture on the Copperbelt, Northern Rhodesia," *Southwestern Journal of Anthropology*, Vol. 15 (1959), pp. 252–53.

the stated objective of early colonial policy. It provided the ideological base for the nineteenth century concepts of the white man's burden and the *mission civilisatrice*. To an unrecognized extent, it was also implicit in the interpretation of the Marxist doctrine of social progress as relevant to the African scene. Since this doctrine predicates a series of predetermined evolutionary stages through which all societies must pass, the Africans, whose cultures are from the Marxist point of view on a "primitive" or "feudal" level, must move through this series of stages to reach the higher status of the industrialized Communist states.

To positions such as these, as to the one which seeks a return to pre-European ways, cultural theory has long provided an essential corrective. Inasmuch as no society is without its own way of life, it never presents a clean slate on which new experience can be written at will. Culture is learned behavior; there is no exclusive franchise for cultural learning. Any people, given the opportunity and motivation, can learn the ways of any other, and can not only grasp but also internalize its values. To be sure, the early experiences of the individual are not erased by learning a new culture. The changes in the traditional customs of a people who experience contact are the end result of what they take over, as this is projected against their earlier patterns. Hence this end result is never identical with the model. It was sheer fantasy on the part of those Africans—a relatively small number, it is true—who believed that they could recapture the "golden age" of their culture which preceded European contact. It was no less fantasy for Europeans— or for that matter, some Africans—to believe that Africans would become European in their thoughts and acts, because African cultures were eroding to their eventual complete disappearance.

African cultural change has been selective. The results of the process of exercising choice, represented in the greater or lesser number of European elements found in a given African setting, and the forms they have taken in this setting, must in each case be regarded as reflecting the historic situation in which this process occurred. What we find not only depends on the opportunity various peoples had to become acquainted with European culture, but also on the degree of intransigence or flexibility with which they faced new cultural experiences. The Masai of Tanganyika and Kenya provided a classical example of cultural rigidity. A comparable group from the same general area were the Pakot, whose resistance to change was explained by reference to the fact that, "Their herding life provides all they need and all they want, and they have found almost nothing in Euroamerican culture that will entice them to abandon their old ways."[19] This contrasts with the receptivity to innovation among the Nigerian Ibo, whose culture provided "alternatives which the individual must decide upon in terms of his own skill and knowledge," so that "he rapidly develops experience in making decisions in which he must estimate his own position and opportunities for success." Since

> culture contact by its very nature introduces new cultural alternatives, . . . the Ibo—traditionally accustomed to thinking, acting, and making decisions in terms of a range of alternatives—are more at home in the culture contact situation than members of other societies with different orientations.[20]

Between these two extremes lay the great range of historic possibilities. Yet the result was in no case a series of cultural mosaics. Especially for the Africans who were born into the changing scene, African and European elements in combination made up their cultural world. In other words, what they learned in their formative years, even though this

[19] Harold K. Schneider: "Pakot Resistance to Change," in *Continuity and Change in African Cultures* (W. R. Bascom and M. J. Herskovits, editors, Chicago, 1959), p. 160.

[20] Simon Ottenberg: "Ibo Receptivity to Change," in *Continuity and Change in African Cultures* (W. R. Bascom and M. J. Herskovits, editors, Chicago, 1959), pp. 138–39.

derived from more than one stream of tradition, was for them a unified tradition. Only the scholar is concerned with historical processes and derivations. Africans, like all human beings, take their cultural setting for granted, living their lives within a framework of accepted values and expectations. This is why any analysis of derivations and processes must, in focusing on change, keep in perspective the factor of cultural integration. Particularly in understanding Africa, both continuity and change must be given full place if we are to grasp the new reality in all its fresh meaning.